Ten Theories of Human Nature

Ten Theories of Human Nature

Fourth Edition

LESLIE STEVENSON

DAVID L. HABERMAN

New York   Oxford

OXFORD UNIVERSITY PRESS

2004

OXFORD UNIVERSITY PRESS

Oxford   New York
Auckland   Bangkok   Buenos Aires   Cape Town   Chennai
Dar es Salaam   Delhi   Hong Kong   Istanbul   Karachi   Kolkata
Kuala Lumpur   Madrid   Melbourne   Mexico City   Mumbai   Nairobi
São Paulo   Shanghai   Taipei   Tokyo   Toronto

Published by Oxford University Press, Inc.
198 Madison Avenue, New York, New York 10016
www.oup.com

Oxford is a registered trademark of Oxford University Press

Library of Congress Cataloging-in-Publication Data
Stevenson, Leslie Forster.
Ten theories of human nature / Leslie Stevenson, David L. Haberman. — 4th ed.
  p.   cm.
Includes bibliographical references and index.
ISBN 0-19-516974-3 (pbk.)
1. Philosophical anthropology.   I. Haberman, David L., 1952–   II. Title.
BD450.S766   2004
128—dc21

                                                                    2003060926

Printing (last digit): 9 8 7 6 5 4 3 2

Printed in the United States of America
on acid-free paper

To my daughters, Sonia and Lydia, who have, of course, taught me much about human nature

L. S.

To my parents, Reuben and Ruth, in many ways the sources of my own human nature

D. H.

Contents

Preface

It is a long time since the summer of 1967, when I first had some of the thoughts that inspired this book. America was riven by the Vietnam War and by race riots in cities, and I was an aspiring but uncertain graduate student of philosophy at Oxford, spending my summer vacation on a cross-continental tour of the United States. Between experiences of the cities of the East and the amazing scenery of the West, and brief encounters with cowboys and Indians, anti-war campaigners and hippies, I remember jotting down some structural comparisons between Christianity, Marxism, psychoanalysis, and existentialism.

In the early 1970s, as a raw young lecturer at St. Andrews University, I found myself faced with large numbers of first-year students who were compelled, under the traditional Scottish system, to take a philosophy course. I wondered what was appropriate for such an audience of conscripts, most of whom would study no further philosophy. My response was to broaden a conventional philosophy of mind course into a critical examination of rival theories of human nature. The first edition of this book emerged from that pedagogical experience. Thirty years have passed since publication, and the book is still, apparently, found useful for many courses in various countries.

It is a rare privilege to be read by so many thousands of students, and I have a corresponding responsibility to update and improve the book as best I can. The differences between successive editions are getting larger, in fact. The second edition made only cosmetic changes, leaving the seven main chapters untouched. In the third edition, I updated my treatment of those seven theories, I added a new chapter on Kant, and David Haberman of the Department of Religion at Indiana University at Bloomington was enrolled to contribute chapters on Confuciansim and Hinduism (thus seven theories became ten).

This fourth edition is still more radically changed. I have at last decided to drop Skinner and Lorenz from the pantheon, and have replaced those chapters by a single long chapter on evolutionary ("Darwinian") theories of human nature. This new chapter contains sections on Skinner and Lorenz, along with various other influential figures, with special critical attention being given to E. O. Wilson. I have written a completely new chapter on Aristotle. And I have added a "historical interlude" to fill the otherwise huge gap in the history of ideas between the ancient world and the Enlightenment: in this section I offer thumbnail sketches of some of the most influential movements and thinkers.

I have also rewritten the other chapters very thoroughly, deepening the treatment (I hope), while still keeping the level introductory. In particular, I have extended my (far from impartial!) account of the Bible, suggesting a distinction between spiritual and supernatural interpretations of Christianity; I have tried to clarify my account of Kant, concentrating on the theme of reasons and causes and adding a comment on his philosophy of history; and I have added sections on Freud as moralist and on Sartre's first and second ethics. David Haberman has also made some clarifications and additions to his chapters on Confucianism and Hinduism.

There are, of course, many plausible candidates for extending the list of theories beyond our chosen ten. In view of the resurgence of the influence of religion in the contemporary world, Islam and Buddhism would be obvious choices, but our editors wanted to keep the theory count to ten (perhaps the fifth edition will be more inclusive). Meanwhile, we can recommend the "Very Short Introductions" on the Koran, Islam, the Buddha, and Buddhism, published by Oxford University Press. (By the standards of that series, the chapters in this book are *very, very* short introductions!)

With the addition of Aristotle and the historical interlude, the center of gravity of the book has perhaps moved backward in time—but that may not be a bad thing! There is a prevailing obsession with being up-to-date with the very latest scientific research or fashionable speculation. But in our rush toward the future, there is the danger of a parochialism of the present that forgets—or is simply ignorant of—the wisdom of the past. I would like to hope that this book will help readers to see presently influential ideas in a more historically informed context, and to evaluate both science-based and religion-based conceptions of human nature in a deeper, more philosophical way.

Comments from various people have suggested more adequate treatment in some places. I hereby thank my St. Andrews colleagues for their reading of the relevant chapter drafts: Sarah Broadie (Plato and Aristotle); David Archard (Marx); Jens Timmerman (Kant and Sartre); Malcolm Jeeves (Darwinian theories); and Gordon Graham, now at Aberdeen (the

Bible). I would like affectionately to remember here my father, Patric Stevenson (1909–1983) for his fastidious attention to matters of style and readability in the first edition, which I hope has rubbed off through me into subsequent editions. I also thank Emily Voigt and Robert Miller of Oxford University Press in New York for their encouragement and support in the writing of this fourth edition.

St. Andrews   L. S.
July 2003

Introduction: Rival Theories and Critical Assessments

This book is meant for anyone who is looking for a "philosophy of life," that is, an understanding of human nature that gives some guidance for how we should live. Such a *prescription* is often based on a *diagnosis* of what tends to go wrong, which in turn presupposes some sort of *ideal* of how life ought to go or how human beings ought to be.

We are using the title phrase "theory of human nature" in a wide sense to cover ancient religious traditions, some classic philosophical systems, and more recent theories that try to use scientific method to understand human nature and find guidance for human life and society. This is to stretch the meaning of the word "theory" beyond purely scientific theories. We could substitute the word "philosophy" in its classical sense of *philo-sophia* (love of wisdom), or perhaps the concept of a "worldview" (derived from the German term *Weltanschauung*) or "ideology" (the beliefs and values by which a certain society or community lives). In our wide sense, a "theory of human nature" encompasses:

1. a background metaphysical understanding of the universe and humanity's place in it;

1

2. a theory of human nature in the narrower sense of some distinctive general claims about human beings, human society, and the human condition;

3. a diagnosis of some typical defect in human beings, of what tends to go wrong in human life and society;

4. a prescription or ideal for how human life should best be lived, typically offering guidance to individuals and human societies.

Only theories in this wide sense that combine such elements offer us hope of solutions to the problems of humankind. For instance, the single assertion that everyone tends to be selfish (i.e., to act only for our own self-interest) is a very brief diagnosis, but it offers no understanding of what makes us selfish and no suggestion as to whether or how we might overcome it. The statement that we should all love one another is a prescription, but it gives no explanation of why we find it so difficult (and no gloss on what sort of "love" of others we should aspire to) and it offers no help in achieving it. The theory of evolution says important things about the place of human beings in the universe, but does not in itself offer any prescription; as a purely scientific, causal explanation of how the human species came into being, it does not attempt to tell us the purpose or meaning of our life—what we should try to do or be.

This book is not a conventional introduction to philosophy in the narrower sense of the academic subject as it is often defined these days, with its divisions of logic, philosophy of language, metaphysics, theory of knowledge, philosophy of mind, ethics, political philosophy, aesthetics, philosophy of religion, and so on. We will touch on topics in many of those areas, but our primary concern is to focus on ten selected systems of thought that offer answers to the sorts of existential, life-relevant questions that motivate many people to study philosophy in the first place. What is our place in the universe? Why are we here? We ask in both the causal sense "What brought us into being?" and the purposive sense "What—if anything—are we here for?" (What should we do, or aim at? What should we avoid?)

It is obvious that much depends on what theory of human nature we accept: for individuals, the meaning and purpose of our lives, what we ought to do or strive for, what we may hope to achieve, or to become; for human societies, what vision of human community we hope to work toward, what sort of social changes we favor. Our answers to these huge questions will depend on whether we think there is some "true" or "innate" nature of human beings and some objective standards of value for human life. If so, what is it, and what are they? Are we essentially products of evolution, programmed to pursue our self-interest, to reproduce our genes, or fulfill our biological drives? Or, is there no such "essential" human nature, only a capacity to be molded by society and its economic, political, and cultural forces? Or, is there some transcendent, objective (perhaps divine?) purpose for human lives and human history?

RIVAL THEORIES

On these fundamental questions there have been, of course, a variety of views. "What is man that Thou art mindful of him . . . Thou hast made him a little lower than the angels, and hast crowned him with glory and honor," wrote the author of Psalm 8. The Bible sees human beings as created by a transcendent God in His own image, with a God-given purpose for human life. There are also the great philosophical systems of Plato, Aristotle, and Kant, which set out supposedly objective standards of value for human lives and societies to aspire to.

"The real nature of man is the totality of social relations," wrote Karl Marx in the mid-nineteenth century. Marx denied the existence of God and held that each person is a product of the particular economic stage of human society in which he or she lives. "Man is condemned to be free," said Jean-Paul Sartre, writing in France in the Second World War. Sartre agreed with Marx's atheism, but differed from him in holding that we are not determined by our society or by anything else, rather every individual person is free to decide what he or she wants to be and do. In contrast, would-be scientific theorists of human nature such as E. O. Wilson have recently treated humans as a product of evolution, with biologically determined, species-specific patterns of behavior.

It will not escape the notice of contemporary readers that these quotations from the Bible, Marx, and Sartre all use the word "man," where the intention was surely to refer to *all* human beings, including women (and children). Such traditional usage has come under criticism for contributing to questionable assumptions about the social and familial dominance of men and the consequent neglect or oppression of women. These are, of course, important issues that involve much more than linguistic usage. We will not address feminist themes head-on in this book: there is no chapter on specifically feminist theories of human nature (which now differ among themselves!). But we will note what our selected "theories" have to say about commonalities and differences between men and women. We will try to avoid sexist language ourselves (but it cannot always be avoided in quotations).

Different conceptions of human nature lead to different views about what we ought to do and how we can do it. If an all-powerful and supremely good God made us, then it is His purpose that defines what we can be and ought to be, and we must look to Him for help. If, on the other hand, we are products of society, and if we find that many human lives are presently unsatisfactory, then there can be no real solution until human society is transformed. If we are radically free and can never escape the necessity for individual choice, then we have to accept this and make our choices with full awareness of what we are doing. If our biological nature predisposes us to think, feel, and act in certain ways, then we had better take realistic account of that in individual choices and in social policy.

Rival beliefs about human nature are typically embodied in different individual ways of life and in political and economic systems. Marxist theory (in some version) so dominated public life in communist-ruled countries in the twentieth century that any questioning of it could have serious consequences for the questioner. We can easily forget that a few centuries ago Christianity occupied a similarly dominant position in Western society: heretics and unbelievers were persecuted and even burned at the stake. Even now, there is in some places a Christian consensus that individuals can oppose only at some social cost. (In many Muslim countries, Islam occupies a similarly dominating position.) In traditionally Catholic countries (like Italy, the Republic of Ireland, and Poland) the Roman Catholic Church has exerted considerable social influence and limits state policy on abortion, contraception, and divorce. In the United States, a certain brand of Protestant Christian ethos underlies much public debate and has influenced government policy, despite the constitutional separation of Church and State.

An "existentialist" philosophy like Sartre's may seem unlikely to have social implications; but one way of justifying modern "liberal" democracy is by the philosophical view that there *are no* objective values for human living, only subjective individual choices. This assumption is highly influential in modern Western society, far beyond its particular manifestation in European existentialist philosophy of the mid-twentieth century. Liberal democracy is enshrined in the American Declaration of Independence, with its acknowledgement of the right of each "man" (i.e., *person*) to "life, liberty and the pursuit of happiness"—which tends to be interpreted as the right of each individual to pursue his or her own *conception* of happiness. It should be noted, however, that those who believe there *are* objective moral standards (whether religious or secular) may still defend a liberal political system if they think it unjust, or unwise, to try to *enforce* those standards. So, although value-subjectivism supports political liberalism, the reverse is not the case.

Outside the Western tradition, there have been other theories of human nature, some of which are still very much alive. Islam, which shares origins with Judaism and Christianity, is undergoing a resurgence of popular strength as the peoples of the Muslim world express their rejection of some aspects of Western culture (and we are thinking here not primarily of terrorists, but of the more moderate defenders of Islamic cultural identity). Islam has spread into the West with immigration and has gained some new adherents there. In India, Hinduism is resurgent, sometimes in fundamentalist or nationalist form. Buddhism, originally an Indian religion, spread into the far East, China, and Japan, and has gained publicity and converts in the West. As the influence of Marx and communism wanes, some in Russia have looked for guidance to their Orthodox Christian past and others to a variety of modern forms of spirituality. And, as China modernizes and looks beyond Marxism for guidance, the ancient Chinese philosophy of Confucius has been looked at again.

We have selected ten theories (philosophies, worldviews, or ideologies) for detailed examination. In each case there will be some critical discussion that will, we hope, encourage readers to think for themselves (and there will be ample recommendations for further reading). We will not endorse any one theory as the "best buy," but will leave our readers to make up their own minds—though there are some suggestions for synthesis in the Conclusion. Before we begin our main business, let us review the prospects for impartial, rational assessment of these controversial matters.

THE CRITICAL EXAMINATION OF RIVAL THEORIES

Many of these theories are (or have been) embodied in human societies and institutions. If so, they are not just intellectual constructions, but ways of life, subject to historical change, to growth and decay. A system of beliefs about the world and human nature that is held by some group of people not in a purely intellectual, academic, or scientific way, but as giving rise to their way of life, has often been called an "ideology."

When a belief is an ideology, used to justify the way of life of a social group, it will be difficult for the members of that community to consider it objectively. There will be strong social pressures to conform to it and acknowledge it. People will feel that their set of beliefs, even if perhaps open to some theoretical difficulties, contains vitally important insights, a vision of essential truths that have practical importance. For many people, to question their theory of human nature is to threaten what gives meaning, purpose, and hope to their life, and thus to cause them psychological discomfort or distress. Inertia, and unwillingness to admit that one is wrong, often play a part here. If one has been brought up in a certain belief and its associated way of life, or if one has converted to it and followed its precepts, it takes courage to question or abandon one's life commitment.

The prospects for impartial, rational, "purely philosophical" examination and evaluation may not seem bright, then. In so many discussions and debates (in public or in private), one feels that people's fundamental positions have already been decided (often by social conditioning of one sort or another) long before, and that all one gets by way of "debate" is a restatement of prejudices on all sides. Thus, one finds people maintaining and defending their favored ideology or theory of human nature (e.g., Christianity or Marxism) in the face of intellectual and moral objections.

First, believers typically look for some way of explaining the objections away. The Christian may say that God does not always prevent evil or answer our prayers, and that what seems bad to us may ultimately be for the best. Human suffering under a political regime has often been excused by its propagandists as the necessary birth-pangs of the new world-order. Preachers and politicians become well practiced at such justification of the ways of God and His Church or of the ruling party and its leader.

Second, the believer can take the offensive by attacking the motivation of the critic. Christians may say that those who persist in raising objections are blinded by sin, that it is their own pride that prevents them from seeing the light. The Marxist may claim that those who do not recognize the truth of Marx's analysis are deluded by the "false consciousness" typical of those who benefit from capitalist society. In the case of Freudian theory, critics of psychoanalysis have often been "diagnosed" as motivated by unconscious resistance to it. Thus a critic's motives can be analyzed in terms of the very theory being criticized.

If a theory is defended by these two devices:

1. not allowing any evidence to count against the theory and always assuming that there must be some way of explaining away putative counterevidence,

2. answering criticism by analyzing the motivations of the critic in terms of the theory itself,

we can say that it is being held as a "closed system." This does not mean, however, that all believers in a theory (e.g., Christians, Marxists, or Freudians) have to hold it in that closed-minded way.

Is it possible, then, to discuss various theories of human nature rationally and objectively, as we are setting out to do in this book? When such theories are embodied in ways of life, belief in them seems to go beyond mere reasoning. The ultimate appeal may be to faith or authority, to community membership, loyalty, or commitment. It seems that there may be no answer to the questions "Why should I believe this?" or "Why should I accept this authority?" that will satisfy someone who is not already a member of the relevant group or tradition or finds themselves attracted to it.

In the contemporary world, rival traditions and ideologies are as influential as ever. Religious, cultic, political, national, ethnic, psychotherapeutic, and gender-based dogmas are asserted with various degrees of aggression or politeness, crudity or sophistication. The media of the so-called "global village" usually seem to bring different cultures together only by way of confrontation, rather than genuine dialogue, mutual listening, and understanding. Many people feel the attractions of certainty, commitment, identity, and membership of a strongly defined community—notably in various forms of "fundamentalism," making appeal to what are seen, rightly or wrongly, as the fundamental, essential, defining themes of one tradition or another (Protestant or Catholic Christianity, Judaism, Islam, Hinduism, Marxism, "free-market-ism," American nationalism, or whatever).

In reaction to this, skepticism and cynicism are very tempting. Nowadays, they tend to take the form of cultural relativism or postmodernism, according to which no particular cultural tradition (or ideology or theory of human nature) can have any more rational justification than any other. One of the most influential prophets of this trend was the nineteenth-century German philosopher Friedrich Nietzsche, who has been described as a "master of suspicion" because he was always ready (like Marx before him and Freud after him) to diagnose an unacknowledged ideological commitment or psychological need behind claims to supposedly "objective" truth or morality. If we jump to the relativist conclusion that there can be no such thing as a true account of human nature, or rational discussion of rival theories about it, the project of this book may seem doomed from the start.

We want to suggest, however, that such despair would be premature. For one thing, not all the theories we discuss are now the ideologies of any identifiable social group, and in those cases, there is less likelihood of their being defended in the closed-minded way. But more importantly, even if a theory is held by many people as a closed system, some degree of rational evaluation is still possible for those who are prepared to try it. We can always distinguish what someone says from their motivation for saying it. Motivation will be relevant if we wish to understand the personality and social background of the speaker. But if we are concerned with the truth or falsity of what a speaker says, and hence with whether there are any good reasons for believing it, then his or her motivation can be ignored. Someone may have admirable motivation for saying something that is nevertheless false, and someone else may be saying something true, even if his or her motivation for saying it is questionable. Criticism is not refuted by dislike of the critic. The most annoying critics are those who are (at least partly) *right!*

So, if the discussion is about whether the theory is true, or whether there are good reasons for believing it, then the objections that anyone produces against it must be replied to on their merits, regardless of motivations. And if motivation *is* considered, to analyze it in terms of the theory under discussion is to assume the truth of that theory, and thus to beg the question (i.e., to argue in a circle). An objection to a theory cannot be rationally defeated just by reasserting part of the theory. The second feature of closed systems—the technique of meeting all criticism by attacking the motives of the critic—is thus rationally unsatisfactory. It is open to us to make the effort to discuss and evaluate on their own merits the propositions that someone asserts (with all due politeness to the assertor).

As to the first feature of closed systems—the attitude of always trying to find some way of explaining away objections—we can always ask whether the proposed "explaining away" is successful. It is not enough just to find some rhetorical flourish, a "one-liner" or "sound bite" that may temporarily surprise critics and allow one to escape with the impression that one has successfully maintained one's position. Rational, philosophical discussion—unlike "debates" in the media—is open-ended, there is always the possibility of making further points and of reexamining what has already been said to see if it can stand up to detailed scrutiny. So, any attempt at "explaining away" can be held up to careful examination, to try to decide whether or not it is really convincing. Many people do not have the time, patience, or willingness to engage in that kind of open-minded debate—but that does not prevent others from trying their best to do so. The ancient Greek philosopher Socrates gave us this method of "Socratic dialogue" (see Chapter 4). Jesus also set an example of being willing to talk and argue seriously with anyone, however socially outcast, with concern for their spiritual well-being.

So we say to the committed (including fundamentalists of various persuasions): we are not asking you to give up your commitment, but to think about it. You can compare it with other theories, considering how far you would agree or disagree with them. You can think about how best you can reply to objections to your own theory. You can think about which parts of your tradition you want to say are really essential, or lay hold of some fundamental truth, and which parts are in some sense optional—perhaps historically important, but not needing to be imposed on everybody. It is up to you, at every stage, to make up (and perhaps change) your own mind about exactly what you want to affirm.

To the uncommitted (including relativists or post-modernists) we say: everybody has to have some sort of theory of human nature or ideology or philosophy to live by; you must have some conceptions of what affects human well-being and some views about what is most worth doing—even if only about what your own long-term well-being or happiness consists in. We invite you to consider these various systems of thought we put before you, to compare your present view (however minimal or relativist it is) with them, and to try to rationally evaluate the differences. No human being who lives at a more than animal level can completely opt out of offering reasons for his or her beliefs and actions.

1

Confucianism: The Way
of the Sages

No other single figure has had more influence on Chinese thought and civilization than Confucius (551–479 B.C.E.). Little is known for certain about this important figure who came to be regarded as "the teacher" in many periods of Chinese history. He was born into the aristocratic yet poor K'ung family in the state of Lu, now part of the province of Shantung. We are told that as a youth he was orphaned early and was very fond of learning. Later in his life he left his home state of Lu and traveled throughout several regions of China offering his service as an adviser to feudal lords; however, he was never successful at obtaining a position that would allow him to put his ideas into practice and so returned to Lu to devote the remainder of his life to teaching. It is useful to keep this failure in mind while considering certain aspects of his teachings. Confucius became honored in Chinese chronicles as the Great Master K'ung, or K'ung Fu-tzu, better known in the West in the Latinized form "Confucius."

By all accounts the text known as *Lun Yu*—usually rendered into English as *The Analects*—is the most reliable source of Confucius's ideas. The *Analects* consists of scattered sayings of the Master that were compiled by his disciples after his death. It is a matter of scholarly debate whether any or all of the *Analects* can be regarded as the actual words of Confucius, and many will argue that some of the chapters are later additions. Although Confucianism is a complex tradition with a long history of development, the *Analects* gives voice to early and central Confucian ideas that continued to define the tradition for many centuries. Therefore, for the purposes of this introduction, I focus exclusively on the *Analects*, treating the text as a whole, and use the name "Confucius" to refer to the source of the sayings recorded in the *Analects*. Two later developments within Confucianism that pertain to theories of human nature are explored toward the end of this chapter.

THEORY OF THE UNIVERSE

The main emphasis in the *Analects* is on humanism, not metaphysics. That is to say, Confucius was concerned primarily with basic human welfare and spoke little about the ultimate nature of the world in which we live. When once asked about worship of gods and spirits, Confucius replied: "You are not able even to serve man. How can you serve the spirits?" (XI.12). And when asked about death he said: "You do not understand even life. How can you understand death?" (XI.12). Avoiding metaphysical speculation, Confucius instead advocated good government that would promote the well-being of the common people and would bring about harmonious relations among citizens. Confucius did, however, recognize that there are forces in the universe that determine our lives. He characterized these by employing two related meanings of the term *ming*: the Decree of Heaven (*t'ien ming*) and Destiny (*ming*).

Confucius insisted that we live in a moral world. Morality is part of the very fabric of the universe; for Confucius, there is something ultimate and transcendent about ethical conduct. He once remarked: "Heaven is author of the virtue that is in me" (VII.23). The concept of the Decree of Heaven was widely accepted in China during Confucius's day. The Decree of Heaven was generally understood to mean a moral imperative for governance, based on the belief that Heaven cares profoundly about the welfare of the common people. Heaven would support an emperor only so long as he ruled for this higher purpose and not for his own benefit. Confucius added to this doctrine by extending the realm of the heavenly mandate to include every person; now everyone—not just the emperor— was subject to the universal law that obliged one to act morally in order to be in harmony with the Decree of Heaven. Ultimate perfection, then, for Confucius, has to do with cultivating a transcendent morality authored by Heaven. It is possible, however, to resist or disobey the Decree of Heaven.

Nevertheless, there are certain dimensions of life that are beyond human control, areas in which human effort has no effect whatsoever. This indeterminate dimension of human life falls under the heading of Destiny, that aspect of Heaven's design that is beyond human comprehension. One's place in life, social success, wealth, and longevity are all due to Destiny. No amount of struggle will make any difference in their outcome; these things are simply determined by one's fate. Whereas the Decree of Heaven can be understood—although with great difficulty—Destiny is beyond comprehension. The distinction between the Decree of Heaven (to which humans can conform or not) and Destiny (which is beyond human agency) is fundamental for Confucius, for if one understands that the material comforts of life are due to Destiny, one will recognize the futility of pursuing them and will devote all one's effort to the pursuit of Heaven's morality. Morality, then—which has nothing to do with social success—is the only worthy pursuit in life. Confucius argued that it is necessary to understand the nature of both the Decree of Heaven (II.4) and Destiny (XX.3), but for different reasons. The Decree of Heaven is the true object of ultimate concern, whereas Destiny is simply to be accepted courageously.

Before we move on to look at Confucius's views of human nature, it is useful to examine another of his concepts: the Way (*tao*). Although the term *Tao* did come to be used in China as an abstract metaphysical principle (especially by the Taoists), for Confucius it primarily meant the "Way of the sages," those ancient rulers of earlier ideal times. The Confucian concept of the Way is linked intimately to the concept of Heaven in that it involves the path of proper conduct. Although it is difficult to discern, the Way of Heaven can be known through the previous actions of the sages. Regarding the sage Yao, Confucius is recorded as saying: "Great indeed was Yao as a ruler! How lofty! It is Heaven that is great and it was Yao who modeled himself upon it. He was so boundless that the common people were not able to put a name to his virtues" (VIII.19). Accordingly, the ancient sages—who modeled themselves on Heaven—become models of the Way to human perfection in the present, the Way to be followed by all people (VI.17). In the end, three related things warrant reverence according to Confucius. He is recorded as saying: "The gentleman stands in awe of three things. He is in awe of the Decree of Heaven. He is in awe of great men. He is in awe of the words of the sages" (XVI.8).

THEORY OF HUMAN NATURE

Confucius seems to have been very optimistic about potential human accomplishments. In fact, the goal of much of Chinese philosophy is to help people become sages. Confucius's remark that "Heaven is author of the virtue that is in me" demonstrates his conviction that human beings have access to the ultimate reality of Heaven's morality. For Confucius, every person is potentially a sage, defined as one who acts with extreme benevolence (VI.30). That is, all human beings have the capacity to cultivate virtue and bring themselves into harmony with the Decree of Heaven. Confucius indicates that the result of following the Way of Heaven is the subjective experience of joy. Optimism regarding human potential, however, is not the same as optimism about the *actual* state of human affairs. The truth is, Confucius went on to attest, that a sage is a very rare being. He declared: "I have no hopes of meeting a sage" (VII.26). Although all human beings are potential sages, in reality this is an uncommon occurrence. Most human beings exist in a dreadful state.

What is it that enables potential sages to be so misled? Confucius said very little directly about human nature, causing his disciple Tzu-kung to remark: "One can get to hear about the Master's accomplishments, but one cannot get to hear his views on human nature and the Way of Heaven" (V.13). His dearth of statements on human nature allowed widely divergent theories to develop in later Confucianism. Despite his lack of explicit statements about human nature, however, it is clear from Confucius's sayings that in certain areas of life human beings exercise a freedom of will. Although we have no control over our Destiny—we cannot, for example, determine our social status or longevity—we are free to reject or pursue morality and proper conduct. That is, we have the ability to resist or conform to the Decree of Heaven, the very source of virtue. While acknowledging that human beings have no significant choice as to the circumstances of the life they live, Confucius stressed that we do have a choice as to *how* we live in any given situation.

While he did not define human nature in any detail, Confucius insisted that all human beings are fundamentally the same. We simply become differentiated due to our different ways of being. "Men are close to one another by nature. They diverge as a result of repeated practice" (XVII.2). What this means, among other things, is that human beings are extremely malleable. We can become almost anything. We are unfinished and impressible, and in need of constant molding to achieve our ultimate end of moral perfection. In accord with modern sociologists and psychologists, Confucius seems to be suggesting that our environment and ways of being significantly determine our character. Thus his great concern with paradigmatic figures—the sages—and the role they play in shaping the ideal human life. Human life without carefully crafted culture produces disastrous results. The subsequent state of problematic social conditions is taken up in the next section.

Two additional matters are worth mentioning in regard to Confucius's views of human nature. First, the ideal moral figure for Confucius is the "gentleman" (*chun-tzu*). This term is decidedly masculine. While the term might be applied in a manner that includes both genders, it is clear that Confucius used the term in an exclusive way. He has little to say about women, and when he does speak of them he frequently does so in unflattering terms. On one occasion, for example, he lumps them together with "small men" and warns that in one's household both are "difficult to deal with" (XVII.25).

Second, although Confucius informs us that human nature is fundamentally uniform, he does not clarify whether this is a good nature that needs to be guarded carefully or a bad nature that stands in need of serious reform. His lack of specificity on this issue spawned much heated debate in later Confucianism. We see what two major thinkers in the Confucian tradition have had to say about this important issue in the last section of this chapter.

DIAGNOSIS

Although the sayings of Confucius are predominantly prescriptive, they give a clear indication of what is wrong with human life. Generally speaking, the human condition is one of social discord caused by selfishness and ignorance of the past. Stated perhaps more succinctly, human beings are out of accord with the Decree of Heaven. Consequently, human interaction is marred by strife, rulers govern with attention only to personal gain, common people suffer under unjust burdens, and social behavior in general is determined by egoism and greed. Such is the dismal state of human beings.

What are the reasons for these distressing circumstances? At least five causes can be discerned in the *Analects*: (1) people are attached to profit; (2) society lacks the respect of filial piety; (3) the connection between word and action cannot be trusted; (4) ignorance regarding the Way of the sages prevails; and (5) benevolence is absent from human affairs. Let us examine these causes one by one.

Confucius said: "If one is guided by profit in one's actions, one will incur much ill will" (IV.12). One of the central tenets in Confucian thought is the opposition between rightness and profit. "The gentleman understands what is moral. The small man understands what is profitable" (IV.16). Ordinary human behavior is driven by a strong concern for the outcome of a particular action with regard to the self. That is, people typically ask, What will I get out of this action? The common aim in action, then, is a selfish one. Actions are generally performed to increase one's wealth or power. This is what Confucius means by action guided by profit. Even if a person does what is right, if the motivation is a nonmoral purpose—say, to gain rank—that person is still guided by profit. Confucius warns in the *Analects*: "It is shameful to make salary your sole object" (XIV.1). Since he believed that morality should be the sole guide for all action, Confucius contended that action guided by profit leads to immoral circumstances and social disharmony wherein all people are selfishly looking out for themselves alone. Material benefits derived from invested labor are not in themselves bad, but the means by which they are obtained is of critical importance to Confucius. "Wealth and rank attained through immoral means have as much to do with me as passing clouds" (VII.16).

Selfish conduct motivated by personal profit implies a lack of true respect for others in a given society. For Confucius, this lack of respect reveals improper relationships within families, which in turn demonstrates a lack of self-discipline. This occurs because individuals have lost their grounding in morality, leading to problems in the family, which is the very basis of a good society. In this sense, Confucianism is very much a tradition of family values. A son who does not know how to treat his father will be a very poor citizen. Corrupt individuals, then, who have not cultivated the personal virtue necessary for proper familial relationships spread ill will throughout society. On the other hand, "It is rare for a man whose character is such that he is good as a son and obedient as a young man to have the inclination to transgress against his superiors" (I.2).

Another problem noted by Confucius is the fact that there is often a difference between what is said and what is done. Confucius said: "I used to take on trust a man's deeds after having listened to his words. Now having listened to a man's words I go on to observe his deeds" (V.10). Confucius recognizes that people are often untrustworthy. Without a direct connection between word and deed there is no basis for trust, since trust rests on the premise that what is said will be done. Without this basic trust, individuals lose the ability to represent themselves sincerely and to rely on others with any degree of confidence. Accordingly, society loses its footing.

Ignorance of the past is also a major cause of the troublesome human condition. What Confucius means specifically by this is an unfamiliarity with the Way of the sages. It was pointed out earlier that the sages model their lives on Heaven, thereby establishing a paradigm for the path to moral perfection. Without knowledge of the Way of the sages, people are cut off from the moral insight of the past. In such a state they become morally adrift and prone to wrong action. Confucius had so much faith in the Way of the sages that he remarked: "He has not lived in vain who dies the day he is told about the Way" (IV.8).

The most important virtue that a human being can possess for Confucius is benevolence (*jen*). To embody benevolence is to achieve moral perfection. This central Confucian idea is represented by a Chinese character that has been explained pictographically as consisting of two parts:

the component for "human" and the component for "two." That is, it represents two people standing together in harmony. Essentially, benevolence has to do with human relationships. Several scholars have argued that *jen* is better translated into English as "human-heartedness" or "humaneness." Regardless, *jen* is a wide-ranging moral term that represents the very pinnacle of human excellence for Confucius. And, according to him, it is definitely within the reach of human beings. "The Master said, 'Is benevolence really far away? No sooner do I desire it than it is here' " (VII.30). The core of a perfected human being, then, is a benevolent heart. Unfortunately, Confucius observes, this virtue is all too rare in the world: "I have never met a man who finds benevolence attractive" (IV.6). Consequently, potential social harmony is replaced with strife.

PRESCRIPTION

The Confucian prescription for the ills of human existence is based on self-discipline. When questioned about the perfect man, Confucius said: "He cultivates himself and thereby brings peace and security to the people" (XIV.42). The ideal ruler for Confucius rules by personal moral example. But just what does self-cultivation mean in this context? The answer to this question can be found by exploring the proposed solutions to the five ills outlined in the preceding section.

To overcome the human tendency to act out of a concern for profit, Confucius proposed "doing for nothing." Specifically, this involves doing what is right simply because it is morally right, and not for any other reason. For Confucius, the moral struggle is an end in itself; through it, one achieves a union of will with the Decree of Heaven. Acting in order to do what is right, rather than what is profitable, can serve also as a shield against life's disappointments. The state of benevolence is characterized by an inner serenity and equanimity and an indifference to matters of fortune and misfortune over which one has no direct control. Righteousness is its own reward, a joyous reward that transcends any particular social situation. Even if all one's efforts go unrecognized, by following the principle of "doing for nothing" one is never discontented. "Is it not gentlemanly not to take offence when others fail to appreciate your abilities?" (I.1). Furthermore, this principle motivates one to keep working for righteousness in a world that has little appreciation for it. Confucius himself is described as one "who keeps working towards a goal the realization of which he knows to be hopeless" (XIV.38). Faith in the Way of Heaven does not depend on results within the social world of rank and recognition. Remember that Confucius himself failed to secure a political position that would have provided him recognition and allowed him to put his ideas into practice. He says in the *Analects* that a man should strive to enter politics simply because he knows this to be right, even when he is well aware that his principles cannot prevail (XVIII.7). This relates to the notion of Destiny discussed in the first section of this chapter. Social success is a matter of Destiny; Confucius therefore concludes that it is futile to pursue it. Moral integrity, however, is within one's control, and in truth it is the only thing in life worth pursuing. One can struggle to understand the ways of Heaven, but it is clear that one should act humanely whatever Heaven sends. Again, it is the cultivation of self that is important, not social recognition. "The gentleman is troubled by his own lack of ability, not the failure of others to appreciate him" (XV.19).

The cultivation of self as a good family member is another of Confucius's prescriptions for a harmonious society. He believed that being a good family member had tremendous influence beyond the boundary of one's immediate family. "Simply by being a good son and friendly to his brothers a man can exert an influence upon government" (II.21). The transformation of society begins with the cultivation of the self within the environment of the family; it then spreads out like ripples caused from throwing a pebble in a still pond. The rules and relationships that govern the family are to be extended to include all of society. Benevolence toward people outside one's family should be an extension of the love one feels for members of one's own family. The most important relationship of all for Confucius is the one between a son and his father. When questioned about filial piety, Confucius advised: "Never fail to comply" (II.5). The manner in which a good son honors a father is by following his ways. "If [after his father's death], for three years, a man makes no changes to his father's ways, he can be said to be a good son" (I.11). This depends, of course, on the virtuous qualities of the father. Confucius is adamant that the father of the family, or by extension the emperor of the state, must rule by moral example. "If you set an example by being correct, who would dare to remain incorrect?" (XII.17).

Confucius was once asked what would be the first thing he would do if he were put in charge of the administration of a state. He replied: "If something has to be put first, it is, perhaps, the rectification of names" (XIII.3). The rectification of names means that there is an agreement between name and actuality. This correction is necessary, because without the agreement between name and actuality, or between word and deed, much is lost. For Confucius, a name carries certain implications that constitute the very essence of the named object. For example, when asked by a duke about good government, Confucius responded by saying: "Let the ruler be a ruler, the subject a subject, the father a father, the son a son" (XII.11). The concept of "son," for example, as we have just seen, is more than a biological designation. The name implies certain attitudes and responsibilities essential to harmonious existence. Moreover, without the connection between word and actuality there is no genuine trust. This is the definition of a lie. After hearing Confucius's remark on good government, the duke exclaimed: "Splendid! Truly, if the ruler be not a ruler, the subject not a subject, the father not a father, the son not a son, then even if there be grain, would I get to eat it?" That is, the word "grain" and the availability of grain are two different things. If there is no connection between them, then one may go hungry because of a locked, or perhaps even empty, granary. Words are easy to produce; if a person or government uses them to conceal the truth, then social chaos ensues. Trust is a critical ingredient of all dependable social interaction. Therefore, the self-cultivating gentleman is "trustworthy in what he says" (I.7) and "puts his words into actions" (II.13).

The antidote for the ignorance of the past referred to in the preceding section is study. Confucianism is a scholarly tradition. In China it is known as the Ju School—the term *ju* comes to mean "scholar"—and is recorded in Chinese sources as the school that delights in study of the Six Classics (*Lui Yi*). From this it is evident that Confucius placed great emphasis on learning. He advised: "Have the firm faith to devote yourself to learning, and abide to the death in the good way" (VII.13). But what is the content of this learning that allows one to abide in the good way? It is clear from the representation of Confucianism just mentioned that the content of Confucian learning is the Classics, a collection of books that constitutes the cultural legacy of the past. Most important for Confucius, the Classics give expression to the Way of the sages and thus grant access to the exemplary conduct that leads to moral perfection. Because of this, study of the Classics is understood to be a vital element in achieving excellence and a sacred enterprise that expands one's nature. It is also an important aspect of good government. "When a student finds that he can more than cope with his studies, then he takes office" (XIX.13).

Excellence is defined by the Confucian tradition primarily as the embodiment of benevolence. The manner in which one comes to embody benevolence constitutes the last of the five solutions being explored. This process really involves three elements: clinging to benevolence at all times while following the "golden rule" and observing the "rites."

Confucius said: "The gentleman never deserts benevolence, not even for as long as it takes to eat a meal" (IV.5). That is to say, one is to be ever mindful of benevolence in everything one does. The Confucian goal is to let benevolence determine all aspects of life, since it is the perfect virtue that denotes the Decree of Heaven. Confucius himself is described in the *Analects* as one who maintained correctness and benevolence at all times (VII.4). But how is one to know what constitutes benevolence?

The practice of benevolence consists in balanced consideration for others and oneself. One measure of the consideration for others is determined by the treatment one desires for oneself. Confucius says: "A benevolent man helps others to take their stand in so far as he himself wishes to take his stand" (VI.30). In other words, this is the golden rule: "Do unto others what you would have done to yourself." Confucius also states this rule in negative form. When asked to define benevolence, he said: "Do not impose on others what you yourself do not desire" (XII.2). In a general sense, then, one's own self becomes a measure of decent conduct. However, Confucius has more to say about the measure of excellent conduct than this. Even if a person's heart is in the right place, it is possible to offend others because of a lack of knowledge about what is appropriate conduct in a particular situation. Knowledge is a key component to ethical action. Specifically for Confucius, this means knowing ritually correct behavior, or the rites (*li*). These consist of regulations governing action in every aspect of life, as well as ceremonial propriety, such as in making offerings to the ancestors. The rites are designed to teach individuals how to act well and are therefore a critical component in moral education. Knowledge of the rites functions as a guide for action beyond the general decency derived from using one's own self as a measure of conduct. Self-interest must finally be harnessed to the rites in order to achieve moral perfection. "To return to the observance of the rites through overcoming the self constitutes benevolence" (XII.1). Observing these rules, a person transcends self-interest. The rites are a body of rules culled from past moral insights and guide action toward perfection. What are the rites based on, and how does one come to know about them? They are based on the Classics, and one comes to know of them through study. Thus, the interconnectedness of Confucius's ideas comes into focus. Moral perfection, or benevolence, is achieved by following the rites, which are known by studying the Classics, which give expression to the Way of Heaven as embodied by the sages.

Perhaps the most significant passage of all those recorded in the *Analects* is one that gives a summary indication of the path to perfection as it is understood in early Confucianism. "The Master said, 'At fifteen I set my heart on learning; at thirty I took my stand; at forty I came to be free from doubts; at fifty I understood the Decree of Heaven; at sixty my ear was atuned; at seventy I followed my heart's desire without overstepping the line' " (II.4). Here Confucius is saying that at fifteen he took up serious study of the Classics. This gave him access to a knowledge of the Way of the sages and, therefore, an awareness of the rites, the institutional form of their perfect demeanor. At age thirty he was able to take a stand in the rites, or to put the proper conduct of the rites into practice. By practicing the rites, he moved at age forty from mere observation of the rites to true understanding of the rites. This led to a concomitant understanding of the Decree of Heaven by age fifty. At sixty Confucius experienced a union of wills with the Decree of Heaven, so that by age seventy he could follow his own desire—now in harmony with the Decree of Heaven—with the result that he spontaneously acted with perfect benevolence.

Indicated here is the salvific path of paradigmatic action. As perfect beings, the sages naturally act with benevolence. Their benevolence is the external expression of a perfected inner state. As such, their benevolent actions become models of and for perfection for Confucians who desire to achieve the accomplished state of a sage. Again, the Way of the sages is available in the Classics; thus the great attention paid to study in the Confucian tradition. What the sages perform naturally becomes the model for the conscious self-discipline that leads to moral perfection. Proper disciplined action is represented in the Confucian tradition as the rites (*li*). From an outsider's perspective, the natural benevolent action of a sage and of a self-disciplined person who follows the rites appear the same, but the internal motive is different. The sage's behavior is the natural expression of an inner perfected state, whereas the disciplined person's behavior consists of studied actions—the rites—that are modeled on the benevolence of the sages. The goal of disciplined action, however, is to achieve a state wherein perfect moral action becomes natural and spontaneous. This is the state of the "gentleman," and this is what is said to have happened to Confucius toward the end of his life. The sages express moral perfection naturally, whereas the gentleman has achieved perfection by modeling his life on the behavior of the sages. The actions of a gentleman and a disciplined Confucian student may also appear the same from the outside, just as a master musician and a disciplined student appear to be making the same moves. But once again, the motives are different in both cases. The master musician has so internalized the fingering chart of the instrument she is playing that she is no longer conscious of it, whereas the student is still consciously following the fingering chart. Likewise, the gentleman has so internalized the Way of the sages that he now acts spontaneously, whereas the Confucian student who "stands in the rites" consciously follows the proper conduct that the rites represent. In either case, by following the rites, both the gentleman and the diligent student have embodied benevolence, the very pinnacle of moral perfection.

As a paradigmatic tradition, Confucianism produces a chain of perfected moral action that makes the benevolent Way of the sages present for the common people and creates moral examples for those who are not involved in the elite tradition of textual study. It should be clear by now that moral perfection for the Confucian tradition is represented by the sages and that, as the ideal of human perfection, the gentleman has achieved moral perfection by studying the Classics and internalizing the Way of the sages. The Confucian practitioner is ideally moving along this same path. Direct observation of present-day human practitioners takes the place of textual study for those unable to read. To the degree that a practitioner can embody benevolence by following the Confucian rites, the Way of the sages is then present for all of society to observe and to follow. In this way, a line of moral perfection reaches back from the time of the sages and continues into the very present. If all people would follow this Way, Confucius believed, individuals would achieve perfection, society would be radically transformed, and benevolence would rule.

LATER DEVELOPMENTS

Because Confucius did not spell out his views on human nature in any detail, a major debate arose within the tradition soon after his death regarding this question: Is human nature originally good or evil? Opposing answers were supplied by two leading figures in the Confucian tradition. Representing the "idealistic wing," Mencius (371–289 B.C.E.) contended that human nature is originally good; representing the "realistic wing," Hsun-tzu (298–238 B.C.E.) argued that human nature is originally evil. Although we cannot possibly do justice to the entire Confucian tradition here, a brief examination of this debate gives further indication of the complexity of this tradition and adds to our overall consideration of human nature.

The writings and ideas of Mencius rank second in the tradition only to those of Confucius, and, above all, his name is associated with his theory of the original goodness of human nature. In a collection of his sayings recorded in a book that bears his name, Mencius articulates his position on the controversy over human nature that came to be regarded as orthodox for the Confucian tradition and normative for much of Chinese culture. In the *Mencius*, Mencius refutes a philosopher named Kao-tzu, who argues that human nature is intrinsically neither good nor bad and that morality therefore is something that has to be added artificially from the outside. "Human nature," Kao-tzu maintains, "is like whirling water. Give it an outlet in the east and it will flow east; give it an outlet in the west and it will flow west. Human nature does not show any preference for either good or bad just as water does not show any preference for either east or west." Mencius, however, is insistent that human nature is innately good. He counters Kao-tzu by explaining: "It certainly is the case that water does not show any preference for either east or west, but does it show the same indifference to high and low? Human nature is good just as water seeks low ground. There is no man who is not good; there is no water that does not flow downwards" (VI.A.2).

The core of Mencius's theory about innate human nature relates to his understanding of the human heart. For Mencius, the thinking, compassionate heart is a gift from Heaven (VI.A.15). This is what defines our essential humanness and sets us apart from animals. Specifically, the heart is a receptacle of four incipient tendencies or "seeds," as Mencius calls them. He maintains that "Man has these four germs just as he has four limbs" (II.A.6). If unobstructed and nurtured carefully, these seeds sprout into the four virtues so greatly prized by the Confucian tradition, as lofty trees grow naturally from small seeds. The four seeds of compassion, shame, courtesy, and sense of right and wrong develop respectively into the four virtues of benevolence, dutifulness, observance of the rites, and wisdom (II.A.6). And Mencius insists that these four seeds "are not welded on to me from the outside; they are in me originally" (VI.6). For Mencius, our original heart identifies us all as potential sages.

Mencius, however, agrees with many of the philosophers of his time that human beings are creatures of desire. Selfish desire in particular threatens to overwhelm the four seeds that define the source of our higher moral nature. The heavenly gift of the thinking heart is therefore recognized to be fragile and can be lost if not used and cultivated. This, of course, is the norm. Mencius says: "Heaven has not sent down men whose endowment differs so greatly. The difference is due to what ensnares their hearts" (VI.A.7). The ensnarement of the human heart, for Mencius, is the source of all evil; thus the great concern for carefully nurturing its innate qualities. "Given the right nourishment there is nothing that will not grow, and deprived of it there is nothing that will not wither away" (VI.8).

All hope for humanity, according to Mencius, lies in the human heart. Our desiring nature is something we share with all animals, but it is our thinking heart—that special gift from Heaven—that sets us up to be benevolent sages. Mencius offers a proof for the innate goodness of all people. "My reason for saying that no man is devoid of a heart sensitive to the suffering of others is this. Suppose a man were, all of a sudden, to see a young child on the verge of falling into a well. He would certainly be moved to compassion, not because he wanted to get in the good graces of the parents, nor because he wished to win the praise of his fellow villagers or friends, nor yet because he disliked the cry of the child" (II.A.6). What Mencius seems to be saying here is that every person in this situation would have an immediate, spontaneous, and unreflective urge to save the child. This reveals a pure impulse for righteousness over selfish profit. Mencius says nothing about the ensuing action. It may be the case that the man involved would, upon any reflection following the "all of a sudden," engage in calculating thoughts of self-interest. Regardless of what follows, however, the momentary urge indicated in this statement is all Mencius needs to demonstrate what he refers to as the seed of compassion. For him, this proves that human nature is intrinsically good.

Mencius's strongest opponent was Hsun-tzu, an important Confucian writer who was born toward the end of Mencius's life. Hsun-tzu held that our interior world is dominated by dynamic impulses of desire. The basic human problem for Hsun-tzu is that human libidinous urges have no clear limit. Nature has given us unlimited desires in a world with limited resources; hence, social strife arises among necessarily competitive human beings. In a text he composed himself, Hsun-tzu writes: "Man is born with desires. If desires are not satisfied for him, he cannot but seek some means to satisfy them himself. If there are no limits and degrees to his seeking, then he will inevitably fall to wrangling with other men" (section 19, p. 89). This view caused him to formulate a position on human nature diametrically opposed to that of Mencius: "Man's nature is evil; goodness is the result of conscious activity" (section 23, p. 157). Hsun-tzu was well aware of Mencius's ideas but insisted that they were wrong. "Mencius states that man's nature is good, and that evil arises because he loses his original nature. Such a view, I believe, is erroneous" (158). Hsun-tzu replaces Mencius's theory of the four seeds with his own theory of four incipient tendencies for profit, envy, hatred, and desire, which if left in their natural state give rise to the four evils of strife, violence, crime, and wantonness. These, he insists, are innate in all humans, so that the path that follows our own nature leads only to evil. "Any man who follows his nature and indulges his emotions will inevitably become involved in wrangling and strife, will violate the forms and rules of society, and will end as a criminal" (157).

Hsun-tzu goes on to compare the criminal-like human being to a warped piece of wood. "A warped piece of wood must wait until it has been laid against the straightening board, steamed, and forced into shape before it can become straight, because by nature it is warped" (164). Surprisingly, Hsun-tzu is rather optimistic about potential human accomplishments, for he too believed that with the proper education and training all people could become sages. "The man in the street can become a Yu [a sage]" (166). What is it, we might ask, that transforms the warped pieces of wood that are human beings into the straight boards of sages, or at least proper citizens? That is, what constitutes the straightening board for human beings? After his statement about warped wood, Hsun-tzu writes: "Similarly, since man's nature is evil, he must wait for the ordering power of the sage kings and the transforming power of ritual principles; only then can he achieve order and conform to goodness" (164). Hsun-tzu here confirms the absolute value of a fundamental Confucian idea; the straightening board consists of the rites, or what is here translated as "ritual principles." For him, the rites are the products of the sheer intellectual activity of the sages and were designed to curb and channel the boundless desires of human beings. When Hsun-tzu says that "goodness is the result of conscious activity," he means a conscious effort to transform oneself by diligently applying oneself to the rites, those guiding principles created and embodied by past sages. Hsun-tzu is clearly an advocate for culture over nature, for the rites are not an essential part of human nature. Everything that is good is a product of conscious human effort. The fact that we have two arms is natural, but virtue comes only with assiduous human effort. For him, the attentive application of the unnatural rites is the key to achieving human perfection. "In respect to human nature the sage is the same as all other men and does not surpass them; it is only in his conscious activity that he differs from and surpasses other men" (161). The sage, then, for Hsun-tzu, is a human being whose nature has been radically transformed by the Confucian rites.

The contrast between Mencius and Hsun-tzu is dramatic. Mencius believed that morality is naturally present in our hearts, whereas Hsun-tzu believed that it is something artificially instilled from the outside. Nevertheless, we observe an agreement in the ideas of Hsun-tzu and Mencius that identifies them both as Confucians. Both agree that the path to sagehood comprises the Confucian rites, those proper modes of action based on the paradigmatic behavior of past sages. For Hsun-tzu, the rites function as a straightening board to transform warped human beings into straight and benevolent citizens, whereas for Mencius, they function more like a racket press designed to keep a stored wooden tennis racket from warping; although innately present, the heart of compassion can become twisted if not reinforced with the constant observance of the rites. Although the two philosophers disagree sharply in theory, they are in complete agreement regarding practice. Human perfection is achieved through a process of following the paradigmatic actions and insights of past sages.

CRITICAL DISCUSSION

We may conclude this introduction to Confucianism with a few comments designed to bring into sharper focus some possible criticisms already hinted at in our discussion. Besides being a system that is rooted in the common decency of the golden rule, Confucianism is a tradition that teaches obedience to superiors. The relevant superiors are the father of the family, the ruler of the state, and the Confucian scholar who makes accessible the Way of the sages. If the heads of the family and state are just men, then all is well. But if such men are unjust, then the entire system is undermined. Confucius himself was aware of this problem and therefore insistent on the moral character of leaders. Nonetheless, his system gives a great deal of power to a few individuals and leaves the majority in a subordinate position.

Confucianism is also a fairly conservative tradition that looks to the past for guidance. This may be seen as an attitude that restricts the creativity of individuals in the present. This made Confucianism a primary target of attack during the Chinese cultural revolution of the late 1960s and early 1970s. Furthermore, it is a system dependent on an elite of literati, the Confucian scholars. We might ask, Do scholars have access to the past in a manner that is free of their own ideological agendas? Confucianism, it has been shown, is based largely on a transcendent view of morality. It may be argued that such a view is simply a way for a certain group to give special privilege to its own view of morality. We might then ask, Whose view of the past and whose view of morality is Confucianism based on? Most historians today contend that no view of the past is completely neutral or apolitical. All historical representations involve issues of power.

Many people seem to be excluded from the Confucian enterprise. The common people are represented as an undifferentiated and generally inept mass, another problem from the perspective of communist China. Women in particular do not seem to be included in Confucius's educational system. His view of human perfection is decidedly masculine, and all in all he has little to say about the potential of women for self-cultivation. When Confucius does speak about women, he does so in derogatory terms, suggesting that they are generally unruly and resistant to legitimate authority. Although the Confucian path to perfection may be expanded by its advocates to include both genders, the *Analects* poses a problem for readers who believe in the equality of the sexes.

Finally, the pragmatic nature of Confucianism has been criticized by other Chinese philosophers, such as the more metaphysically minded Taoists. The Taoist philosopher Chuang-tzu, for example, criticized the Confucians for their reduction of reality to only that which concerns human social affairs. Chuang-tzu reversed Hsun-tzu's assessment of what is valuable by advocating nature over culture. As a nature mystic aware of the immensity of life in all its forms, Chuang-tzu believed that the Confucians occupied a tragically small world. He also characterized Confucians as people overly concerned with utilitarian matters and countered this preoccupation with a celebration of the usefulness of uselessness. Over the course of time, however, Confucianism has proven to be a much more attractive system to Chinese thinkers for establishing virtuous human society than the more abstract metaphysical thought of Taoism.

Although Confucianism was discredited in China in the early twentieth century by the collapse of the imperial system and was a primary target of the cultural revolution (which identified it with everything that had been wrong with the older system), it has experienced somewhat of a revival, especially since the death of Mao Zedong in 1976. The revival, known as New Confucianism, has been carried out by a group of scholars who aim to modernize Confucianism rather than abandon it altogether. The modernization involves a process of weeding out those aspects of the older Confucian culture that are deemed problematic from a modern perspective, such as the subordination of women. An exemplary figure of this new movement is Tu Weiming, a professor currently at Harvard University who has explored Confucian thought for its application to the contemporary quest for more socially just and ecologically harmonious ways of living. He sees Confucianism as a positive resource for thinking about ways to overcome the destructive side of modernization that threatens both human communities and the natural world. In this new form, Confucianism is once again making significant contributions to considerations concerning the big questions of the day.

FOR FURTHER READING

Basic text: *The Analects* (many translations and editions). I have quoted from the excellent translation by D. C. Lau, *Confucius: The Analects* (London: Penguin, 1979). This is a very readable and reliable text that includes a valuable introduction. Another readily available translation is that by Arthur Waley, *The Analects of Confucius* (New York: Macmillan, 1938; New York: Vintage, 1989).

Mencius: I have quoted from the translation by D. C. Lau, *Mencius* (London: Penguin, 1970). This edition also includes an excellent introduction.

Hsun-tzu: I have quoted from the translation by Burton Watson, *Hsun Tzu: Basic Writings* (New York: Columbia University Press, 1963).

For more on Confucianism, see *Thinking through Confucius* by Roger T. Ames and David L. Hall (Albany: State University of New York Press, 1987).

To gain a better understanding of the place of Confucianism in Chinese philosophy, see *A Short History of Chinese Philosophy* by Fung Yu-lan (New York: Macmillan, 1948; New York: Free Press, 1966); *Disputers of the Tao* by A. C. Graham (Lasalle, Ill.: Open Court, 1989); and *The World of Thought in Ancient China* by Benjamin I. Schwartz (Cambridge, Mass.: Harvard University Press, 1985).

For more on New Confucianism and the writings of Tu Weiming, see *Confucian Thought: Selfhood As Creative Transformation* (Albany: State University of New York Press, 1985).

2

Upanishadic Hinduism: Quest for Ultimate Knowledge

An introductory examination of Hinduism can be very challenging, since there is no founder, no clear historical beginning point nor central text, as we find in most other religious traditions. Hinduism is an extremely diverse tradition that consists of a wide range of practices and beliefs, making the task of generalization nearly impossible. The term "Hinduism" itself is largely a Western construct designed simply to refer to the dominant religion of the majority of the people who inhabit the South Asian subcontinent. Therefore, in many ways, it is absurd to attempt to represent Hinduism with a single text, for no particular text is accepted as authoritative by all people who might identify themselves as Hindus, and many think of their religion as being grounded in a way of action, rather than a written text. Nevertheless, if one were to seek a "foundational text" to represent significant tenets of Hindu philosophy, a good selection would be one of the principal Upanishads. The group of texts known as Upanishads have played a decisive role throughout Hindu religious history; they have defined central philosophical issues in India for centuries and continue to be a major source of inspiration and guidance within the Hindu world today. One of the objectives of this chapter is to give a sense of the wide range of interpretive possibilities that emerge from early Hindu texts, demonstrating specifically how practices as diverse as world renunciation and forms of worship that embrace the world itself as divine are justified by the same texts.

The earliest Upanishads were composed in northern India in the seventh or eighth century B.C.E. The term "Upanishad" means literally to "sit near" but has come to mean "esoteric teaching," for these texts represent secret teachings passed on to groups of close disciples by forest-dwelling meditation masters. The Upanishads, which contain highly speculative thought about the ultimate nature of reality, are among the greatest intellectual creations of the world. Although the Upanishads do not present a single philosophical system but rather give voice to exploratory and often contradictory reflections, their overall theme is one of ontological unity, the belief that everything is radically interconnected. The oldest and largest of the Upanishads is the *Brihad Aranyaka Upanishad* ("The Great and Secret Teachings of the Forest"). This text is not the product of a single author but is a compilation of a number of conversations between teachers and students. The *Brihad Aranyaka Upanishad* has a great deal to say about the ultimate nature of the world and the true identity of human beings, and thus provides a good starting point for exploring important issues within Hindu philosophy.

THEORY OF THE UNIVERSE

We observe in the *Brihad Aranyaka Upanishad* an ardent metaphysical search for the absolute ground of all being. One of the central philosophical tenets of the Upanishads is that there is a single, unifying principle underlying the entire universe. At the level of ultimate realization, the world of multiplicity is revealed to be one of interconnected unity. The attempt to identify that unifying principle can be seen in a famous passage involving the philosopher Gargi Vacaknavi and the great sage Yajnavalkya (3.6). Gargi opens an inquiry into the ultimate nature of the world, challenging Yajnavalkya to identify the very foundation of all existence. She asks the sage: "Since this whole world is woven back and forth on water, on what, then, is water woven back and forth?" Yajnavalkya responds initially: "On air, Gargi." But Gargi is not satisfied with this answer. "On what, then, is air woven back and forth?" Yajnavalkya supplies another answer, and then another, and still another as Gargi presses him to identify increasingly fundamental layers of reality. Finally, the sage reveals to her that the entire universe is woven back and forth on what he calls *"brahman."* At this point he claims that he can go no further; *brahman* is declared to be the end of Gargi's search. Although other entities were suggested as the possible foundation of all being (e.g., space [4.1.1] and water [5.5.1]), these were rejected, as the one ultimate reality and absolute ground of all being came to be identified as *brahman*. *Brahman* was declared to be the highest aim of all metaphysical inquiry: "All the vedic learning that has been acquired is subsumed under '*brahman*' " (1.5.17).

The term *brahman* is derived from a Sanskrit root that means to "grow," "expand," or "increase." Although in early usage it was associated with sacred utterances, over the course of time it came to be identified with the very force that sustains the world. During the time of the Upanishads, it settled into its principal meaning of "ultimate reality," the primary cause of existence, or the absolute ground of being. Brahman was identified as the fine essence that pervades the entire universe. It is the totality of all reality, both manifest and unmanifest. Another famous passage from the *Brihad Aranyaka Upanishad* well portrays the metaphysical quest for the unitary ground of being that ends in *brahman* (3.9.). Since this passage yields keen insight into Hindu theology, I quote it in full.

The passage opens with the searcher Vidagdha Shakalya questioning the sage Yajnavalkya about the number of gods in existence. "How many gods are there?" he asks. Yajnavalkya responds first: "Three and three hundred, and three and three thousand." Not satisfied with this answer Vidagdha continues.

> "Yes, of course," he said, "but really, Yajnavalkya, how many gods are there?"
> "Thirty-three."
> "Yes, of course," he said, "but really, Yajnavalkya, how many gods are there?"
> "Six."
> "Yes, of course," he said, "but really, Yajnavalkya, how many gods are there?"
> "Three."
> "Yes, of course," he said, "but really, Yajnavalkya, how many gods are there?"
> "Two."
> "Yes, of course," he said, "but really, Yajnavalkya, how many gods are there?"
> "One and a half."
> "Yes, of course," he said, "but really, Yajnavalkya, how many gods are there?"
> "One."

When asked by Vidagdha to identify this "one god," Yajnavalkya concludes: "He is called '*brahman*'."

Although divinity expresses itself in multiple forms, ultimately it is One. Here again, we witness philosophical inquiry into the ultimate nature of reality that ends with the discovery of the single unifying principle called *brahman*. But if reality is one, how—and why—did it become many? Creation stories maintained by any tradition tell us much about that tradition. We find in the *Brihad Aranyaka Upanishad* an account of creation that provides answers to these questions and serves as a model for much Hindu thought.

"In the beginning there was nothing" (1.2.1). Yet a great deal can come from nothing, for much of the Hindu tradition holds that the entire universe came out of this original nothingness. Like the modern "Big Bang" theory, this text describes an expansion from an original dimensionless point of infinite unity; yet, unlike the Big Bang theory, this account of creation tells us *why* the expansion occurred.

In the beginning there was nothing but the single unitary principle, *brahman*. However, because it was alone, it was lonely and "found no pleasure at all" (1.4.2). In this state of loneliness, it desired another and so divided itself into two parts, a male and a female. Departing from the original state of abstract neutrality, the male and female pair began to interact sexually, and from this was born the entire universe of diverse forms. Thus, the original point of undifferentiated unity divided itself and, exploding outward, produced the phenomenal world of multiple forms. The *Brihad Aranyaka Upanishad* calls this "*brahman*'s super-creation" (1.4.6). This account of creation expresses the true nature of reality and the ultimate aim of beings within that reality. We will have occasion to refer to this story later, but the important point is to realize that it accounts for the multiplicity of the world, while recognizing in a fundamental way the radical interconnectedness of the world. The original unity is never lost; it simply takes on the appearance of multiple forms.

This theory of the origin of the universe recognizes the simultaneity of unity and diversity. The One reality differentiates itself through what the text calls "name and visible appearance" (1.4.7). The world we experience with our senses, then, is a single reality, though it is clothed with a variety of names and appearances. This is aptly expressed in the following verse:

> The world there is full;
> The world here is full;
> Fullness from fullness proceeds.
> After taking fully from the full,
> It still remains completely full. (5.1.1)

Here we have a portrait of divinity that is simultaneously immanent and transcendent. *Brahman* is not only *in* the world, it *is* the world; there is also a dimension of *brahman* that is completely beyond the world of multiple forms. This is asserted in the *Brihad Aranyaka Upanishad* as a teaching about the two aspects (*rupa*) of *brahman* as the form and the formless: "the one has a fixed shape (*murta*), and the other is without a fixed shape (*amurta*)" (2.3.1). *Brahman* as all forms is everything that is solid and transitory, whereas *brahman* as the formless is ethereal and unchanging. A good way to approach this philosophy is to reflect on the double meaning of the phrase "Nothing ever remains the same." The world of concrete things is in constant flux and always changing; things never remain the same. On the other hand, the no-thingness from which all comes is eternal and unchanging; it ever remains the same. It is important to remember, however, that these are not two separate realities but the same reality seen from different perspectives. The world of forms is pervaded by the unified *brahman* as salt pervades the water in which it is dissolved: "It is like this. When a chunk of salt is thrown in water, it dissolves into that very water, and it cannot be picked up in any way. Yet, from whichever place one may take a sip, the salt is there! In the same way this Immense Being has no limit or boundary and is a single mass of perception" (2.4.12).

Before we move on to examine what the *Brihad Aranyaka Upanishad* has to say about human nature, one additional important point should be mentioned. Several passages insist that *brahman* is inexpressible and therefore impossible to define. We are told, for example, that "it is neither coarse nor fine; it is neither short nor long; it has neither blood nor fat; it is without shadow or darkness; it is without air or space; it is without contact; it has no taste or smell; it is without sight or hearing; it is without speech or mind; it is without energy, breath, or mouth, it is beyond measure; it has nothing within or outside of it; it does not eat anything; and no one eats it" (3.8.8). That is, *brahman* is completely beyond the world we experience with our senses. This is often expressed in the text by saying that *brahman* is "not this, not that (*neti neti*)."

On the other hand, there are passages that identify *brahman* with everything we experience with our senses: "Clearly, this self is *brahman*— this self that is made of perception, made of mind, made of sight, made of breath, made of hearing, made of earth, made of water, made of wind, made of space, made of light and the lightless, made of desire and the desireless, made of anger and the angerless, made of righteous and the unrighteous; this self is made of everything" (4.4.5). In direct contrast to the "not this, not that" view, this passage continues: "He's made of this. He's made of that." These two different ways of describing *brahman* led to divergent understandings of the world and the self, which in turn resulted in significant differences in religious practice. Two of the most important interpretations of the Upanishads are explored in the final section of this chapter.

THEORY OF HUMAN NATURE

The recognition that all of life is interconnected has clear implications for a theory of human nature. According to the *Brihad Aranyaka Upanishad*, our kin are not only fellow human beings but all other beings as well. This text teaches that the essential self of a human being is radically connected to all beings: "The self within all is this self of yours" (3.5.1). The ultimate self—referred to in the Upanishads by the term "*atman*"—is not, therefore, an autonomous unit operating independent of other beings but rather a part of this larger interrelated network of reality. "This very self [*atman*] is the lord and king of all beings. As all the spokes are fastened to the hub and the rim of a wheel, so to one's self are fastened all beings, all the gods, all the worlds, all the breaths, and all these bodies" (2.5.15). The text makes it very clear that the true self not only animates all beings but is inseparable from the whole of reality (2.5.1–14). The self is all, and all is the self.

The Upanishads certainly recognize a self that is transitory and separate from other selves. That is, the self as ego (*ahamkara*) is identified with the body and its social environment. This is the self we immediately think of when someone asks us who we are. This is also the self we ordinarily invest with great meaning and strive to preserve. This, however, is neither the ultimate self nor the true identity of a human being. The essential self is defined as the *atman*. Our ordinary self is simply a finite, conditioned mask covering our true and infinite nature.

Some passages in the *Brihad Aranyaka Upanishad* suggest that the *atman* is undefinable; it is not to be identified with anything: "About this self (*atman*), one can only say 'not—, not —.' He is ungraspable, for he cannot be grasped. He is undecaying, for he is not subject to decay. He has nothing sticking to him, for he does not stick to anything. He is not bound; yet he neither trembles in fear nor suffers injury" (3.9.28). Other passages, however, identify the *atman* with everything: "Clearly, this self is *brahman*—this self that is made of perception, made of mind, made of sight, made of breath, made of hearing, made of earth, made of water, made of wind, made of space, made of light and the lightless, made of desire and the desireless; this self is made of everything. Hence there is this saying: 'He's made of this. He's made of that'" (4.4.5). Note the seemingly contradictory nature of these two statements, which might be used to support very different notions of the self and the world. In either case, the text goes on to define the *atman* as the immortal, unchanging self; it "is beyond hunger and thirst, sorrow and delusion, old age and death" (3.5.1).

A central teaching of the Upanishads is that the true self is that eternal dimension of reality that is somehow not different from the highest reality of *brahman*: "And this is the immense and unborn self, unageing, undying, immortal, free from fear—the *brahman*" (4.4.24). Since the *atman* is identified with *brahman*, it too is defined as the very source of all life, the root of all existence: "As a spider sends forth its thread, and as tiny sparks spring forth from a fire, so indeed do all the vital functions, all the worlds, all the gods, and all beings spring from this self [*atman*]. Its hidden name is: 'The real behind the real,' for the real consists of the vital functions, and the self is the real behind the vital functions" (2.1.19). In sum, the *Brihad Aranyaka Upanishad* teaches that one's essential self transcends individuality, limitation, suffering, and death.

Another common designation we find for the *atman* is that it is the "inner controller" of all life (3.7.2–23). This designation is connected to perhaps the most notable characterization of the *atman* we find in the *Brihad Aranyaka Upanishad*. The *atman* is not an ordinary object of consciousness but rather the subject of consciousness, or the silent witness of consciousness. The *atman* is the knower of all knowledge, or the "perceiver of perception." "When, however, the Whole has become one's very self [*atman*], then who is there for one to smell and by what means? Who is there for one to see and by what means? Who is there for one to hear and by what means? Who is there for one to greet and by what means? Who is there for one to think of and by what means? Who is there for one to perceive and by what means? By what means can one perceive him by means of whom one perceives this whole world? Look—by what means can one perceive the perceiver?" (2.4.14). As the perceiver of perception, the *atman* is not an object of consciousness and therefore cannot be known in any ordinary way, for it is declared to be consciousness itself. Although there is a great deal of similarity between Upanishadic Hinduism and early Buddhism, many Buddhists tend to reject the idea that consciousness is identical to an essential self. Nonetheless, the Upanishads identified our true self as that which enables us to be conscious beings, namely all-pervasive consciousness. The primary aim of the Upanishads is to bring about a shift in identity from the transient ego self associated with the body to the eternal and infinite self that is not different from the All. In other words, the goal is to realize that the *atman* is *brahman*, although the task of delineating the details of this equation was left to later writers.

According to the Upanishads, our present life is just one in a long, long series of death and rebirth. When our present life ends, we are reborn in a new body. "It is like this. As a caterpillar, when it comes to the tip of a blade of grass, reaches out to a new foothold and draws itself onto it, so the self [*atman*], after it has knocked down this body and rendered it unconscious, reaches out to a new foothold and draws itself onto it" (4.3.3). That is, as a caterpillar moves from one blade of grass to another, so we move from one body to another. Although some later philosophers insisted that it is a different type of self that constitutes the individual self that undergoes reincarnation, reincarnation seems to have been assumed in the Upanishads.

Informed by this assumption, two paths are outlined in the *Brihad Aranyaka Upanishad* as possible postdeath experiences (6.2.15–16). The first option is the path of return to this life. After death, people's bodies are placed on the cremation fire. Those who performed religious sacrifices designed to enhance worldly life pass into the smoke. From the smoke, they pass into the night and eventually end up in the world of the ancestors. From there they pass into the moon, where they are turned into the rain, by which they return to the earth. Reaching the earth, they become food. The food is eaten by a man and then offered in the fire of a woman, where people take birth once again. This is the ongoing cycle of death and rebirth that defines life for most people. Enjoyment of the cycles of existence is presented here in a positive light.

There is another path, however, for the forest-dwelling meditation masters who have achieved the highest knowledge. After death, these are placed on the cremation fire and pass into the flames. From the flames, they pass into the day and eventually reach the world of the gods. From there they pass into the sun. The sun in much Hindu mythology represents the doorway out of this world, and, indeed, we are told that those who achieve the highest knowledge go on from the sun to reach the world of *brahman*, from which they never return to worldly life. This is one of the earliest representations of *moksha*, or "liberation" from the ongoing cycle of death and rebirth. Although these two paths are presented simply as the two postdeath possibilities in the *Brihad Aranyaka Upanishad*, some later Upanishads insist that the path of no return is far superior to the path of return. According to the more ascetic Upanishads, return to this world is an indication of one's failure to achieve ultimate knowledge of one's self. A very special kind of knowledge, then, is declared to be the culmination of a successful human life.

DIAGNOSIS

The main problem with human existence is that we are ignorant of the true nature of reality. "Pitiful is the man, Gargi, who departs from this world without knowing this imperishable" (3.8.10). We see from this statement that all success rests on knowing the imperishable *brahman*, of which we are a part. It is extremely difficult to know, however, since it is that "which sees but can't be seen; which hears but can't be heard; which thinks but can't be thought of; which perceives but can't be perceived. Besides this imperishable, there is no one that sees, no one that hears, no one that thinks, and no one that perceives" (3.8.11). Without knowledge of the unified and infinite *brahman*, one perceives only the ordinary objects of consciousness and therefore suffers the fate of identifying completely with the dying world of fragmentary and transitory forms. "With the mind alone must one behold it—there is here nothing diverse at all! From death to death he goes who sees here any kind of diversity" (4.4.19).

Ignorance of the true nature of reality is tantamount to ignorance of the true nature of our own selves. Or, stated in different terms, the human predicament consists of a severe identity problem: we don't know who we really are. We identify ourselves with the fragmented, seemingly disconnected phenomenal world of diversity, instead of with the One *brahman*. We are creatures of infinity stuck in highly conditioned and finite personalities. While in reality we are kin to the immense universe, we spend our lives overwhelmed and blinded by the limited projects of our own ego. The result of this is alienation: from others, from the very source of life, from the One, and even from our own true self. The human condition is thus an ongoing experience of fragmentation, isolation, and loneliness. Consequently, our social worlds are riddled with crime and hostile conflict, informed by belief in our own individuality, and we are plagued with existential anxiety, rooted in an investment in the disconnected, transitory self.

The life of the lone individual is anything but free, according to the Upanishads. Life grounded in the belief in a separate self is heavily conditioned and determined. The determining factors are identified as *karma* in the *Brihad Aranyaka Upanishad*, the first text to mention this concept so important to later Hindu thought. The sage Yajnavalkya talks about *karma* in this way: "What a man turns out to be depends on how he acts and on how he conducts himself. If his actions are good, he will turn into something good. If his actions are bad, he will turn into something bad. A man turns into something good by good action and into something bad by bad action" (4.4.5). Ordinary human life, informed by the belief in an autonomous self, is revealed to be highly contingent, conditioned by forces determined by previous actions. Yajnavalkya continues: "A man resolves in accordance with his desire, acts in accordance with his resolve, and turns out to be in accordance with his action." What this means is that we are psychologically programmed in such a way that under normal circumstances free action is impossible. We act out of desire, which itself is the result of some prior action recorded in the unconscious mind. That desire manifests itself as a resolve for action. The subsequent action leaves an impression in the mind, which then goes on to determine the nature of another desire, the root of future action. Here, then, is a picture of the human predicament as a cycle of psychological bondage. A great deal of Hindu yoga and meditation aims to free us from this limited and conditioned state.

PRESCRIPTION

The Upanishads are generally optimistic about the possibility of attaining ultimate freedom. The *Brihad Aranyaka Upanishad*, however, does not outline a single prescriptive path. A major task of later systematic writers was to articulate a coherent interpretation of this and other Upanishads and to delineate a specific path leading to the ultimate state that those texts describe. As we shall see, the divergent interpretations that emerged differed greatly about the nature of the world and the self.

Generally speaking, the Upanishadic path to freedom involves acquiring a special kind of knowledge. Ordinary knowledge will not cut the chains of our bondage. "Into blind darkness they enter, people who worship ignorance; And into still blinder darkness, people who delight in learning" (4.4.10). The Upanishadic texts do not disparage all learning but rather sound a note of caution about the limits of conventional knowledge. What this passage seems to be saying is that it is dangerous to rely too heavily on ordinary knowledge. Ordinary information is fine for operating in the conventional world of multiple forms; however, it is worthless for knowing the ultimate nature of reality and the self.

The *Brihad Aranyaka Upanishad* makes it clear that one must finally let go of any attachment to ordinary ways of knowing. The text tells us that one "should stop being a pundit and try to live like a child. When he has stopped living like a child or a pundit, he becomes a sage" (3.5.1). That is, after gaining significant exposure to the scriptures and becoming an expert in the scholarly sense, one should abandon any reliance on learning and try to return to the simple and spontaneous state of a child. This still, however, does not give clear indication of how one is to achieve ultimate knowledge and freedom. Only in very general terms does the *Brihad Aranyaka Upanishad* recommend a path of withdrawing from ordinary ways of being and meditating continually on the *atman*. This vagueness is characteristic not only of this text but of other Upanishads as well. It remained for later commentators to spell out in detail exactly what the final state involves and how it can be attained.

DIVERGENT INTERPRETATIONS

One of the greatest disagreements within Hinduism occurs between those who view ultimate reality as an impersonal absolute and those who emphasize a personal relationship with ultimate reality. (A concomitant question is: Is the world ultimately real or not?) Not surprisingly, these two radically different stances have led to widely divergent interpretations of the *Brihad Aranyaka Upanishad*. A complete introduction to later Hinduism would involve a description of an expansive array of religious practices, including domestic rites, temple rituals, pilgrimages, yogic discipline, and so forth, as well as the beliefs that inform these diverse practices. Although such a task is impossible within the limitations of this chapter, the ideas of two leading figures from the Hindu tradition—Shankara and Ramanuja—are examined to indicate the wide range of practices and beliefs that are included under the rubric of Hinduism. Both are identified as Vedanta philosophers, where "Vedanta" means literally the "end of the Vedas," that is, the culmination of the revealed books of wisdom known as the Vedas. This term is taken primarily to refer to the teachings of the Upanishads but also includes the *Bhagavad Gita* and the *Brahma Sutra*. Although there are also schools of Hindu philosophy that are not Vedanta, Shankara and Ramanuja represent two of the most influential schools of Hindu thought and practice. Since both Shankara and Ramanuja wrote commentaries on the *Brahma Sutra*, a text that further investigates the concept of *brahman* introduced in the Upanishads, we can use these two works to explore this fundamental divergence in interpretation.

Shankara's Advaita Vedanta

Shankara (788–820) is one of the best-known Hindu philosophers in India and in the West. Although his philosophical system of Advaita ("Non-Dualism") informs the activities of only a small minority of Hindus and has tended to overly dominate Western understandings of Hinduism, it represents an important philosophical position within the Hindu world and constitutes one of the most popular rationalizations for the act of religious renunciation.

What does it mean to know *brahman*? Perhaps the most pressing question that remained from Upanishadic speculation was: What is the relationship between the ultimate reality of *brahman* and the world of multiplicity we experience with our senses? A concomitant question arose: What is the status of a personal God and the individual soul? Shankara was one of the first Indian philosophers to formulate a consistent and singular viewpoint based on the Upanishads that addressed these important questions. His is a philosophy of unity that ultimately devalues all diversity. For Shankara, *brahman* is the only truth, the world is ultimately unreal, and the distinction between God and the individual soul is only an illusion.

Brahman, for Shankara, is the sole reality. It is the absolute undifferentiated reality, one without a second (*advaita*) and devoid of any specific qualities (*nirguna*). Since he understands the highest realization of *brahman* to be a state in which all distinctions between subject and object are obliterated, he concludes that the world of diversity must finally be false. Shankara recognizes that the Upanishads speak of two aspects of *brahman*, one with qualities (*saguna*) and one without (*nirguna*), but he maintains that the former is simply the result of perception conditioned by limiting factors. "Brahman is known in two aspects—one as possessed of the limiting adjunct constituted by the diversities of the universe which is a modification of name and form, and the other devoid of all conditioning factors and opposed to the earlier" (1.1.12). In fact, Shankara claims that all apparent distinctions within *brahman* are the result of the superimposition of the frames of reference of the viewer. This brings us to one of the most important concepts in his philosophy: the theory of illusion, or "*maya*." *Maya* is the process by which the world of multiplicity comes into being; it is the force by which the formless takes form. *Maya* both conceals and distorts the true reality of *brahman* and is manifest epistemologically as ignorance (*avidya*). Its workings cannot be explained in words, since language itself is a product of *maya*. Since all diversity is finally false for Shankara, *maya* is the major obstacle to the highest realization of ultimate knowledge.

What this means is that the world we experience with our senses is not *brahman* and therefore not ultimately real: "The senses naturally comprehend objects, and not Brahman" (1.1.2). By this Shankara certainly does not mean that the world is a figment of our imagination. He was a staunch opponent of subjective idealism. For him the world has an apparent reality; that is, it is existentially real. He writes: "It cannot be asserted that external things do not exist. Why? Because they are perceived. As a matter of fact such things as a pillar, a wall, a pot, a cloth, are perceived along with each act of cognition. And it cannot be that the very thing perceived is non-existent" (2.2.28). Shankara does recognize the category of the nonexistent and gives as a stock example "the son of a barren woman." Our world, on the other hand, has an apparent reality, and in this sense it "exists." However, since the experience of the world is devalued by the ultimate experience of *brahman* in which all distinctions are obliterated, it cannot be the absolute reality. Just as the contents of a dream are devalued upon waking, so too the experience of the world is devalued upon the waking of ultimate enlightenment. The stock example used to explain this is the snake and the rope. A person erroneously perceives a rope to be a snake in dim light. The fear that the person subsequently feels is real enough, existentially. However, when the light of knowledge illuminates the "snake," it is discovered to be a rope all along. The snake was merely superimposed onto the rope, giving the snake an apparent reality. So too—as the illustration is applied—the world and *brahman*. The world of multiplicity is ordinarily superimposed onto the nondual *brahman*, with the result that we live in an illusory world. The experience of the world, however, is revealed to be false in the ultimate knowledge of *brahman*. This theory allows philosophers to disassociate the problematic world from the true reality, just as reflections of the moon in various pots of water are finally disassociated from the moon.

The same argument is applied to two other important differentiated entities: the personal God and the individual soul. Shankara defines the personal God as *brahman* with attributes. But since all attributes are the product of the limiting factors of ignorance, God, too, is finally declared to be an illusion. Worship of the personal God, however, is highly beneficial, for although God is not the highest reality, it is the highest reality conceivable for creatures still enmeshed in the cosmic illusion of *maya*. That is, the personal God is a necessary component of spiritual experience, since it provides a transition between the world and *brahman* for those who are still attached to the world. In the end, however, one must give up this sense of separateness and reintegrate all gods back into one's self.

A related concept for Shankara is the individual soul (*jiva*). By now it should be clear that all diversity for Shankara is considered to be the result of illusory perception, so it will come as no surprise to learn that he ultimately rejects the individual soul as illusory. Although the *jiva*, or individual soul, involves a higher level of realization than the ego-identity associated with the body, in the final analysis it, too, is unreal. The true self for Shankara is the *atman*, defined as pure consciousness. Like the world and God, the individual soul is merely an apparent reality, whose appearance is the result of viewing the self through the limiting factors of ignorance. He writes that the self "is endowed with eternal consciousness, . . . it is only the supreme Brahman Itself, which while remaining immutable, appears to exist as an individual soul owing to association with limiting adjuncts" (2.3.18). Though in everyday experiences we feel ourselves to be agents of our own actions, this, too, is an illusion. This means that the true self is eternally free from the conditioning effects of *karma*; to be free one needs only to realize that bondage is a mental construct. Shankara also maintains that the self is beyond all experience, since this involves a difference between the experiencer and that which is experienced. Therefore, at the highest level of realization, the individual soul, the subject of all experience, disappears as an illusion; the true self is declared to be identical with *brahman*, the absolute unified ground of being.

The goal of all spiritual endeavor for Shankara is the realization of this ultimate fact. The highest level of the knowledge of *brahman* involves the obliteration of all distinctions between the knowing subject and all known objects in the state of absolute identity. A favored metaphor for the ultimate experience so conceived is the reemergence of all drops of water back into the single undifferentiated ocean. This is how Shankara interprets the Upanishadic quest for ultimate knowledge.

But what are the essential components of a path designed to accomplish this ultimate feat? In the first section of this chapter we encountered the *Brihad Aranyaka Upanishad*'s creation myth, which recounts how the world of multiple forms came into being out of desire, a desire for another. The essential element in the story for Shankara is the unity that preceeds the diversity produced by desire. Since desire is associated with the creative force that divides the original oneness, eradicating desire is a necessary step toward the process of reunification. This brings us to the idea of renunciation. The highest spiritual path, according to Shankara, consists of a meditative practice designed to lead one to the insightful realization that "I am *brahman*." He calls the practice of meditating on and realizing the true self "*samadhi*." An important prerequisite to this practice, however, is a withdrawal from ordinary social and domestic activities and a retreat from our ordinary investment in the data of the senses. That is, one of the most prominent consequences of Shankara's theory is the move toward the practice of world renunciation. Shankara is credited with founding an important order of renouncers (*sannyasis*) known as the Dashanamis. These are men who embark on the path by performing their own funeral rite, thereby indicating the end of their former identity and the beginning of full-time participation in a celibate religious community and meditation on *brahman* as the impersonal absolute.

Ramanuja's Vishishta Advaita Vedanta

Diametrically opposed to the views of Shankara is the perspective of those Hindus—especially the Vaishnavas (worshippers of God in the form of Lord Vishnu)—for whom the personal nature of the divine is an ultimate attitude and not an illusion to be transcended. One of Shankara's most determined and well-known opponents was Ramanuja (1017–1137), an important theologian and chief interpreter of Vedanta for the southern Indian devotional movement known as Shri Vaishnavism. His philosophical system is designated Vishishta Advaita ("Non-Dualism of the Differentiated"), since it takes differentiated things to be real, and understands them to be attributes of a nondual reality. Ramanuja's philosophy values both unity and multiplicity, a stance that results in a very different view of the nature of God, the world, and the self.

In his commentary on the *Brahma Sutra*, Ramanuja criticizes Shankara for his refusal to acknowledge any qualities or distinctions in the nondual reality of *brahman*. Like Shankara, Ramanuja accepts the Upanishadic assertion that *brahman* is the sole reality; however, for him, *brahman* means God, who is endowed with innumerable excellent qualities. "The word 'Brahman' primarily denotes that supreme Person who is the abode of all auspicious qualities to an infinite degree and is free from all worldly taint. This supreme Person is the only Being the knowledge of whose real nature results in liberation" (1.1.1, p. 1). Thus Ramanuja does not make a distinction between *brahman* and God, as does Shankara. Rather, Ramanuja interprets Upanishadic descriptions of *brahman* as "without qualities" to mean the absence of certain kinds of qualities: qualities that are negative or binding. In effect, he reverses Shankara's privileging of *brahman* without qualities (*nirguna*), arguing that *brahman* with qualities (*saguna*) is the higher form. Specifically, Ramanuja resists Shankara's conceptualization of *brahman* as pure undifferentiated consciousness, contending that if this were true, any knowledge of *brahman* would be impossible, since all knowledge depends on a differentiated "object." "Brahman cannot be, as the Advaitins say, non-differentiated pure Consciousness, for no proof can be adduced to establish non-differentiated objects" (1.1.1, pp. 19–20).

The particular kind of experience for which we should aim, according to Ramanuja, is a blissful knowledge of *brahman* as the Lord with infinite and amazing qualities or, stated more simply, the love of God. But for this relationship to be possible, there must be a distinction between the knowing subject or the one who loves (the individual soul), and the known object or the beloved (the Lord). Many of the devotional theologians within Hinduism remark that they do not want to become sugar (Shankara's goal); instead, they want the blissful experience of tasting sugar (Ramanuja's goal). This means that difference must be taken seriously, and this implies a very different picture of the world of sense experience than the one we encountered in Shankara's Advaita system.

The world is real, for Ramanuja, and was created out of God's desire to become manifold. That is, the world is the result of a real transformation of *brahman*. The stock example used to explain this viewpoint is the transformation of curds from milk. Curds that are produced from processing milk are both different and nondifferent from their source. This view is more widely accepted by Hindus than is Shankara's view that the world is ultimately an illusion. It implies that the creative process that resulted in multiplicity is not finally to be overcome but rather is to be appreciated for what it truly is, the product of God's creative activity. Like Shankara, Ramanuja connects the desire of the one to become many with the concept of *maya*, but instead of conceptualizing *maya* as "illusion," as does Shankara, Ramanuja takes it to be the "creative power" of God. "The word Maya does not mean unreal or false but that power which is capable of producing wonderful effects" (1.1.1, p. 73). The world, then, is viewed in a much more positive light, and in fact Ramanuja goes on to characterize it as the "body of God." He maintains that *brahman* "is the creator, preserver, and destroyer of this universe, which It pervades and of which It is the inner Ruler. The entire world, sentient and insentient, forms its body" (1.1.1, p. 55). That is, the conditioned and transitory world is an attribute of the unconditioned and eternal God, as the transitory body is an attribute of the eternal soul. The world is therefore different from God, yet it is also inseparably connected to God, as an attribute is connected to its substance.

This is also the case with the individual soul (*jiva*). It, too, is considered to be part of the body of God, and it is in this manner that Ramanuja interprets the Upanishadic identity of *brahman* and the true self. Whereas Shankara ultimately characterized the individual soul as a false illusion, for in his view all distinction is obliterated in the final experience of *brahman*, Ramanuja maintains that it is real and eternal. As a part of *brahman*, the soul is both different and nondifferent from the whole (2.3.42, p. 298). The world of matter and individual souls enters into God at the time of dissolution and separates from God at the time of creation. Rejecting Shankara's claim that the true self is pure consciousness beyond all experience, Ramanuja maintains that the true self is a special enjoyer of experience (2.3.20, p. 285). In its highest state, it is the eternal, blissful knower of *brahman*.

The path to freedom and the blissful experience of *brahman* is well represented in the following passage. "This bondage can be destroyed only through Knowledge, i.e., through the Knowledge that Brahman is the inner ruler different from souls and matter. This Knowledge is attained through the Grace of the Lord pleased by the due performance of the daily duties prescribed for different castes and stages of life, duties performed not with the idea of attaining any results but with the idea of propitiating the Lord" (1.1.1, p. 80). Far from renouncing the world of action, a very particular way of acting is indicated here that is linked to the *karma-yoga* of the *Bhagavad Gita*, the other major Vedanta text. *Bhagavad Gita* 2.47 states that one in pursuit of ultimate liberation should act in a manner that avoids both an attachment to the results of action and the abandonment of action. That is, as a path of action, *karma-yoga* is situated between two modes of behavior current in Hindu religion. On the one hand, the path of Vedic sacrifice—and ordinary action, for that matter—is a mode of action wherein the act is performed with a controlling concern for the outcome of the action. Why, after all, do we do anything if it is not for the result we expect to achieve by performing the act? Much religious activity follows the same logic; a religious act such as Vedic sacrifice is performed to obtain some desired result. In accord with the *Bhagavad Gita*, however, Ramanuja holds that such action reveals a fundamental ignorance and serves only to bind us further. Life, according to Ramanuja, is a cosmic play (*lila*), wherein God is the ultimate Playwright (2.1.33, p. 237). The ordinary human urge to control the outcome of all our actions is tantamount to an effort to usurp the role of the Playwright. Moreover, insisting on a particular outcome of action in a world everabundant as *brahman* is like walking into an extraordinary store filled with an amazing assortment of candies with a fixed desire for a certain kind of candy bar, one that, as it turns out, happens not to be there. The result is suffering and bondage in a potentially wonderful situation. What, then, to do? The answer certainly does not lie in abandoning all action, for that is the other mode of behavior to be avoided. Following the *Bhagavad Gita*, Ramanuja insists that one should engage in the action that comes to one according to one's own life situation. World renunciation is simply another attempt to establish control and cannot lead us to the state of blissful enjoyment. Instead, Ramanuja advises us to surrender completely to God, for only then are we free to enjoy the marvelous show that is the world. Whereas Shankara renounces the world, Ramanuja demonstrates how to live in it freely.

Although Ramanuja has little to say about the worship of concrete forms of God in his commentary on the *Brahma Sutra*, he belongs to a devotional community in which this type of meditation is the central religious practice. Acts directed to pleasing the Lord instead of one's egoistic self are often enacted in the context of worship of concrete forms or bodies of God, either in a temple or at a home shrine. Informed by such texts as the *Brihad Aranyaka Upanishad*'s conversation wherein Vidagdha asked Yajnavalkya how many gods there are, these concrete forms are considered to be multiple forms of a single, nondual divinity. *Brahman* is understood to be fully present in these special bodies, which are limited forms of the infinite that God compassionately assumes for the purpose of granting accessibility to embodied human beings with ordinary senses. The limited forms are like the defining frame placed around certain works of art that serve to allow focused perception of something that might have otherwise been missed. A great deal of Hindu practice involves the loving service of such concrete forms of God. Whereas Shankara saw these acts as preliminary to the higher business of *samadhi* meditation, for Ramanuja, loving acts directed toward God are supreme. Loving devotion implies a very different attitude toward human emotions than we observe in Shankara. Since the world is real for Ramanuja, everything in it—including human emotions—can be used as fuel for the spiritual life.

The goal of such devotional acts is a kind of union with God, wherein the liberated soul lives in the loving presence of the Lord but does not dissolve into undifferentiated oneness with Him. This is often conceived of in Vaishnavism as an eternal and blissful existence in God's heavenly abode of Vaikuntha. Here "the released self abides as an enjoyer of the supreme Brahman" (4.4.20, p. 493).

We observe, then, two radically different religious sensibilities arising from—or at least being justified by—the same Upanishadic texts. For Shankara the nondualism of the *Brihad Aranyaka Upanishad* means that the world of multiplicity and everything connected with it is, in the final analysis, an illusion. With the dawn of true consciousness, the world, the individual self, and even God are revealed to be unreal. Participation in the ordinary world, then, is viewed as a hindrance to the highest spiritual life. The consequence of this view is a religious life that values world re-nunciation and is suspicious of anything based on ordinary human senses. Ramanuja, on the other hand, interpreted the nondualism of the *Brihad Aranyaka Upanishad* to mean that there is a single cause to everything but that the multiple effects of that single cause are real. Ultimate reality is understood to be God as the Inner Controller of the manifold world and the individual soul. The consequence of this position is a religious life of devotional activity that views the world positively and uses the or-dinary senses to pursue a blissful experience of the differentiated *brahman*. Although world-renouncers can still be found in almost all religious centers in India today, devotional practices in temples and home shrines dominate the Hindu tradition.

CRITICAL DISCUSSION

The Vedanta philosophy represented by Shankara and Ramanuja is a tex-tual tradition. What this means specifically is that Vedanta philosophers—though they insist that the final proof of anything must be experience—rely heavily on scriptures such as the *Brihad Aranyaka Upanishad*, which they take to be authoritative. Many philosophers today would not accept scripture as a reliable source of truth. Moreover, Vedanta philosophy rests on the transcendental claims of the Upanishads, repre-sented by the concept of *brahman*. Obviously, this too makes it suspect for secular philosophers, for whom the idea of transcendence is highly problematic. This is, after all, what makes Vedanta a "religious" philos-ophy. The philosophical traditions of India differ from many of those in the West on this exact point, for much of Hindu philosophy is intended to be of practical assistance to spiritual experience.

In contrast to many of the other theories represented in this book, Vedanta philosophy appears to have little to say about social and politi-cal struggles and reforms or about practical morality. Although some recent defenders of Vedanta philosophy have denied this accusation, it holds a certain amount of truth. The writings of Vedanta philosophers are preoccupied with achieving a higher knowledge and freedom and with metaphysical concerns regarding the nature of ultimate reality, the world, and the self. *Brahman* for Shankara, for example, has little to do with the ordinary world and transcends all normative distinctions, and the true self is beyond the categories of good and evil. It should be pointed out, however, that Shankara insists that there are moral consequences of all actions for people living in the conditioned world of *maya*. Selfless, compassionate acts erode false boundaries and lead to higher realization, whereas egoistic, violent acts reinforce false boundaries and lead to further bondage. Moreover, although in theory Ramanuja's system values the world, sometimes in practice it is the case that worldly particulars are valued only so far as they lead to the knowledge of God, and not in themselves.

Although women participate actively in the metaphysical discussions of the *Brihad Aranyaka Upanishad*, and although there is no textual evidence to suggest that they were in any way excluded from the higher goals expressed in that text, women are excluded from Shankara's order of renouncers and are never allowed to serve as temple priests in Ramanuja's tradition of Shri Vaishnavism. Although Ramanuja opened his tradition to women and the lower classes, Vedanta philosophy in general, and Shankara's school in particular, tends to be very elitist. It requires a knowledgeable religious practitioner who is well educated in scripture, at least in its expectations for the highest realization. In classical Indian society, this deters all but those who occupy the upper classes. Those denied such preparation by birth are likewise often denied the opportunity for the highest achievement—at least in this lifetime.

FOR FURTHER READING

Basic Text: *Brihad Aranyaka Upanishad* (many translations and editions). All quotations are from the translation by Patrick Olivelle, *Upanisads* (New York: Oxford University Press, 1996). This is a very readable and reliable text that includes a valuable introduction. Other readily available translations are those by Robert E. Hume, *The Thirteen Principal Upanishads* (New York: Oxford University Press, 1971), and by R. C. Zaehner in *Hindu Scriptures* (New York: Knopf, 1966).

Shankara's commentary on the *Brahma Sutra*: Few reliable translations exist. I have quoted from one of the most available English translations: Swami Gambhirananda, *Brahma-Sutra-Bhasya of Sri Shankaracarya* (Calcutta: Advaita Ashrama, 1977).

Ramanuja's commentary on the *Brahma Sutra*: Few reliable translations exist. I have quoted from one of the most available English translations: Swami Vireswarananda and Swami Adidevananda, *Brahma-Sutras, Sri Bhasya* (Calcutta: Advaita Ashrama, 1978).

For an overall introduction to Indian philosophy, see M. Hiriyanna, *Outlines of Indian Philosophy* (Bombay: George Allen & Unwin, 1973).

For more on the philosophy of the Upanishads, see Paul Deussen, *The Philosophy of the Upanishads* (New York: Dover, 1966).

For more on the *Brahma Sutra*, see S. Radhakrishnan, *The Brahma Sutra: The Philosophy of Spiritual Life* (London: George Allen & Unwin, 1960).

For more on Shankara's Advaita Vedanta, see Eliot Deutsch, *Advaita Vedanta: A Philosophical Reconstruction* (Honolulu: University Press of Hawaii, 1969).

For more on Ramanuja's Vishishta Advaita Vedanta, see John Carman, *The Theology of Ramanuja* (New Haven: Yale University Press, 1974).

For more on the worship of concrete forms of divinity within Hinduism, see Diana Eck, *Darsan: Seeing the Divine Image in India* (New York: Columbia University Press, 1996).

3

The Bible: Humanity in Relation to God

This chapter will examine ideas about human nature and destiny in the Bible. The Hebrew Bible, or Old Testament, consists of a variety of writings—creation stories, histories of the Jewish people, their ancestry and laws, the Psalms and wisdom literature, and the prophetic writings—dating from about the eleventh century to the second century B.C.E. It is recognized as the authoritative Word of God by both Jews and Christians. The much shorter New Testament, mostly written in the first century C.E., is distinctive of Christianity and not accepted by Judaism. I will therefore treat these separately. (Quotations will be from the Revised English Bible.)

In both testaments there was a complex historical process by which certain texts became recognized as religiously authoritative and worthy of inclusion in "the canon" of sacred scripture. There was some disagreement about *which* texts should count as canonical; and even now the status of the Old Testament Apocrypha remains disputed.

Judaism as it exists today as a world religion has developed not only from the Hebrew Bible but from the Rabbinic tradition that compiled the Talmud from about the second century C.E. (*after* the birth of Christianity). I will not attempt to deal with post-Talmudic Judaism, but will confine my attention to the Hebrew Bible.

Christianity has had a continuous and complex history of development since the first century C.E., through the early Church Councils that formulated the Creeds, the emergence of the Papacy, the schism between Rome and Orthodoxy in the eleventh century, the Reformation in the sixteenth century, and the many more developments and splits that followed. And we should not forget the early versions of Christianity, which never came within the Papal ambit and which still survive in the Coptic churches of the Middle East, Africa, and India. I will not attempt to deal with all this, but will concentrate on the text of the New Testament.

The third great monotheistic world religion of Semitic origin is Islam, which originated in the Arabian peninsula with the visions of the prophet Muhammed in the seventh century. Islam recognizes as forbears Abraham and the succession of Old Testament prophets leading up to Jesus, but claims that Muhammed is the last and greatest of the prophets and that the Qu'ran is the uniquely authoritative message of God ("Allah"). But it would take another chapter, and different expertise from mine, to do justice to Islam.

There are obvious problems in interpreting and assessing ideas from the Bible. On the one hand, believers (of one tradition or another) treat it as sacred text, as revealing the nature and will of God Himself; some treat every sentence as infallibly authoritative, and many appeal to it for ethical guidance. Judaism and Christianity (like Hinduism, and Confucianism in traditional Chinese society) are not mere theories; they are living religions that interpret and guide the lives of their adherents. They are not attributable to a single thinker (Moses is not now believed to be the author of the Pentateuch, the first five books of the Hebrew Bible; Jesus is central to Christianity, of course, but even if he can be credited with many of the sayings attributed to him in the Gospels, he did not leave any writings, though St. Paul certainly did). And Judaism and Christianity have developed notoriously diverse and rival versions.

On the other hand, there has developed, especially over the last two centuries, a great body of expertise in the ancient languages of Hebrew, Aramaic, and Greek, and in the archaeology, history, and sociology of the communities that produced the biblical texts, so that there is now a huge industry of academic study and interpretation. The texts are of different dates, written and edited by different hands, produced and used for different purposes. And, of course, they have been used by theologians down the centuries to support rather different theological positions. To say there is a Judeo-Christian belief in X, a Hebrew conception of Y, or a New Testament view of Z is to risk oversimplification.

It will be impossible to please everyone—the believers with their various versions of faith and the scholars with their academic controversies.

There cannot be such a thing as an objective, neutral approach to the Bible, innocent of all preconceptions. So it is perfectly fair for the reader of this chapter to ask where I am "coming from," what my preconceptions are likely to be. All right then: I was brought up in an Anglican home, but started to question the fundamentals. Converted to an evangelical form of Christianity as a student, I soon began to diverge from it and came to think of myself as an atheist for the next quarter-century or so. Then I sampled the Quaker approach and was attracted by the faith's spirituality and ethical/social commitment without dogma or creed, so I joined the Religious Society of Friends, which understands Christianity as "not a notion, but a way."

In this chapter I will first examine the background "theory of the universe" that is common to Judaism and Christianity (and Islam), namely, the monotheist conception of God. We can hardly avoid this eternally debated topic here, but I will attempt only a brief review of it, for my main agenda is with the Hebrew and Christian conceptions of human nature. I will examine these in turn, under the headings of theory, diagnosis, and prescription. I will suggest a distinction between "spiritual" and "supernatural" versions of Christianity, and I will touch on some of the difficulties that face the latter.

METAPHYSICAL BACKGROUND: THE JUDEO-CHRISTIAN CONCEPTION OF GOD

The opening three chapters of Genesis, the first book of the Hebrew Bible, tell of the divine creation of the whole world, including human beings. The story continues with the descendants of Adam (Chs. 4–5), the flood and Noah's ark (Chs. 6–9), Noah's descendants and the tower of Babel (Chs. 10–11). All this is told as *universal* human history. God's call of Abram to become the ancestor (renamed Abraham) of His chosen people, the Jews, begins at Chapter 12, and all the rest of the Hebrew Bible relates to the subsequent history of "the children of Israel."

Let us consider how God is represented in the opening universal chapters. In Genesis 1–2:3 the Hebrew word for God is *elohim*, a plural form, whereas in the second version of the creation story in 2:4 ff. God is also referred to as "JHWH," a singular form (with consonants only, usually read as "Jahweh"). Scholars have concluded that the book of Genesis has been put together from at least two sources. The text we have, whatever people may believe about its ultimately divine inspiration, is surely a result of human editorial processes long ago. In these early chapters, then, the English translation with the proper name "God" may be misleading, for it is not clear that the conception invoked is of a single superhuman person. The opening verses might be translated as "In the beginning the gods (or the divine powers) created the heavens and the earth. . . . "

God (or the divine powers, but it is simpler to carry on with the singular form) is represented as uttering words of command, such as "Let there be light," which are immediately fulfilled. It sounds as if God does not need to physically do anything in order to create—He does not get His hands dirty (if He has hands at all!)—He just gives the command and the result follows. In the traditional interpretation, God creates *ex nihilo,* he does not work on preexisting material like Plato's demiurge in the *Timaeus,* but calls everything into existence in the first place. The Hebrew God is a language user: He has conceptions of things before they come into existence and He gives new names to things when they exist ("God called the dry land earth," 1:10, etc.). It is as if God is the mental or conceptual power behind everything. However, some verses do represent God as physically acting on matter, for example, "God . . . separated the water under the vault from the water above it . . . " (1:7), so there is some ambiguity on this point.

At each stage of creation, God "saw that it was good" (1:10, etc.). He is represented as making judgments of value, not arbitrarily choosing what is to be called "good," but recognizing, in what He has created, the application of a preexisting, objective standard of value. The point is reinforced at the end of the sixth "day" of creation, when God "saw all that he had made, and it was very good" (1:31). There is a fundamental point made here about the intrinsic goodness of all that exists, including human beings (at least, before the Fall).

However, things soon go wrong. In Chapter 3 we are told of the first human disobedience by Eve and Adam; in Chapter 4 Cain murders his brother; and in 6:5–7 God bitterly regrets His creation of human beings because of their great wickedness, and angrily (vengefully?) resolves to wipe out not just humans, but all living things—until Noah finds favor in His eyes and is allowed to save his family and other animals (6:8–9:19). God is represented as moodily changing His mind, first about the worthwhileness of the whole business of creation, then about His decision to extinguish the human race (6:7). This characterization hardly fits with later theological conceptions of God as omnipotent, omniscient, and perfectly good!

In the preceding fragment (Genesis 6:1–4), there is an intriguing reference to "the sons of the gods" having intercourse with human females and to "the Nephilim" (apparently a race of giants) being on the earth in those days. This confirms that the text is a compilation of several ancient stories containing different conceptions of the divine.

In subsequent books, God is frequently represented as *speaking* to individual people: to Adam and Eve (Genesis 2–3), to Noah (6:13), to

Abraham (12:1 ff., 22:1 ff.), to Jacob (31:3), repeatedly to Moses (notably from the burning bush, Exodus 3:4 ff., and when delivering the Ten Commandments on Mount Sinai, Exodus 31, 34), to Joshua (Joshua 1:1 ff.), to Samuel (1 Samuel 3:4 ff.), to Elijah (1 Kings 17:2 ff., 19:13), and to Job (Job 38:1). Typically, God tells individuals what action to take in their circumstances. Moses is represented as having a particularly intimate relationship with God, talking with him face to face, as one man speaks to another (Exodus 33:11); yet Moses was afraid to look at God (3:6) and, later, he is not allowed to see God's face (33:20)—note the implication that God is (in principle) visible and has a face! More usually, God is represented as having a voice, but not a body or a locatable spatial presence (although Job is said to *see* God with his own eyes, Job 42:5).

The Psalms are a collection of prayers, typically addressed to God. They are poetic in form, and some of what they say about God obviously has to be taken as metaphorical: for example, God as "a shield" (Psalm 3:3), the heavens as "the work of His fingers" (8:3), "the Lord's throne in heaven" (11:4), "the Lord is my lofty crag" (18:2), "smoke went up from his nostrils . . . he flew on the back of a cherub . . . he loosed arrows, he sped them far and wide" (18:8–14), "the Lord is my shepherd . . . you have richly anointed my head with oil" (23:1–5), and so on. But with much else of the talk of God, it is not clear whether we should take it metaphorically or literally, for example, the Lord's anger may flare up in a moment (Psalm 2:12), "he answers from his holy mountain" (3:4), he has "heard my weeping" (6:8), "the Lord passes sentence on the nations" (7:8), "it is God who girds me with strength" (18:32), "you are he who brought me from the womb" (22:9), and so on.

By the time of the prophets (the books of Isaiah, Jeremiah, and those that follow), God is usually represented as speaking through an intermediary—the prophet who has a vision (Isaiah 1:1) or receives the word of the Lord (Jeremiah 1:4 ff.) and then delivers the message to the people using phrases like "Thus says the Lord. . . . " Typically, the prophets foretell what is about to happen and interpret the events of human history—past, present, and future—in terms of God's will. Predictions of invasion and destruction, of enslavement and exile, and of return, rebuilding, and restitution are expressed in terms of God's purposes, whether punishment for disobedience, disloyalty, and sin or merciful forgiveness.

In the so-called wisdom literature, such as Proverbs, Ecclesiastes, and (in the Apocrypha) the Wisdom of Solomon, there is noticeably less explicit talk of God. Scholars detect Egyptian or Greek influences in these writings, but the first two, at least, are generally accepted as part of the Old Testament canon. "The fear of the Lord is the foundation of knowledge," we are told at the beginning of Proverbs (1:7), but the rest of the book hardly mentions Him. In The Wisdom of Solomon, wisdom is personified, almost deified—and in female gender: "The spirit of wisdom is kindly towards mortals . . . " (1:6) ". . . Like a fine mist she rises from the power of God . . . She is but one, yet can do all things . . . age after age, she enters into holy souls" (7:25–27). We will say that such talk of wisdom is personification (like the personification of "Aphrodite" as the goddess of love in Greek thought, or of "Virtue" as a female person in poetry and paintings). But what about the talk of God? Is it also personification, a mere figure of speech? (Put the opposite way, though, is wisdom any less real than God? Wisdom is often noticeable by its absence, but in some people its presence can be recognized.)

In the third edition of this book, I wrote that God can hardly be treated as a mere symbol in the Bible, that much else may be poetry, parable, symbol, allegory, or myth—but not God Himself, who is obviously conceived of as the supreme Reality. Now I am not so sure. Where should we draw the line between symbolic or metaphorical talk of God and realistic, literal talk of Him? When God is described as having a face, nostrils, breath, arms, hands, and fingers, contemporary believers take all that as metaphor, poetry, or picture-thinking. They tell us that God does not have a body. Artists like Michelangelo and William Blake painted God as a bearded European man of a certain age (and thereby exerted a stranglehold over our imaginings that still persists), but theologians now say those are mere pictorial images and that anyone who thinks *that* is the sort of God that the Judeo-Christian tradition believes in is missing the point. (We may feel some sympathy with the forbidding of graven images at Exodus 20:4 and with the Islamic ban on representational art.)

We are typically told that the biblical God is not supposed to be, or to have, a material body. He is not one object among others in the universe, He does not occupy a position in space, or last for a certain length of time. Nor is He to be identified with the whole universe, the sum total of everything that exists—that is pantheism, not theism. God is said to be transcendent as well as immanent: although in some sense present everywhere and all the time, He is also thought of as beyond the world of things in space and time (Psalm 90:2, Romans 1:20). God is not supposed to be like the unobservable entities (atoms, electrons, magnetism, quarks, superstrings, etc.) that scientific theory invokes to explain what we can observe through our senses: He is not a scientific postulate. The existence and actions of God are surely not empirical hypotheses to be tested by observation and experiment.

Yet God is not a mere abstraction like numbers, shapes, and the other objects of mathematics. He is supposed to be a personal Being who creates us, loves us, gives us guidance, enters into agreements or covenants with individuals or nations, judges us, and may redeem or save us. So, although lacking a body, He is still thought of as *a person*, a superhuman mind endowed with intelligence, knowledge, desires, and purposes; capable of anger, love, and forgiveness; of intentions, actions, and some kinds of intervention in the world, whether by "speaking" to people in their minds or perhaps more directly by miraculous exertion of His omnipotent power to change the course of physical events. But His significance is at least as much moral as cosmological: belief in Him is supposed to affect how we conceive of ourselves and how we ought to live.

Much thought and debate, both at the popular level and at more intellectual levels, have assumed that the traditional biblical talk of God has to be interpreted realistically, at face value, as implying the existence of a superhuman person. If He is not an embodied person (that, we agree, is too crude and makes the mistake of taking metaphors literally), then we have to think of Him as a *dis*embodied person with superhuman properties of omniscience, omnipotence, and total benevolence—a conception of someone who is greater and better than anything or anyone we can conceive of (as Anselm put it).

But this conception runs the risk of avoiding empirical falsification at the cost of metaphysical obscurity. Can we really make sense of the notion of a disembodied person, especially one with those idealized superlative properties? Of course we can utter the relevant *words*, and seem to understand something by them. But what is meant by the claim that there *exists* such a supernormal person? It is not, we agreed, an empirical hypothesis that might even yet be confirmed or disconfirmed by some new, esoteric bits of scientific evidence (though there are still some who tend to take it that way). What, then, is the point of the speech-act of asserting this metaphysical claim?

This is not a book about the philosophy of religion and the main business of this chapter is the biblical account of human nature. I can only leave the reader with the suggestion that there is a nonliteral, less naively realist way of interpreting the biblical talk of God, taking it as an overarching picture or metaphor—or perhaps a recipe for generating many metaphors. It provides a scheme of interpretation that many people, from biblical times to the present day, have found helpful, useful, or illuminating in the effort to understand and express their experience of life— its ups and downs, its delights and disasters, its loves and hates, its moral failures, its illuminations, and its new possibilities. Others, however, have discarded the theistic scheme of interpretation or have never used it. Perhaps the difference between theism and atheism is not so much a question of metaphysical fact concerning the existence of a supernormal but incorporeal person, but rather a question of how helpful, useful, and il-

luminating a person finds theistic figures of speech in talking about life—
and the answer can be a matter of degree.

THE HEBREW THEORY OF HUMAN NATURE

The Hebrew conception of humanity sees us as existing primarily in relation to God, who has created us to occupy a special position in the universe: God said "Let us make human beings in our image, after our
likeness, to have dominion over . . . all wild animals . . . " (Genesis 1:26).
The question immediately arises whether we should read this story literally, as narrating historical events that occurred at some specific time in
the distant past, or as mythology, which may poetically express important truths about the human condition, but not at the level of history or
science. Probably the original writers, editors, readers, and listeners did
not make any such distinction, but it is a question we cannot avoid now.

Two large difficulties face any attempt to see literal truth here. One is
that the text itself displays internal inconsistencies, for there are *two* stories of the creation of human beings in Genesis, each of which gives an
entirely different account at several points, most notably on the creation
of woman. The first story has God creating men and women simultaneously, and in the plural (1:27). The second story has God first creating a
single man (2:7), then fashioning a woman out of a rib taken from the
man (2:22).

The other difficulty, of course, is the inconsistency of the literal text
with the results of science—specifically cosmology, geology, and evolutionary biology—which give different accounts of the origin of the material universe in the Big Bang; the formation of galaxies, stars, and the solar
system; the origin of seas, continents, and atmosphere; and the eventual
evolution of humans from lower forms of life. There is even a contradiction with common sense, for how did Cain (elder son of Adam and Eve)
find a wife (4:17), if *all* humans are descended from that first couple?

I propose that only symbolic readings of the creation stories can be
taken seriously. It is now widely—though not universally—accepted that
they are myths (perhaps symbolic of deep religious truths), so there need
be no incompatibility with science. Anyone who asserts the historical existence of Adam and Eve as the unique ancestors of all humanity is in
my view insisting on an overly literal interpretation of scripture.

What can it mean to say that we are made in the image of God? The
believer will say that human beings are unique in that we have something
of the rationality and personhood of God. But that statement can be turned
around to say that our conception of the perfect rationality and moral personhood of God is an idealization from our own imperfect rationality and

morality. We can agree that we are (imperfectly) rational beings and that we are also persons, we have self-consciousness, freedom of choice, and the capacity for loving personal relationships, as well as the capacity for hatred and vice.

What can it mean to say that human beings are made to have dominion over the rest of creation? We have (for better or for worse) a certain degree of power over nature: at the time of Genesis, people in the Middle East were already domesticating animals and growing food by agriculture, they had passed beyond the hunter-gatherer stage.

Although human beings are thus seen as having a special role compared to the rest of creation, we are also seen as continuous with nature. The first human was made of "dust from the ground" (Genesis 2:7), that is, of the same matter that composes the rest of the world. "God breathed into his nostrils the breath of life." (Are we to take *that* literally? Does God breathe?!) It is a recurring *mis*interpretation of the biblical account of human nature that it involves a distinction between material body and immaterial soul or spirit. The Hebrew word translated as spirit, *ruach*, also means wind or breath and need not be interpreted as referring to a separable Platonic soul, but rather the property or function of being alive, perhaps more like Aristotle's nonsubstantial conception of soul (see Chapter 5). Dualism of body and soul is a Platonic idea that is *not* to be found in the Old Testament (or in the New). Nowadays we are so influenced by the distinction between body and soul that we have inherited from Plato and Descartes that we tend to read it into the Bible, although it is not really to be found there.

According to the biblical conception, we are *persons*, importantly different both from inanimate matter and from other animals. Our personhood, however, does not involve the possession of an immaterial entity detachable from the body. There is no firm expectation of life after death expressed in the Hebrew Bible. The Jews did not develop any belief in an afterlife until shortly before the time of Jesus, and even then they did not agree about it (the Gospels mention the Sadducees, who denied the idea of resurrection).

The relation of women to men in the Hebrew scheme of things is somewhat ambiguous from the start. As we have seen, one creation story suggests equality of the sexes, while the second implies that the male is the primary form of humanity. Moreover, in the story of human disobedience, "the Fall," the woman is represented as first giving in to temptation and then persuading her husband to do the same (Genesis 3:6). Ever since, there has been a tendency to see women as somehow more subject to sin and as tempting men to sin. And there is an early association of sexuality with sin, because as soon as Adam and Even disobey God's prohibition, "the eyes of both of them were opened, and they knew that they were naked; so they stitched fig-leaves together and made themselves loincloths" (3:7). As punishment for disobedience, God decrees, *inter alia*, that wife will desire her husband, but he will be "master" of her (3:16). In the stories of Abraham and his descendants, there is a tremendous emphasis on the importance of producing *male* heirs (typical of many human cultures to the present day). And, of course, God Himself is almost always described in masculine terms.

Probably the most crucial point in the biblical understanding of human nature is the notion of freedom, conceived of as the choice between obedience to God's will, faith in Him, love for Him, or disobedience, faithlessness, and pride. The necessity for choice between obedience or disobedience, good and evil, is presented in Genesis 2:16–17, where God forbids Adam to eat from the tree of knowledge of good and evil. (But why should knowledge of good and evil be a *bad* thing, one wonders? Isn't it precisely what one would expect of human maturity? Perhaps the thought is that there is a primeval stage of innocence, before moral distinctions are understood, in early childhood—and maybe also in early human evolution.)

Greek thought puts great store in the intellect, our ability to attain knowledge of truth (including moral truth); the highest fulfilment of human life was thought by Plato and Aristotle to be attainable only by those who are able to gain such rational knowledge. The Judeo-Christian tradition, in contrast, puts the emphasis on human goodness, a matter of basic attitude—of "heart" or will rather than mind or intellect—which is something open to all, independent of intellectual ability.

There is thus a democratic impetus, an ideal of the equality of all finite human beings before God, implicit in the Bible. (Though it can, of course, be questioned how well Jewish and Christian practice has lived up to this ideal.) The concern with human goodness is not just with right action: it is at least as much with the foundation in human character and personality from which such actions will flow. And, in a way, it goes beyond the conceptions of human virtue offered by Plato and Aristotle, for the biblical writers see the only firm foundation for human goodness as faith in the transcendent yet personal God. The idea is that God created us for fellowship with Himself, so we fulfill the purpose of our life only when we love and serve our Creator.

There are various dramatic exemplifications in the Old Testament of this ultimate requirement of obedient submission to God rather than use of the intellect to reason things out and make one's own judgments about truth and morality. One is in the story of Abraham being commanded by God to sacrifice his only son Isaac (Genesis 22). God rewards Abraham for being a "godfearing" man, ready to give up even his own child in response to divine requirement; so God promises that he will be the patriarch of innumerable descendants. A different response to the situation would be to reject any such killing of an innocent child as immoral and to conclude that any such "command" could not really come from a good, loving God. Even if it was only given as "a test of faith," what sort of God would play such a trick? A more anthropological interpretation is that this story shows the early Jewish tradition rejecting the practice of child sacrifice prevalent in some neighboring religious cultures.

Another famous case of faith being preferred to reason is in the book of Job, where Job and his interlocutors struggle with the problem of undeserved suffering. Job is a blameless and godfearing man, but Satan persuades God to test Job by letting him be subjected to catastrophic losses and afflictions (Job Chs. 1–2). Despite all the efforts of Job's would-be comforters, no reasoned explanation of his suffering is offered (Chs. 3–37). In the end, God Himself simply appears, asserts His power and authority, and Job submits (Chs. 38–42). The answer, such as it is, seems to lie in adopting the appropriate attitude of humility before God (or fate, or the laws and accidents of nature) rather than in attaining some kind of intellectual insight.

DIAGNOSIS: HUMAN DISOBEDIENCE

Given this picture of humanity as made by God, the diagnosis of what is basically wrong with humankind follows. We misuse our God-given freewill, we choose evil rather than good, we are infected with sin, and we therefore disrupt our relationship to God (Isaiah 59:2). But the Fall need not be thought of as a particular historical event: the story of Adam and Eve eating the forbidden fruit can be read as a symbol of the fact that although we are free, there is a fatal flaw in our nature that makes us liable to sinful misuse of our freedom.

Genesis 3:14–19 represents certain familiar features of human life as results of the Fall—punishments imposed by God for disobedience—such as the necessity to work to get food, the pain of childbirth, and even death itself. We can all wish for a life in which these things were not necessary, and we may fantasize about a primeval Eden or a heavenly Paradise after death, in which there is no tension between inclination and necessity, desire and duty. It seems odd, however, to conceive of these fundamental biological features of life as the result of human moral failings.

Identifications and condemnations of human sinfulness recur throughout the Old Testament. Cain and Abel, the two sons of Adam and Eve, begin the fratricidal history of humanity when Cain murders his brother.

In Genesis 6:5–7, God regrets His creation of human kind—until Noah finds favor. In Genesis 11:1–9 God is depicted as confusing the original single language of humanity because humankind was growing too proud and had tried to build the tower of Babel up to the heavens.

Throughout the subsequent history of the children of Israel there are repeated prophetic denunciations of their disloyalty and unfaithfulness to God, pride, sinfulness, selfishness, injustice (see Exodus 32, Numbers 25, 1 Samuel 19, 2 Samuel 11, Isaiah, Jeremiah, Amos, etc.).

PRESCRIPTION: GOD'S COVENANTS AND REGENERATION

The Hebrew prescription is based on God, just as much as the theory and diagnosis. If God has made us for fellowship with Himself, and if we have turned away and broken our relationship to Him, then we need God to forgive us and restore the relationship. Hence the idea of salvation, of a regeneration of humanity made possible by the mercy, forgiveness, and love of God. In the Old Testament, we find the recurring theme of a "covenant," a quasi-legal agreement like that between a powerful conqueror and a subject state, made between God and His chosen people. One covenant was with Noah (Genesis 9:1–17), another with Abraham (Genesis 17), and the third, most important, covenant is with the "children of Israel" led by Moses, by which God redeems them from their bondage in Egypt and promises that they will be His people if they keep His commandments (Exodus 19).

But none of these covenants seems to be totally effective: sin does not disappear from the face of the earth (nor has it still, we may want to add!). There is even a danger of spiritual pride, if a nation conceives of itself as comprising "God's chosen people" and feels justified in conquering and oppressing its neighbors. The Hebrew Bible records genocide by the children of Israel as they took over "the Promised Land," and God is even represented as ordering it (Joshua Chs. 8–11). There is a tension between the exclusive tribalism—worshipping Jahweh as the God of Israel as opposed to the gods of other peoples—that characterizes the early stories of the deliverance from Egypt and the conquest of Canaan, and the later, universal tendency—worshipping the God of *all* humankind—that appears in the prophets ("I have formed you, and destined you to be a light for peoples," Isaiah 49:8).

When the people failed to obey God's commandments and laws, there arose the prophetic idea of God using the events of history, especially defeat by neighboring nations, to punish them for their sin. But there is also a promise of God's merciful forgiveness, and His regeneration of not just the people of Israel, but the whole of creation. The second Isaiah, in particular, uses ecstatic language (unforgettably set to music in Handel's *Messiah*) to express this vision of God's forgiveness, redemption, and new creation: "Then will the glory of the Lord be revealed, and all mankind will see it" (40:5); "You will go out with joy and be led forth in peace, before you mountains and hills will break into cries of joy. . . ." (55:12); "See, I am creating new heavens and a new earth!" (65:17). Thus the hope arose amongst Judaism for the coming of a God-appointed savior, "the Messiah," which Christians identify in Jesus.

THE NEW TESTAMENT

The Jewish rabbi, or religious teacher, Jesus of Nazareth did not write anything—nothing that we know of, anyway. Like Socrates (see Chapter 4), Jesus exerted a magnetic personal influence on his disciples and interlocutors, and an indirect influence down the centuries through the writings of his followers. The new religion of Christianity developed out of their reactions to his life, teachings, crucifixion, and alleged resurrection. The first Christian documents were letters ("Epistles") of St. Paul (and others) to the early Christian communities. Most of these are reckoned to predate the compilation, between 70 and 100 C.E., of the four Gospel narratives of Jesus' life and death.

For Christians, the coming of Jesus changed their conceptions both of God and of human nature. The God of the Old Testament now became for them God the Father, and Jesus is identified as somehow embodying or instantiating God, or being one with God (John 10:38), so that he can be described as "God the Son." The threefold Christian conception is completed with the recognition of God the Holy Spirit (anticipated as far back as Genesis 1:2, but powerfully experienced by the apostles on the day of Pentecost, according to Acts 2:1–5). All this was later summed up in the paradoxical formulation of the doctrine of the Trinity: "three persons in one God."

Because of the enormous influence of Christianity in Western civilization down to our own time, the word "Christian" is often used in honorific ways. Until recently, it was shocking or foolhardy to declare oneself *not* a Christian (in some circles, it still is). But what *are* we to mean by the word? What criteria does someone have to satisfy to count as a Christian? And why is this question regarded as so important? Surely its importance relates to a cultural inheritance that has been widespread in the West: an assumption that "we" are Christian and that we need to define what Christianity is to distinguish ourselves from others. (Notoriously, further divisions are made when various brands of Christianity differentiate themselves from rivals.)

Whatever connotations the term "Christian" has come to have, it at least involves some theological claim about Jesus. To be a Christian, it is hardly enough to say that Jesus was a supremely good man or a person of great spiritual insight—for atheists and members of other faiths may say such things. The most central Christian claim is that there was a unique revelation of God in this particular historical figure, a person who lived, preached, and was crucified in Roman-occupied Palestine in the first century. This is traditionally expressed in the doctrine of *incarnation*: that Jesus is both human and divine, the eternal Word of God made flesh (John 1:1–18). The later credal formulations of this in Greek philosophical terms ("two natures in one substance") are perhaps optional. But the basic idea of incarnation, that God was *uniquely* present in Jesus, seems definitive of Christianity—if anything is.

THE NEW TESTAMENT ON HUMAN NATURE

Jesus also expanded the conception of human nature for Christians by showing that in some sense human nature can become divine. But what can that possibly mean? In Romans 8:1–12, Paul makes a crucial contrast between "the spirit" and "the flesh," the latter term was the traditional translation in the Authorized Version (the Revised English Bible has "our old nature," and the Jerusalem Bible has "human nature"). A similar distinction is attributed to Jesus in John 3:5–7 (also 6:63):

> In very truth I tell you, no one can enter the kingdom of God without being born from water and spirit. Flesh can give birth only to flesh, it is spirit that give birth to spirit. You ought not to be astonished when I say "You must all be born again."

There is a tendency for us to interpret this in metaphysically dualist terms, as the distinction between incorporeal soul and physical body. But Paul's distinction seems to be not so much between soul and body (mind and matter), nor between our spiritual nature and our human nature (which would suggest that our human nature is intrinsically bad, contrary to the idea of humanity being made in the image of God), but rather between regenerate and unregenerate humanity, redeemed and unredeemed human nature. The fundamental contrast here is between two ways of living:

> Those who live on the level of the old nature have their outlook formed by it, and that spells death; but those who live on the level of the spirit have the spiritual outlook, and that is life and peace. (Romans 8:5–6)

Of course, it is tempting to identify "the flesh" with our biological nature—our bodily desires, especially our sexuality (compare Plato's conflict between Appetite and the higher parts of the soul, in Chapter 4). But it is a misinterpretation of the Christian conception of human nature to identify the distinction between good and evil with that between our mental and physical nature. Desires for wealth or fame or power are more mental than physical, but Jesus' teaching condemns these as worldly rather than spiritual (see "the Sermon on the Mount" in Matthew Chs. 5–7) and for Paul, too, they are surely part of "living on the level of the old nature."

It has to be admitted, however, that the ascetic view that our sexual desires are intrinsically evil has had a strong influence in the history of Christianity. We can find this tendency in Paul (see 1 Corinthians Ch. 7, where he describes marriage as second best to celibacy), and it was made more influential by Augustine. Paul is especially scathing about homosexuality (Romans 1:27), as were Jews in general, but it is not clear that this is essential to Christianity rather than a cultural attitude of the time. It is notable that Paul does not condemn the institution of slavery (1 Corinthians 7:20–24).

On the question of equality between the sexes, we should note that in the Gospel stories Jesus treats women with great respect. However, he did not choose any women to be his disciples: in that way Jesus was presumably a man of his time, a Jewish rabbi. Paul said that in Christ there is no such thing as Jew and Greek, slave and freeman, male and female (Galatians 3:28), yet he seemed to support patriarchy when he wrote that wives must be subject to their husbands (Ephesians 5:22). Paul displays an obsession with the covering of women's hair in church, whose cultural context is obscure to us now (1 Corinthians 11:3–10). Much Christian thought has found females theologically problematic ever since—witness the continuing controversies about the ordination of women.

Is the distinction between living on the level of the old nature and living on the level of the spirit to be made purely in this life, or does it also involve life after death? Here we encounter a divergence between what might be called a purely spiritual interpretation of Christianity and a supernatural or eschatological version (the word "eschatological" means to do with the end of the world, "the last things"). Jesus is said to have proclaimed the coming of "the Kingdom of Heaven" or "the Kingdom of God" (Matthew 4:17, Ch. 23, Mark 1:15). But it is not clear whether this means a psychological, a political, or a metaphysical change (and apparently it was not clear to Jesus' hearers). The phrase "eternal life" (or "everlasting life") is used in the Gospel of John, where Jesus is represented as offering eternal life to whoever will believe in him (John 3:16), to those who are "born again." But we need not jump to the conclusion that these phrases mean the continuation of human life after death. Could they mean a new and better way of living in *this* life, a way that relates properly to eternal truths and values?

Some of Jesus' sayings and Paul's writings can be taken in this way. Consider this vivid passage in Galatians 5:16–25:

> What I mean is this: be guided by the Spirit and you will not gratify the desires of your unspiritual nature. . . .
>
> Anyone can see the behavior that belongs to the unspiritual nature: fornication, indecency, and debauchery; idolatry and sorcery; quarrels, a contentious temper, envy, fits of rage, selfish ambitions, dissensions, party intrigues, and jealousies; drinking bouts, orgies, and the like. . . .
>
> But the harvest of the Spirit is love, joy, peace, patience, kindness, goodness, fidelity, gentleness, and self-control, against such things there is no law. Those who belong to Christ Jesus have crucified the old nature with its passions and desires. If the Spirit is the source of our life, let the Spirit also direct its course.

This passage confirms our interpretation of the old or unspiritual nature as the source of selfish and worldly passions as well as bodily debaucheries. It is in some ways more specific than Paul's oft-quoted hymn to "love" (*agape*, traditionally translated as "charity") in 1 Corinthians Chapter 13, which is easily sentimentalized. And it is clear that we are not merely being reminded here of what is right and wrong, we are being told of a fundamental transformation of mind, from which ethical behavior will flow.

In the New Testament, love of God, and life according to His will, is open to all regardless of intellectual ability (1 Corinthians 1:20). Jesus famously summed up the Old Testament law in two injunctions: "Love the Lord your God with all your heart, and with all your soul, and with all your strength, and with all your mind; and your neighbor as yourself" (Matthew 22:34–40, Mark 12:28–31, Luke 10:25–28; anticipated in Deuteronomy 6:5 and Leviticus 19:18). The "love of neighbor" that is meant here is different from mere human affection, it must be divine in nature: " . . . let us love one another, because the source of love is God. Everyone who loves is a child of God and knows God, but the unloving know nothing of God, for God is love" (1 John 4:7–8).

"Eternal life" implies *at least* a Spirit-inspired, divinely loving life in this world, but it is impossible to ignore that the New Testament also lays great stress on resurrection, a last judgment, eternal punishment for the wicked, and everlasting life for all believers (Matthew 7:21–23, 13:36–43, and Chs. 24–25). Traditionally, the resurrection of Jesus after his death on the cross has been proclaimed as God's guarantee that there is a life after death for everyone—or at least for "the saved." We are offered hope of a regenerate, spiritual life: "For anyone united to Christ, there is a new creation" (2 Corinthians 5:17). But this is seen as a lifelong process that looks beyond to life after death for its completion (Phillipians 3:12–14). The Christian expectation of resurrection is made quite explicit in 1 Corinthians Chapter 15.

THE NEW TESTAMENT DIAGNOSIS OF SIN

The doctrine of original sin does not imply that we are totally and utterly depraved. It means that nothing we can do can be *perfect* by God's standards: "All alike have sinned, and are deprived of the divine glory" (Romans 3:23). We find ourselves in inner conflict. We often recognize what we ought to do, but somehow we fail to do it. St. Paul expresses this vividly in Romans 7:14 ff., he even personifies sin (rather like the Freudian *id*), saying "It is no longer I who perform the action, but sin that dwells in me" (7:17), thereby threatening to excuse the sinner from responsibility—which was surely not his intention! John also contrasts slavery to sin with being set free by knowing the truth in Jesus (John 8:31–36).

As we have seen, sin is not basically sexual in nature: sexuality has its rightful place in marriage. The true nature of sin is mental or spiritual; it consists in pride, in the preference for our own selfish will against God's will, and our consequent alienation from Him. But this surely does not mean that all self-assertion is sinful. Nietzsche characterized Christianity as recommending "slave morality" in praising meekness and self-abasement and discouraging vigorous human self-assertion and living life to the fullest. A superficial reading of the Beatitudes (Matthew Ch. 5) may suggest this. "Blessed are the poor in spirit," Jesus said, but it is not obvious how we are to understand those mysterious words. Some of the stories of Jesus (such as his expulsion of the money changers from the temple) and of Paul suggest no inhibition on clear moral judgment, righteous anger, and resolute action.

The Fall of humanity is seen as involving the whole creation (Romans 8:22): everything falls short of the glory of God. But one wonders if it is necessary to personify evil in the concept of Satan or demonic powers—though those notions certainly appear in the New Testament (Matthew 4:1–11, Mark 5:1–13, Acts 5:3, 2 Thessalonians 2:3–9, Revelation 12:9). And it is Manichean, not biblical, to believe in twin and equal powers of good and evil: for Jew and Christian alike, God is ultimately in control of all that happens, despite the manifold appearances of evil in the world.

PRESCRIPTION: GOD'S SALVATION IN CHRIST

Scholars and theologians have long debated what Jesus' conception of himself was. In the gospels he is represented as making dramatic theological claims about himself, especially in the Fourth Gospel, where he claims to be the Messiah (John 4:25–26), the Son of God (5:16–47, see also Matthew 16:15–17), the bread which comes down from heaven (John 6:30–58), and to have existed before Abraham was born (8:58). But the Gospels were compiled after Jesus' death, by writers who were already believers in his divine status. It is in the earlier writings of Paul that we find the earliest written formulations of the Christian theory of incarnation and salvation. The central claim is that God was uniquely present in Jesus of Nazareth and that God uses Jesus' life, death, and resurrection to restore us to a right relationship with Himself:

> . . . as the result of one misdeed [*Paul is thinking of Adam's Fall*] was condemnation for all people, so the result of one righteous act [*i.e., Jesus' death on the cross*] is acquittal and life for all. For as through the disobedience of one man many were made sinners, so through the obedience of one man many will be made righteous. (Romans 5:18–19)

Paul writes with great eloquence and conviction, and his language has acquired great authority for many, but if we stop to think about what he is saying here, it seems to run counter to our ordinary convictions about responsibility and blame. How can it be fair to blame all humanity for a misdeed of one man long ago (supposedly, Adam)? How can it be right to acquit or "make righteous" the whole of sinful humanity because of the obedience of another man (Jesus)? There is a mysterious theological theory of *atonement* involved here, that the particular historical events of the life and death of Jesus are the means by which God reconciles the whole of creation to Himself (Romans 5:6–10, 2 Corinthians 5:18–21).

For Christians, it apparently is not enough to say that Jesus provides an example of someone being prepared to suffer death rather than go against his most fundamental values—Socrates and other historical figures (including the Christian martyrs) also provide such examples, but they are not divinized in the same way. Paul and other Christian writers (Hebrews Ch. 10) are obviously influenced by Old Testament ideas of sacrifice, but not many theologians are now prepared to interpret Christ's "saving work" as a propitiatory sacrifice—as if God requires blood to be shed (any blood, even that of the innocent) before he will be prepared to forgive sins. But how, then, is the crucifixion of a Jewish religious teacher under the Roman governor Pontius Pilate in Jerusalem in about the year 30 supposed to effect a redemption of the whole world from sin?

The Christian prescription is not complete with this mysterious "saving work" of Jesus Christ. It needs to be accepted by each individual person and to be spread throughout the world by the Church. But there is some obscurity about just what is required from individuals to be "saved." Baptism became the traditional ritual for becoming a Christian, but that is only an outward and visible sign of an inward and spiritual change. There are familiar, constantly invoked phrases for the latter: being "born again," "believing in Christ," having "faith in Christ," "being justified by faith alone," and many variations on these. But what do these phrases really mean? Do they require a propositional belief in a theological claim that Jesus is the Son of God, and also that his death atones for the sins of the world? Or do they mean rather a personal relationship of trust in Jesus as a religious authority, a "guru," a revealer of God, a guide to life, a source of spiritual life? But how can people who have never met Jesus in the flesh have a personal relationship with him? What can that mean other than treating him—or, more precisely, the written representations of Jesus that we are left with—as a supremely inspiring example of self-less living, life "in the spirit"?

A traditional problem arises over the parts played by human beings and God in the drama of salvation. The fundamental conception is that redemption can only come from God, through His offering of Himself in Christ. We are "justified" in the sight of God not by our own good works, but by faith (Romans 3:1–28), by our mere acceptance of what God does for us. We are saved by this free grace of God, not by anything that we can do ourselves (Ephesians 2:8). Yet, just as clearly, there is an assumption that our will is free: it must be by our own choice that we accept God's salvation and allow its regeneration of our lives. The New Testament is full of exhortations to repent and believe (e.g., Acts 3:19) and to live the life of the Spirit. There is thus a long-standing tension between the view that salvation is entirely due to God's grace and the insistence that something crucial depends on our freely chosen response (see the mention of Augustine and Pelagius in the Historical Interlude).

SPIRITUAL OR SUPERNATURAL VERSIONS OF CHRISTIANITY?

The doctrines of incarnation, atonement, resurrection, and the end of this world are a problem to human rationality, and their formulation has provoked much debate in the Christian tradition. How can one particular human being be a member of the transcendent, eternal Godhead? The doctrine of the Trinity—that there are three persons in one God—multiplies the conceptual problems. The standard thing to say is that these are mysteries rather than contradictions, that human reason cannot be expected to understand the infinite mysteries of God, that we can only accept in faith what God has revealed of Himself to us. But this kind of statement from within the perspective of faith does nothing to answer the difficulties of the unbeliever or the puzzled.

Unlike early Judaism, Christianity developed a clear expectation of life after death. But this is not the Greek idea of the survival of an incorporeal soul. The Christian Creeds express belief in the resurrection of the *body*, and the main scriptural warrant for this is in 1 Corinthians 15:35 ff., where Paul says that we die as physical bodies but are raised as "spiritual bodies." It is not clear what a spiritual body is supposed to be, but Paul does use the Greek word *soma*, which means body. Christians claim that the resurrection of Jesus was both a real, observable event in history and a unique act of God. (The idea of the Virgin Birth is almost as miraculous, but is perhaps less crucial.) And Jesus' resurrection is supposed to show the possibility of a similar resurrection for everybody.

Is it meant that there will be a time in the future of this world at which the general resurrection will take place? Paul says "we shall all be changed, in a flash, in the twinkling of an eye, at the last trumpet-call" (1 Corinthians 15:51–52), and Peter predicts that on "the day of the Lord . . . the heavens will disappear with a great rushing sound" (2 Peter 3:10). Jesus himself is reported as predicting the imminent end of the world (Matthew Ch. 24). Paul keeps reminding his readers that the time is short, and in 1 Thessalonians 4:16–17 he writes his most vivid description of what he expects to happen:

> . . . when God's trumpet sounds, then the Lord himself will descend from heaven; first the Christian dead will rise, then we who are still alive shall join them, caught up in the clouds to meet the Lord in the air. Thus we shall always be with the Lord.

Paul seems to envisage a cataclysmic divine event that will dramatically and visibly intrude into our time and space.

The book of Revelation is full of vivid descriptions of such eschatological events, including strange beasts, battles, and tortures, and displaying an obsession with numbers. (To my mind, it is like the script for a science-fiction movie, with lots of special effects, and in very poor taste—even the description of the new Jerusalem in Chapter 21 seems more interested in its jewelry and its dimensions than its spiritual qualities. In my humble opinion, I would question its place in the canon!) In any case, it is clear that early Christians had, right or wrong, a definite expectation of an end to human history, a taking up of humanity into a metaphysically different kind of existence. It would be nice to think that all will then be "saved," but many passages foresee a last judgment and a final division between the saved and the damned (Revelation destines some for "the second death" at 21:8).

How can we understand this eschatological prediction or vision? (Are we meant to *understand* it at all? Unless we understand it, though, how can we believe it?) If bodies are resurrected, then presumably, as *bodies* of some kind, they have to occupy space and time. Now, it is surely not meant that they exist somewhere in our physical universe—that at some large distance from the earth there exist the resurrected bodies of St. Paul, Napoleon, and Aunt Agatha! That would make it a scientific hypothesis, to be tested empirically. So it seems that what we have to try to make sense of is the idea that there is a space in which resurrected bodies exist, but with no spatial relations with the space in which we live.

The question of time is at least as difficult. Is it meant that there is a system of events with no temporal relation to the events of this world? Or is the resurrection world timeless, in which case what sense can be made of the idea of resurrected *life*? For life, as we understand it, is a process in time. Is a life that literally goes on forever even an *attractive* prospect? The answer is, I suggest, not obvious. If, on the other hand, resurrected life is not in time, what sense can we make of it—how can persons live a *personal* life, doing things, communicating with others, but in a timeless state?

Many thinking Christians may acknowledge such intellectual problems. But they remain practicing members of a Christian community and in some sense "accept" or "go along with" the orthodox doctrines because of what they find in the life and worship of the Church and in reading the Bible— a certain growth in the spiritual life. They may say that Christianity is not just a theory, it is a way of life. Possibly we can reach some degree of agreement on what counts as "spiritual growth," in terms of the sort of "fruits of the spirit" mentioned in Galatians 5 and 1 Corinthians 15. But any claim that such spiritual growth can be achieved only by accepting the metaphysical, supernatural, and eschatological claims of New Testament Christianity (rather than those of Judaism, Islam, Hinduism, Buddhism, or even scientific naturalism) is highly disputable.

FOR FURTHER READING

There are now several different English translations of the Bible. One excellent version for present purposes is the *Oxford Study Bible: Revised English Bible with the Apocrypha,* edited by M. J. Suggs et al. (Oxford University Press, 1992). This version contains explanatory footnotes and helpful essays on the historical, sociological, literary, and religious background of the biblical texts.

In the Very Short Introduction series published by Oxford University Press, see the titles on the Bible by J. Riches, on Judaism by N. Solomon, on Theology by

D. F. Ford, on Paul by E. P. Sanders, and on Atheism by J. Baggini. There is also a title on Jesus, by H. Carpenter, formerly in OUP's Past Masters series.

For more on Christian understandings of human nature, see Reinhold Niebuhr's classic *The Nature and Destiny of Man* (New York: Charles Scribner's Sons, 1964); E. L. Mascall, *The Importance of Being Human* (New York: Columbia University Press, 1958), which presents a neo-Thomist view; *Man: Fallen and Free*, edited by E. W. Kemp (London: Hodder & Stoughton, 1969), which presents an interesting variety of essays, including a notable summary by J. A. Baker of the Old Testament view; and J. Macquarrie, *In Search of Humanity* (London: SCM Press, 1982; New York: Crossroad, 1983), which presents a more existentialist view.

For a feminist critique of Christianity, while retaining theism, see Daphne Hampson, *After Christianity* (London: SCM Press, 1996).

Books on philosophy of religion are countless. One comprehensive set of readings is *Philosophy of Religion: Selected Readings*, edited by M. Peterson et al. (Oxford University Press, 1996).

C H A P T E R

4

Plato: The Rule of Reason

Let us start our examination of nonreligious (or not explicitly religious) theories of human nature by considering the philosophy of Plato (427–347 B.C.E.). Although it dates back nearly two and a half millennia, Plato's pioneering thought is still of great contemporary relevance. He was one of the first to argue that the systematic use of our reason can show us the best way to live. A clear conception of human virtue and fulfillment, based on a true understanding of human nature and its problems, is in Plato's view the only way to individual happiness and social stability.

PLATO'S LIFE AND WORK

A short sketch of Plato's background will help us understand the origin of his ideas. He was born into an influential family in the Greek city-state of Athens, which enjoyed economic prosperity through its empire and trade, and at one stage developed a remarkably democratic system of government, which we now honor as the first experiment in democracy. We remember Athens above all as a center of unprecedented advances in the arts and intellectual inquiries, including sculpture, drama, history, mathematics, science, and philosophy. One of its greatest figures was the ethical philosopher Socrates, whose teaching deeply impressed Plato. But these thinkers lived in a politically disturbed period in Athens: the war with Sparta ended in disastrous defeat, and a period of tyranny ensued. When a new faction came to power, Socrates came under suspicion because of his association with certain people. He was brought to trial and condemned to death in 399 B.C.E. on a charge of subverting the state religion and corrupting the young.

Socrates' method of arguing and teaching was akin in some ways to that of the "Sophists" of his day. These self-styled experts offered, for a fee, to impart certain kinds of skill; in particular the art of rhetoric (i.e., persuasion by public speaking), which was important for political advancement in Athens. (The Sophists could be described as the public relations consultants of their time!) They also discussed ethics and politics. Athenians were aware of the variety of beliefs and practices in various cultures around the Mediterranean, so they were confronted with the question of whether there is any criterion of truth in these matters. The Sophists often expressed skepticism about whether moral and political values were anything more than arbitrary conventions. What we now call "cultural relativism" was thus a tempting option at this early stage of thought.

Unlike the Sophists, Socrates charged no fees for his teaching, and he concerned himself with fundamental philosophical and ethical questions. His great inspiring idea was that we can come to know the right way to live, if only we will use our reason properly. He has been called "the grandfather of philosophy," not so much for any conclusions he reached, but for pioneering the method of using rational argument and inquiry in an open-minded, nondogmatic way. Famously, Socrates claimed superiority to unthinking people only in that he was *aware* of his own ignorance about so many difficult matters, whereas they thought they knew. He was adept at showing by persistent questioning that they did not know what they claimed to know. Plato's early dialogues (especially the *Apology*) portray Socrates as believing that "the unexamined life is not worth living," and as making his fellow Athenians think about their lives in ways they would not otherwise have done. Socrates felt called with a kind of religious intensity to disturb people's mental complacency; so it is not surprising that he found himself a focus of hostility, even to the point of death.

In all this, Socrates deeply influenced Plato, who was shocked at the execution of his inspirational teacher. Although disillusioned with contemporary politics, Plato retained Socrates' faith in rational inquiry; he was convinced that it was possible to attain knowledge of deep-lying truths about the world and about human nature, and to apply this knowledge for the benefit of human society. Socrates did not leave any writings—his influence was entirely oral. Plato himself expressed some skepticism about the value of books, tending to agree with Socrates that actual dialogue was the best way to get people to think for themselves and perhaps change their approach to life. However, Plato did write extensively, often with great literary skill, and his works are amongst the first major treatises in the history of philosophy. They are in conversational form, typically with Socrates taking the leading part in the argument. Most scholars think that in the early dialogues such as *Apology, Crito, Euthyphro,* and *Meno,* Plato was mainly expounding Socrates' ideas, whereas in later works (which tend to be longer and more technical) he was expressing his own distinctive theories. Plato founded the Academy in Athens, which can be described as the world's first university.

One of the most famous and widely studied of Plato's texts is the *Republic,* a lengthy, complex, and closely argued dialogue between several characters; it is traditionally divided into ten books (which do not always make natural divisions of the argument). As the title suggests, one main theme is an outline of an ideal human society, but the central argument concerns the problems and fulfilment of individual human beings. In this work, Plato touches on many topics, including metaphysics, theory of knowledge, human psychology, morals, politics, social classes, the family, education, and the arts. I will concentrate on the *Republic* here, with occasional reference to other dialogues. I will incorporate some critical points along with my exposition. (There is a traditional page-numbering system for Plato's texts: my references are to *Republic* unless otherwise stated.)

METAPHYSICAL BACKGROUND: THE THEORY OF FORMS

Although Plato mentions God, or the gods, at various places, it is not clear how literally he takes such talk (he is hardly a believer in the polytheism of Greek popular religion). When he does talk of "God" in the singular, he does *not* mean the biblical conception of a personal Being who appears to or communicates with individual people and intervenes in human history. Plato has in mind a rather more abstract ideal: in the *Philebus* and *Laws,* God or the divine is identified with reason (*logos*) in the universe. (The prologue of the Gospel of John, "In the beginning was the word (*logos*) . . . " shows the influence of this Platonic idea.) In the *Timaeus,* Plato gives a creation story that differs from the biblical doctrine of God's creation out of nothing in that Plato's "divine wisdom" organizes the world out of preexisting matter and can only do the best he can with this somewhat recalcitrant material.

What is most distinctive of Plato's metaphysics, however, is his theory of "Forms" (the Greek word is *eidos*). But it is a matter of difficult philosophical interpretation to say what exactly this amounts to, for Plato hardly presents it as an explicit theory, nor does he argue for it in any very systematic way. It is mentioned or assumed at crucial points in various dialogues, though to Plato's credit we also find him wrestling with difficulties in it, in the *Parmenides*. We have to remember that he was a pioneer in philosophy, struggling to express and clarify fundamental ideas for the first time in human thought.

Plato realizes that human knowledge is not simply a matter of mere passive observation of things and events in the world around us. As he argues in the *Theaetetus*, our knowledge involves understanding, in that we actively interpret the stimulations we receive through our sense organs, we apply concepts to organize and classify what we perceive, using our mental powers as well as our sense organs (see the related remarks on Kant's epistemology in Chapter 6). Plato's Forms can be identified with concepts, at least as a first approximation to understanding him. I will present four main aspects of the Forms here: logical or semantic (to do with meanings and concepts), metaphysical (to do with what is ultimately real), epistemological (to do with what we can know), and moral or political (to do with how we ought to live).

The logical or semantic aspect of the Forms is their role as concepts or principles of classification that constitute the meaning of general terms. What justifies our application of one word or concept such as "bed" or "table" to many particular beds or tables? These are Plato's own examples at *Republic* 596, where part of his point is that craftsmen making things must have a concept of what they are trying to make. But the "one over many" structure applies to any general concept. We recognize things in the world as falling under natural kinds: species of animal and plant; kinds of metal, rocks, and liquids. Even with simple sensory qualities, such as redness or heat, there are many things that are red, and many others that are hot, but one concept of each quality. And, at 507, Plato distinguishes the many different good things and beautiful things from the single Forms of Goodness and Beauty.

The "nominalist" view about concepts or universals is that there is nothing that all instances of a concept literally have in common—at best, there may be some similarities between them. The view traditionally labelled "Platonic realism" is that what makes particular things count as Fs is their resemblance to, or "participation in," the Form or Idea of F, understood as an abstract entity, something existing in its own right and different from all the individual instances of it. At *Republic* 596, Plato's view seems to be that for each general word there is one Form. But elsewhere he suggests that only some special kinds of words or concepts, those that pick out genuine unities (including what we would now call "natural kinds") express what he would call a Form. He is reluctant to accept, for example, that there are Forms corresponding to the terms "mud," "dirt," or "barbarian" (the latter was used for all non-Greeks, like our word "foreigner").

An important metaphysical aspect of the Forms is that Plato thinks of them as more real than material things, in that they do not change, decay, or cease to exist. Material objects get damaged and destroyed, but the Forms are not in space or time, and they are not knowable by the senses, only by the human intellect or reason (485, 507, 526–27). Plato's grand metaphysical theory is that beyond the world of changeable and destructible things there is another world containing these unchanging eternal Forms. The things we can perceive are only distantly related to these ultimate realities, as he suggested by his haunting image of the typical human condition as people chained like prisoners, facing the inner wall of a cave in which all they can see are mere shadows cast on the wall, and know nothing of the real world outside (515–17). If Plato were alive today, he might be quick to point out how well his image applies to so many of us who rely for our (supposed) knowledge of the real world on watching television, movies, and computer screens!

Most people may be concerned only with shadows, and ignorant of ultimate reality, but Plato thought that by a process of education it is possible for human minds—or, at least, the more able of them—to attain knowledge of the world of Forms. The epistemological aspect of his theory is that only this intellectual acquaintance with the Forms properly counts as knowledge. Plato discusses the nature of knowledge in several dialogues, but in the *Republic* we find the thesis that only what fully and really exists can be fully or really known: perception of impermanent objects and events in the physical world is only "belief" or "opinion," not knowledge (476–80). (Plato elaborates on the mechanics of his cave story to make it fit the more detailed structure of his theory of knowledge: his prisoners see the shadows cast from a fire by artifacts carried about within the cave, whereas outside there are more real objects, which themselves cast shadows by the light of the sun.)

One of the clearest illustrations of the theory of Forms comes from the geometrical reasoning with which Plato was familiar, and which Euclid was to systematize later. Consider how in doing geometry we think about lines, circles, and squares, although no physical object or diagram is *perfectly* straight, circular, or equal-sided. What we count as straight or equal for practical purposes, to some degree of approximation, will not be so by a more precise standard—irregularities or differences can always be found if things are examined closely enough, perhaps by a microscope. Yet we can prove theorems concerning geometrical concepts—straight lines without thickness, perfect circles, exact squares—with complete certainty, by deductive arguments. Similarly, we know truths of arithmetic that are quite independent of the vagueness or impermanence of the material things we count. ("1 + 1 = 2" is not disproved by the merging of two water droplets!) We thus seem to attain knowledge of exactly defined, unchangeable mathematical objects, namely patterns or Forms that material things imperfectly resemble. Like many other philosophers since, Plato was deeply impressed by the certainty and precision of mathematical knowledge, and he took this as an ideal to which all human knowledge should approximate. He therefore recommended the teaching of mathematics as a vital means toward detaching our minds from mere perceptible objects.

It is the moral application of the theory of Forms that plays the most important role in Plato's conception of human nature and society. We can distinguish many particular courageous actions or just dealings from the general concepts or Forms of Courage and Justice. In the early dialogues Plato depicts Socrates seeking an adequate general definition of such virtues and never being satisfied with mere examples or subclasses of them. We have to distinguish these ideals from the (often complicated and messy) reality of particular human beings in real-life situations. Often an action or a person may be right, just, or admirable in one way but not in others (e.g., doing the best thing for one friend or relation may involve neglecting another). But Plato holds that the ethical Forms set absolute standards of value for us (472–73). Just as no material object is perfectly square, perhaps no human being or society is perfectly good.

For Plato, the Form of Goodness is preeminent in the world of Forms: it plays an almost God-like role in his system, being described as the source of all reality, truth, and goodness. He compares its role in the world of the Forms to that of the sun as the source of all light in the world of material things (508–9). Plato's twin images of sun and cave—concerned with the source of light and the notion of coming to "see the light"—give us a memorable pictorial presentation of the theory of Forms.

It is crucial to Plato's whole philosophy that we can, by the proper use of our faculty of reason, both come to know what is good and actually become good. In this he was following the lead of his role model Socrates. In some of the early dialogues (*Protagoras* and *Meno*), Plato portrays Socrates arguing for what seems to have been the historical Socrates' own doctrine, that to *be* virtuous, to be a good human being, it is enough to *know* what human virtue is. All the virtues are said to be identical at root, in that one cannot possess any one of them without having the others; and this unique human goodness is identified with knowledge in the wide sense of wisdom, not mere store of information, or intellectual virtuosity.

Socrates is thus committed to the doctrine that nobody knowingly or willingly does what he or she thinks to be wrong. But this surely conflicts with all-too-obvious facts about human nature: we often know quite well what we ought to do, and yet somehow or other we don't get around to doing it—indeed, we sometimes find ourselves unwilling to do it. We shall see later how Plato attempts to cope with this difficulty.

The theory of Forms is Plato's answer to the intellectual and moral skepticism or relativism of his time. It is one of the first and greatest expressions of the hope that we can attain reliable knowledge both about the world as a whole and about the proper conduct of human life and society. Yet we may well suspect that Plato has overintellectualized the role of reason and knowledge. He makes a good case that we all need to use our reason in exercising prudent self-control, moderating our emotions and desires, their expressions and fulfillments. But in the central metaphysical sections of the *Republic* (Books V–VII) Plato insists on a highly theoretical conception of reason as consisting in a special kind of knowledge of the Forms which is open only to a trained intellectual elite. It is not very plausible that such specialized philosophical thinking is either necessary or sufficient for human goodness.

THEORY OF HUMAN NATURE: THE TRIPARTITE STRUCTURE OF THE SOUL

Plato is one of the main sources for the dualist view, according to which the human soul or mind (these terms are here used synonymously) is a nonmaterial entity that can exist apart from the body. According to Plato, the soul exists before birth, it is indestructible, and will exist eternally after death. His main arguments for these doctrines are in the early dialogues. In the *Meno,* Plato tries to prove the preexistence of the soul, arguing that what we call learning is really a kind of "recollection" of an acquaintance our souls supposedly had with the Forms before birth (a version of the Eastern doctrine of reincarnation). People of average intelligence like a slaveboy, can be brought to understand mathematical propositions (the simpler ones, anyway!) and to realize why they must be true, by having their attention called to the steps of a proof. Plato says, plausibly enough, that the mental ability to recognize the validity of the inferential steps and the necessity of the conclusion must be innate. But then he makes the much more disputable claim that such innate abilities can only be explained by the human soul's knowledge of the Forms in a previous life. We would now offer evolutionary explanations of innate human abilities (see Chapter 10).

In the *Phaedo,* Plato presents a number of other arguments that the human soul must persist after the death of the body. He tries to disprove the materialist theory of the earlier Greek atomists (such as Democritus) that the human soul is composed of tiny particles that dissipate into the air at death. He also argues against the conception (which Aristotle later developed in more detail, see Chapter 5) that the soul is a kind of "harmony" of the living human body and brain, like the music made by an instrument when properly tuned and played. Plato's arguments are sometimes intricate and apparently playful, but they repay careful study: we can learn a lot by trying to specify exactly where they go wrong.

Plato held, with the intensity of a religious belief, that it is the immaterial soul, not the bodily senses, that attains knowledge of the Forms: he compares the soul to the divine, the rational, the immortal, indissoluble and unchangeable. The soul is the higher element in human nature, the body the lower. The preoccupation of the philosopher or wise person should be the care of his or her soul; and since the soul is immortal, this is also a preparation for death and the life after death. In the famous scene at the end of the *Phaedo*, in Socrates' last conversations in prison before drinking the hemlock, Plato presents his hero as looking forward to the release of his soul from all bodily cares and limitations. The doctrines of the immateriality and immortality of the soul also appear at the end of the *Republic* in "the myth of Er" in Book X (608–20). This has seemed to many commentators to be an ill-fitting appendix to a philosophical work, but Plato seems to have found it appropriate at certain points to resort to more literary, less argumentative, means of communication. This is ironic, given his suspicion of the rhetorical power of the arts such as poetry.

What is really central to Plato's main moral discussion in the *Republic* is his theory of the three parts of the soul (435–41). Although this is expressed in terms of "the soul," we need not interpret it as involving metaphysical dualism: we can take it as a distinction between three different aspects of our mental nature. We can recognize the existence of internal conflicting tendencies in ourselves, even if we take a materialist, evolutionary view of human beings as one kind of animal with a well-developed brain. (I will concentrate here on Plato's tripartite theory, but we should note that in the *Philebus* and *Laws* he presents human nature as divided *two* ways between reason and pleasure; and he says more about pleasure in the *Gorgias* and *Protagoras*.) Echoes of Plato's threefold distinction can be found in many thinkers since (e.g., in Freud, see Chapter 8).

At this point in Plato's thought we can see him acknowledging the implausibility of the Socratic doctrine that nobody willingly (or clearsightedly, or wholeheartedly) does what he or she believes to be wrong. He wrestles with both the theoretical question of how such inner conflict is possible and the practical problem of how one can achieve inner harmony. Let us first examine his arguments for the tripartite structure.

Consider an example of mental conflict or inhibition, such as when someone is thirsty but does not drink the available water because he believes it is poisoned or because of some religious asceticism—quite often we do not (or not immediately) gratify our bodily urges. But conversely, we sometimes find ourselves giving way to the temptations of the proffered cigarette, the second cream cake, the third glass of wine, or the seductive charmer, even though we know that the consequences are likely to be bad for us. Bad habits can notoriously become addictive: gluttony (or, these days, anorexia), alcoholism, drug dependence, habitual search for new sexual partners. Plato argues that where there is any kind of internal conflict, there must be two different elements with contradictory tendencies. In the case of the thirsty man, there must be one part that makes him want to drink and a second that forbids him; the first Plato calls "Appetite" (under which he intends to include all the physical urges, such as hunger, thirst, and sexual desire), and the second he calls "Reason."

So far, Plato is on familiar ground. But he argues for the existence of a third element in our nature by examining different cases of mental conflict. His first example may seem rather weird: a story of someone who felt a fascinated desire to look at a pile of corpses and yet was disgusted with himself for having such a desire (440). Plato claims that to explain cases like this we need to recognize the existence in ourselves of a third element that he calls "Spirit" or passion. His argument for this is not very explicit, but it seems to be that because there is an *emotion* of self-disgust involved, not just an intellectual recognition of the irrationality or undesirability of the desire, Spirit must be distinct from Reason.

We surely have to agree that emotion is different both from bodily desires and from rational or moral judgment. Love is not the same as lust, but on the other hand it is more than a mere intellectual judgment about the admirable qualities of the beloved. Anger, indignation, ambition, aggression, and the desire for power are not *bodily* desires, nor are they mere judgments about the value or disvalue of things, although they involve such judgments. Plato goes on to remark that children (and even animals) show Spirit before they display Reason; and anyone who has dealt with children can confirm this from experience of their high spirits, delights and frustrations, stubbornness, and (sometimes) aggression and bullying.

Plato asserts that Spirit is usually on the side of Reason when inner conflict occurs. But if it is a genuinely distinct element in the mind, there must presumably be cases where it can conflict with Reason. Plato quotes a line of Homer "He smote his breast, and thus rebuked his heart" in brief confirmation of this. And we can surely add examples from our own experience—occasions when we have felt emotions of anger, jealousy, or love that we judge unreasonable, undesirable, or even immoral. Perhaps there can even be cases in which one is pulled in *three* directions by the different elements—for example, by lust, romantic love, and reasoned judgment about who would be the best partner!

Plato presents his threefold theory in vivid, even crude, images. In the *Phaedrus* at 253–54 (a dialogue mainly about love) he compares the soul to a chariot, pulled by a white horse (Spirit) and a dark horse (Appetite), driven by a charioteer (Reason) who struggles to keep control. At *Republic* 588 Plato describes a person as composed of a little man, a lion, and a many-headed beast. This obviously involves an infinite regress—a person within a person, and so on—but Plato was too good a philosopher not to notice this and he must have been offering the picture only as an image.

Is Plato's tripartite anatomy of the soul adequate? It can be seen as an interesting first approximation, distinguishing some elements in human nature that can conflict with each other. But it is hardly a rigorous or exhaustive division, even if one redescribes the parts in modern terms as intellect, emotion, and bodily desire. In particular, it is not very clear what Plato's middle element of Spirit amounts to. Emotions are part of our human nature, of course, but Plato seems also to have had in mind human desires or drives that are not *bodily* appetites but not exactly emotions either, such as self-assertion, ambition, and desire for money, status, or power. And where does the will come into the story? Doesn't Plato still have to accept that it is one thing to recognize or judge (with one's reason) what one ought to do, and another to do it, or try to do it? A different tripartite distinction of mental faculties that has become standard, especially since the advent of Christianity, is as follows: reason, emotion, and *will*. Perhaps we need to distinguish at least five factors in human nature: reason, will, nonbodily motivations or drives, emotions, and bodily appetites.

Much of Plato's discussion seems to be conducted with men rather than women in mind, but he had views about the sexes that were strikingly original in his time. In Greek society, women played almost no part in public life and were usually confined to their reproductive role and household duties. The philosophical discussions of love in the Platonic dialogues are all about male homosexual love, which was socially accepted then. In the *Republic* (449 ff.), however, Plato argues that there is no role in society that need be restricted to either sex. He allows that some women are athletic, musical, philosophical, and even "high-spirited." (The mind boggles! He meant courageous, and therefore suitable for military service.) Plato still patronizingly assumes that men are on average better than women at everything, but he thinks that the only absolute distinction is the biological one (that males beget children and females bear them) and that any other differences are only matters of degree. He is therefore prepared to admit women of appropriate talent to the ruling class.

One other main feature of Plato's theory of human nature should be emphasized: we are social creatures (i.e., to live in society is natural to human beings). Human individuals are not self-sufficient, we each have many needs that we cannot meet by ourselves. Even food, shelter, and clothing can hardly be obtained without the help of others. A desert island individual would have to struggle for survival and would miss out on the distinctively human activities of friendship, play, art, politics, learning, and reasoning. Manifestly, different people have different aptitudes and interests; there are farmers, craftsmen, soldiers, administrators, and so on, each fitted by nature, training, and experience to specialize in one kind of task; division of labor is therefore essential in society (369–70).

DIAGNOSIS: DISHARMONY IN SOUL AND SOCIETY

Reason, Spirit, and Appetite are present to some degree in every person. Depending on which element is dominant, three kinds of people exist. The main desire of each type is, respectively: knowledge, reputation, or material gain. Plato describes them as, philosophic, victory loving, and profit loving (581). He has a very clear view about which of the three elements should rule: it is Reason that ought to control both Spirit and Appetite (590). But each has its proper role to play, and there should ideally be harmonious agreement between the three aspects of our nature, with Reason in overall command. Plato expresses this in an eloquent passage at 443:

> Justice . . . isn't concerned with external actions, but with a man's inward self. The just man will not allow the three elements which make up his inward self to trespass on each other's functions or interfere with each other, but by keeping all three in tune, like the notes of a scale . . . will in the truest sense set his house in order, and be his own lord and master, and at peace with himself. When he has bound these elements into a single controlled and orderly whole, and so unified himself, he will be ready for action of any kind . . .

And just as the reasoning part of the soul ought to direct and control the other parts, so those people with the most highly developed "reason" (which includes moral wisdom, as we have seen) ought to rule society in the interests of everyone. A well-ordered, "just" society will be one in which each class of person plays their distinctive role, in harmony with each other (434).

Plato describes this ideal condition of human beings and society by the Greek word *dikaiosune,* which has traditionally been translated as "justice." But, when applied to individuals, the word does not have its modern legal or political connotations. There can be no exact English translation: "virtue," "morality," "proper functioning," "well-being," or even "mental health" may help to convey what Plato had in mind. At 444, he says that virtue is a kind of mental health or beauty or fitness, and vice a sort of illness or deformity or weakness. His fundamental point is that what is good or bad for us depends on our human nature, the complex of factors in our psychological makeup.

The theory of the parts of the soul (with the background theory of Forms as objects of knowledge) thus defines Plato's ideals for individual and social well-being; and when he looked at the facts of his own day he found that they were very far from ideal. One wonders whether his judgment of our present condition would be any less harsh. Many people still do not show much "inward harmony" or controlled coordination of their desires and mental powers. And many human societies do not manifest the orderliness and stability that Plato sought.

The problems of human individuals that Plato diagnoses are intimately related to the defects in human societies. One cannot simply attribute to him either the conservative or right-wing view that social problems are due to individual wrongdoing, or the liberal or left-wing view that individual vices can be blamed on faults in the social order. Plato would say, I think, that the two are interdependent: an imperfect society tends to produce flawed individuals, and troubled or badly brought-up individuals contribute to social problems.

Plato devotes Book VIII of the *Republic* (543–76) to a systematic classification of five kinds of society, beginning with the ideal outlined earlier that he calls an "aristocracy" (meaning a meritocracy, an aristocracy of talent rather than birth), and going on to diagnose four types of imperfect society, which he calls "timarchy," "oligarchy," "democracy," and "tyranny." Plato also describes a kind of defective individual supposedly typical of each society. He offers an account of how each political stage can arise by degeneration from its predecessor and how each individual character may be formed as a result of problems in the previous generation (concentrating on relations between fathers and sons).

In a "timarchic" society such as that of ancient Sparta, honor and fame—especially in warfare and hunting—are valued above all. Reason and philosophical understanding are neglected, and Spirit plays the dominant role in society and in members of the ruling class (545–49). Something similar was true of feudal society in premodern Europe.

In an "oligarchy," the older class divisions break down, money making becomes the dominant activity, and political power comes to lie with the wealthy. Plato expresses disgust for the resulting type of character, who

> . . . establishes his appetitive and money-making part on the throne, setting it up as a king within himself, . . . and makes the rational and spirited parts sit on the ground beneath appetite, one on either side, reducing them to slaves. . . . He won't allow the first to reason about or examine anything except how a little money can be made into great wealth. And he won't allow the second to value or admire anything but wealth and wealthy people or to have any ambition other than the acquisition of wealth or whatever might contribute to getting it. (553)

(Plato would obviously not be too keen on the free-for-all competition of contemporary capitalism!)

"Democracy" may arise by the poor majority seizing power. In the *Republic,* Plato took a very jaundiced view of democracy as he understood it, influenced no doubt by his experience of the arbitrariness and instability of Athenian democracy, in which every adult male citizen (but not women or slaves!) could vote in the meetings that decided policy, and government positions were often filled by lot (555–57). Plato thought it absurd to give every person an equal say, when most people—in his view—do not know what is best. He criticizes what he labels the "democratic" type of person as lacking in discipline, pursuing mere pleasures of the moment, indulging "unnecessary, spendthrift" desires (the *successful* money maker, for all his faults, at least has to exert some self-control):

> A young man . . . associates with wild and dangerous creatures who can provide every variety of multicolored pleasure in every sort of way.
> . . . seeing the citadel of the young man's soul empty of knowledge, fine ways of living, and words of truth . . . [these desires] finally occupy that citadel themselves.
> . . . and he doesn't admit any word of truth into the guardhouse, for if someone tells him that some pleasures belong to fine and good desires and others to evil ones and that he must pursue and value the former and restrain and enslave the latter, he denies all this and declares that all pleasures are equal and must be valued equally. (559–61)

Anarchy, Plato thinks, is the sequel to the chaotic and unbridled liberty of democracy: permissiveness spreads, fathers and teachers lose authority. (He is horrified at the idea of liberating women and slaves!) There then arises a desire for restoration of some sort of order, and usually some forceful, unscrupulous individual emerges, wins absolute power, and becomes a tyrant (565–69). The tyrannical character, as Plato diagnoses it, is not so much the tyrant himself (who has to exercise some intelligence and self-control to gain and maintain his power), but the person who is completely dominated by his own appetites, especially sexual desires. He will stop at nothing, he will sacrifice possessions and money, family relations and friends in the frenzied pursuit of his lusts (572–76).

In this series of social diagnoses and character sketches, one may feel that the analogies between individual and society are sometimes overstretched. But each sketch shows notable sociological and psychological insight, and their contemporary applications are obvious. Plato concludes that each type of person and society departs further from the ideal, reaching a deeper level of degradation and unhappiness. He is clear that the money-making, pleasure-seeking, and lust-dominated people are far from happy, and this is part of his case why "justice" or "morality" is in the interests of the individual.

PRESCRIPTION: HARMONY IN SOUL AND SOCIETY THROUGH EDUCATION AND GOVERNMENT BY THE PHILOSOPHER-KINGS

Plato has said that "justice" or well-being is essentially the same thing in both individual and society—a smooth working together of the parts within the soul or the classes in the state (435); and the lack of such harmony is injustice. But there is some ambiguity in the *Republic* about whether individuals can change themselves independently of any institutional reforms or whether social change must precede individual improvement and make it possible. (This is a problem that is still with us.) One main purpose of Plato's argument is to answer the challenge put in the mouth of the cynical Thrasymachus (in Book I) by showing that it is, after all, in the long-term interest of the individual to be just or moral. Plato does this by reconceptualizing what justice is, insisting that, since it is a harmony of the three elements in our souls (Book IV), it is bound to make each one of us a happier, more fulfilled human being (Book IX).

But how can such harmony be attained? Plato remarks at 444 that virtue and vice are the result of one's actions: so it seems that what we make of ourselves is, at least to some extent, up to us (an existentialist theme, see Chapter 9). In the famous speech of Socrates in the *Symposium* (200–212) Plato outlines a route by which our love (*eros*) can be gradually transformed from erotic desire for beautiful bodies, through admiration of beauty of soul, and eventually to love of "absolute" or divine beauty, the Form of beauty itself. But this presupposes "instruction in the things of love"—and who is qualified to provide it?

Here the social element comes into Plato's story: he lays great stress on appropriate education as the most important way to produce virtuous, harmonious, well-balanced, "just" people (376–412, 521–41). Plato was one of the first to see education as the key to constructing a better society. And by "education" he does not mean just formal schooling, but also upbringing, including all the social influences on someone's development. In some places (377, 424–25) he anticipates Freud's emphasis on the importance of early childhood (see Chapter 8). Plato goes into considerable detail about the kind of education he envisages, and formal academic study is by no means at the center (but is reserved for an elite subgroup at an appropriately mature age). What Plato sees as vital for everyone is a training of the whole person—Reason, Spirit, and Appetite together. He therefore recommends gymnastics, poetry, and music as elements of the common curriculum. We may find the details of his educational scheme amusingly archaic, but the idea that the "character-forming" foundations are more important than academic superstructures remains as realistic as ever.

But how is education to be instituted? It requires a clear conception of what is being aimed at, a whole theory of human nature and human knowledge, in fact. Moreover, it needs elaborate social organization and resources. This is one main reason why in the *Republic* Plato offers a prescription that is radically political:

> There will be no end to the troubles of states, or of humanity itself, till philosophers become kings in this world, or till those we now call kings and rulers really and truly become philosophers, and political power and philosophy thus come into the same hands. (473)

Plato is well aware that this sounds absurdly unrealistic, but, given his understanding of the Forms, human knowledge, and human nature, we can see his rationale for it. If there is such a thing as the truth about how we ought to live, then those who have such knowledge are the only people who are properly qualified to govern society. Philosophers are, in Plato's conception, those who have come to know the ultimate realities, including the true standards of all value, so if *they* were to govern society, the problems of human nature could be solved.

To produce lovers of wisdom, fit to be philosopher-kings or "Guardians," the higher stages of education will be open only to those with sufficient mental ability. At an appropriate age, they will study mathematics and then philosophy, the disciplines that lead the mind toward knowledge of the Forms and a love of truth for its own sake. The elite thus produced would prefer to continue with their intellectual studies, but Plato expects them to respond to the call of social duty and apply their expertise to the running of society. After experience in subordinate offices, some of them will be ready for supreme power. Only such lovers of wisdom and truth will be impervious to the temptations to misuse power, for they will value the happiness of a right and rational life more than material riches (521).

The way of life of these Guardians is to be spartan, in something like the modern sense of the word (Plato seems to have derived some of his ideas from the Greek state of Sparta). They are to have no personal property and no family life. The state is to select which Guardians are suitable for breeding, and organize "mating festivals." The resulting children are to be brought up communally by nurses and precautions are to be taken to ensure that no parent recognizes his or her own child (457–61). Here Plato goes flatly against the psychological need for strong emotional bonds between children and the adults who bring them up (normally their parents). As a high-born Greek male, he obviously had no experience of child care and children's needs!

Plato's view that his trained Guardians will be such lovers of truth and goodness that they can be trusted never to misuse their power seems naively optimistic. He ignores the wisdom of the adage that power corrupts—and absolute power corrupts absolutely. There is surely a need for constitutional checks and balances to guard against exploitation or tyranny. Plato asks "Who is qualified to wield absolute power?" But should we not rather ask "How can we ensure that nobody has absolute power?"

What if well-educated, supposedly knowledgeable people disagree about questions of morals and politics—as we know they often do. Is there any way of showing who is right? Plato hopes to use rational argument, and he is one of the great philosophical pioneers in doing so. But when someone thinks they know the ultimate truth about such questions of value and policy, they may be intolerant of anyone who disagrees and may feel justified in forcing their view on others (as the history of religious and political controversies bears witness).

What of the rest of society—the nonelite? There are many different economic and social functions that need to be performed, and a division of labor is the natural and efficient way of organizing this. Plato makes a threefold division of society (412–27), parallel to his theory of the soul. Besides the Guardians, there is to be a class traditionally called the "Auxiliaries," who play the roles of soldiers, police, and civil servants: they will put the directions of the Guardians into effect. The third class would contain the workers—farmers, craftsmen, traders, and all those who produce and distribute the material necessities of life. The division between these three classes will be very strict; Plato says that the "justice" or well-being of the society depends on each person performing his own proper function and not interfering with others (432–34).

> The object of our legislation is not the welfare of any particular class, but of the whole community. It uses persuasion or force to unite all citizens and make them share together the benefits which each individually can confer on the community; and its purpose in fostering the attitude is not to enable everyone to please himself, but to make each man a link in the unity of the whole. (519–20)

Plato seems more concerned with the harmony and stability of the whole society than with the well-being of the individuals in it. We may be in favor of "community spirit," and of each person contributing something to the well-being of society, but Plato seems to envisage rather more than this in his strict class division and his insistence that each person fulfill his allotted function and that alone. This is what he calls "justice" in the state, but it is plainly not what *we* mean by the term, which implies equality before the law and some degree of social justice, or fair shares for all. If a worker is not content to be a worker, to accept a strictly limited share of economic goods and have no say in politics, then Plato's state would forcibly compel him to remain in his station. But what is the point of such a rigidly organized society unless it serves the interests of the individuals in it?

Plato's republic has an authoritarian, even totalitarian, character. He has no compunction about censorship—he proposes to exclude poets and other artists from his ideal society, on the grounds that they appeal to the lower, nonrational parts of our nature (605). Plato's hostility to poetry may be more understandable when we realize that until his time it was almost the only source of common conceptions of ethics, and he was fighting for the appeal to reason. He would surely be horrified at the pervasive and almost unregulated influence of the media and the entertainment and advertising industries on everyone in contemporary society from early childhood onward. We may not like Plato's solution of state censorship, but he calls our attention to the continuing problem of how truth and goodness can be presented and inculcated amid a welter of competing cultural and economic interests and influences.

In the *Republic*, Plato dismisses democratic constitutions rather quickly, and we may think, unfairly. He was thinking of Athenian-type democracy in which every citizen had a vote on major decisions. Even if electronic voting systems might make this technically feasible nowadays, it would surely result in unstable government, subject to the changing whims of an enormous population easily influenced by collective emotion and "rhetoric" or clever advertising, which was Plato's criticism of Athenian democracy. However, the most crucial feature of modern democracies— that a government must submit itself for reelection within a fixed period of time—provides a means for peaceful change that is absent from the *Republic*. It should be noted that in the *Statesman* and the *Laws*, Plato advocates the rule of law and endorses democracy, for all its imperfections, as the best kind of constitution given human nature as it is.

The *Republic* is one of the most influential books of all time. I have concentrated on this one work; the reader should remember that Plato wrote much else, developing and changing his views over time. Socrates and Plato started a tradition of rational inquiry into how we should live. Nothing, I suspect, would please them more than to know that some of us still carry this on.

FOR FURTHER READING

Basic text: Plato's *Republic*. There are many translations, but the one that has recently earned most praise for readability and liveliness is by G. M. A. Grube, revised by C. D. C. Reeve (Indianapolis: Hackett, 1992).

The *Republic* is a lengthy and complex work; some readers may prefer to approach Plato via his shorter dialogues, such as the *Euthyphro, Apology, Crito, Phaedo, Meno* or *Protagoras*.

There is an excellent thematic introduction to ancient philosophy in Julia Annas's *Very Short Introduction* (Oxford University Press, 2000).

For an introduction to Plato's thought see, in the Past Masters series, R. M. Hare, *Plato* (Oxford University Press, 1982). This is also available as the first part of a trilogy entitled *Founders of Thought* (Oxford University Press, 1991), which also contains introductions to Aristotle and Augustine.

There is a deeper philosophical discussion of the *Republic* in a work by Julia Annas, *An Introduction to Plato's Republic* (Oxford University Press, 1981). This combines scholarship with clear-sighted attention to the main moral argument, its foundation in claims about human nature, and its continuing contemporary relevance (see especially the summing up in Ch. 13).

For a classic attack on Plato's political program, see K. R. Popper, *The Open Society and Its Enemies*, 4th ed. (London: Routledge, 1962).

For a very full scholarly treatment of Plato's moral philosophy, see Terence Irwin, *Plato's Ethics* (Oxford University Press, 1995).

5

Aristotle: The Ideal of Human Fulfillment

ARISTOTLE'S LIFE AND WORK

Aristotle (384–322 B.C.E.) lived in the next generation after Plato, and also spent much of his life in Athens, so the brief historical background sketched in Chapter 4 applies here too. He joined Plato's Academy at the age of seventeen, and the influence of Plato on his thought is obvious. Although Aristotle was deeply impressed by the views of his mentor, he was capable of criticizing them on important points (which is the ideal relationship between philosophical teacher and pupil!).

Aristotle left Athens in 347, probably for political reasons, and for a few years he became a tutor to the Greek warlord who became famous as Alexander the Great, the world conqueror (but who demonstrated little sign of having learned from his academic mentor!). Aristotle came from a medical family and he did extensive research on the structure of animals and plants. This experience of empirical scientific work shows its influence in his writings, which, despite their abstractness, display a more this-wordly spirit compared with Plato's yearning for transcendence. He returned to Athens in 335 and founded the Lyceum, which continued the tradition of systematic intellectual inquiry started by Plato's Academy. In the last year of Aristotle's life, political infighting forced him out of Athens once again.

The corpus of Aristotelean texts that have come down to us cover an amazing range—logic, metaphysics, epistemology, astronomy, physics, meteorology, biology, psychology, ethics, politics, law, "poetics" (theory of the arts)—and in many of these subjects Aristotle was a pioneer. There was no clear distinction between philosophy and science in those days: Aristotle was interested in formulating the fundamental concepts and principles in every area. He studied what we now recognize as the sciences of astronomy, physics, biology, and psychology, laying down foundations that remained largely unquestioned until the seventeenth century. Apparently, many more of his writings have not survived: the talents and energy of the man were prodigious! The texts available tend to be abbreviated and allusive lecture notes rather than polished, elegant literary works like Plato's dialogues. Aristotle's writing is abstract, technical, and systematic: he can be described as a philosophers' philosopher.

However, the *Nicomachean Ethics*, the main work in which Aristotle discusses human life, its ideals, and its vicissitudes, is relatively accessible. My references will be to this text (using the standard numbering, prefaced by "NE"), unless otherwise indicated. It is not easy reading (no substantial philosophy is), but, like Plato's *Republic*, it deals with profound issues of how to live, it is not overly lengthy, and is reasonably well organized; in some passages it rises to a sort of eloquence. The *de Anima*, a shorter and more technical work, is also important for Aristotle's view of human nature.

METAPHYSICAL BACKGROUND: FORMS AS PROPERTIES, AND THE FOUR KINDS OF QUESTION

Aristotle sometimes talks of gods, but he does *not* mean the biblical concept of a personal Being who has a plan for human history and reveals Himself to particular people. Though he may have paid outward respect to popular Greek polytheism (Zeus, Hera, Athena, et al.), at *Metaphysics*, XII.8, 1074b1 ff., Aristotle says these are anthropomorphic myths for the common people. He did have a concept of a single supreme god, for in the *Physics*, Book VII, he argues that there must be a single unmoved mover, a changeless cause of all the processes of change in the universe. (St. Thomas Aquinas turned this into one of the "Five Ways" of proving the existence of the Christian God.) Moreover, Aristotle held that "it is the function of what is divine to think and use its intellect" (*Parts of Animals*, IV. 10, 686a29), but the kind of thought attributed to the Aristotelean god is intellectual contemplation, not any sort of *care* about human affairs. The unmoved mover is more a concept of scientific theory than an object of worship or obedience (hence my avoidance of a capital "G" in designating it).

Aristotle was influenced by Plato's theory of Forms, but severely critical of it. We saw in Chapter 4 how Plato proposed that what makes particular things count as Fs is their "participation in" the Form of F, understood as an abstract entity existing apart from all the instances of it. Aristotle opposes this separation of the Forms and rejects Plato's metaphysical picture of another world containing the eternal Forms, beyond the world of changeable material things. His own view (standardly labeled "Aristotelian realism") is that there really is something common to all things to which a general concept F can correctly be applied, namely the property (or Aristotelian Form) F—but this common property exists *in the things that have it*, not separately in some other world. This makes Plato's image of the cave dwellers inappropriate: for in Aristotle's understanding of our human situation, our need is not to find a way out of the cave into a different world, but to discern more clearly what is already before our eyes.

Talk of Forms as properties in things rather than as separate entities seems to bring us back to robust common sense, but when such talk is probed philosophically, it becomes problematic. And Aristotle sees this. In what sense is it the *same* property (e.g., of catness, or being a cat) that is found in all cats? If we use a noun like "property" (or "Form"), a word with a singular and a plural, we seem to commit ourselves to thinking of the property as a mysterious kind of *thing*, which can be wholly and completely present in many different things at the same time. Aristotle realizes that we need to distinguish different *categories*—things or substances are fundamentally different from properties or qualities, and we have to say different sorts of things about each.

Do we find the same one-many structure in the use of all general terms, or is the detail different in other cases? Aristotle notices that we often use words in extended ways that do not carry exactly the same meaning in every case. One of his standard examples is the adjective "healthy": we talk of healthy people, food, exercise, climate, a healthy complexion, having a healthy respect for something, and so on, and it is obvious that we do not mean to say that all these are healthy in the primary sense (applicable to people) of having well-functioning bodies that are likely to live long.

Aristotle applied this lesson to value terms, and especially to the most general value term "good." He was aware that different subjects require various methods of study and degrees of precision, so that ethics differs from mathematics in the sorts of results that are possible (NE1094b12–29). He questioned whether all good things are good in some unitary sense, involving a separate Platonic Form of the Good. In NE I.6 (1096a12–1097a14), Aristotle gives a rapid salvo of technical arguments against the

Platonic view (introduced by a declaration that friendship with Plato is dear, but the truth is even dearer!). One of his basic points is that we recognize *several* things as good in themselves, that is, as worth having or pursuing for their own sake, not for the sake of anything else (e.g., pleasure, honor, wisdom), but when we ask what makes such different things all good, there seems to be no general answer we can give, for wisdom surely is good in an irreducibly different way from the way in which honor (or pleasure) is good. (This would seem to rule out even a single Aristotelian Form of goodness, a property that all good things possess!)

Another methodological and metaphysical lesson that Aristotle bequeathed to us is traditionally called "the doctrine of the four causes." In the *Physics*, II.3, 194b16, he distinguishes four questions we can ask about anything, with their corresponding answers or explanations:

1. What is it made of? Its matter ("the material cause")
2. What is it? Its form; the sort of thing it is ("the formal cause")
3. What brought it into existence? Its cause in the modern sense ("the efficient cause")
4. What is it for? Its purpose or function ("the final cause")

Aristotle seems to have assumed that all four questions always have an answer. With respect to the fourth, this commits him to a "teleological" view of the whole universe, according to which everything has a definite purpose or function, a goal that it serves or somehow strives toward. Human artifacts like beds, knives, and telephones have purposes for which they were constructed; and the organs of plants and animals, such as roots, hearts, and eyes, have functions, as Aristotle well understood from his biological studies. As for *whole* animals and plants, although it is odd to speak of them existing "for" some purpose, we have an idea of what counts as a mature, flourishing specimen of each species. (More controversially, Aristotle tries to do something like this for the human species.) But we do not think of inanimate natural objects—rocks, mountains, rivers, glaciers, beaches, clouds, sun and moon, planets, stars, and galaxies—as existing for a purpose (unless, of course, you believe that God created each of them with a particular end in view). And we do not think there is some "natural," mature, or best state of these things that they tend to grow toward in favorable conditions. Aristotle seems to have overextended the scope of teleology, then, but otherwise his distinction of four sorts of questions is a useful clarification of our thought.

In such ways, Aristotle repeatedly teaches us not just to latch onto the first idea that occurs to us or the first theory we hear of (which is the lazy way in philosophizing), but to think more carefully, to examine a suitably varied set of cases, to take the trouble to recognize the complexity of the world and of our ways of thinking and talking about it, and to be open-minded, without factional spirit, in our consideration of general theories. He can be honored as a founding father of the kind of "analytical" philosophy exemplified in the thought of Ludwig Wittgenstein in the mid-twentieth century.

THEORY OF HUMAN NATURE: THE SOUL AS A SET OF FACULTIES, INCLUDING RATIONALITY

As we have seen, Plato defended the dualist view, according to which the human soul is an immaterial substance that can exist apart from the body after death. Aristotle radically undermines this whole way of thinking in a subtle way that I will now try to explain.

On this topic it is Aristotle the biologist who makes a vital contribution to philosophy. He sees human beings as one kind of animal, albeit a very special kind, uniquely capable of rational thought. And he sees animals (by which we mean not just mammals, but reptiles, birds, insects, crustaceans, etc.) as one main class of living things, plants being the other. All life thus forms an enormous hierarchy of orders, genera, and species, each with its own distinguishing features. The main outline of this tree-like branching structure was recognized long ago from empirical observation by early biologists such as Aristotle himself and was further refined by Linnaeus in the eighteenth century, before Darwin came up with the theory of evolution, to explain how the hierarchy relates to a historical lineage of descent (see Chapter 10).

Aristotle outlines his approach in his groundbreaking short treatise traditionally known by its Latin name, *de Anima* ("Of the soul"), and which is the first book on psychology. Straight away we should be aware of the problems in using the word "soul" to translate the Greek *psyche*. One danger is that "soul" has strong religious connotations of piety and immortality, deriving from both Christianity and Plato. But Aristotle lived four centuries before Christianity and he offers an entirely different conception of *psyche* from Plato. We can substitute "mind" for "soul," but that only replaces one four-letter noun by another. The crucial difference in the Aristotelian conception is that the soul or mind is not thought of as a thing or substance at all (not even an *immaterial* substance). Strictly, Aristotle's view would be best expressed by not using *any* noun to translate *psyche*, but to say instead that living things are "ensouled"; that is, they have certain distinctive ways of existing and functioning.

Technically, Aristotle applies his general distinction of matter and form to this case, and says that the soul is the "form" of a living thing. But

"form" here does not mean Platonic Form, nor does it have the more ordinary meaning of shape; rather it means what makes something the *fundamental sort* of thing it is (the second, "formal cause," in the list of four
questions). What, then, makes something alive? This question is not meant
in the sense of what brought it into being (which would be the third, "efficient" cause), but, rather, what is it for something to be alive, what criteria does anything have to satisfy to count as a living thing?
Remembering that plants as well as animals are alive, we can say that the
criteria are metabolism and reproduction. The first is what Aristotle called
"self-nourishment, growth, and decay" or "the nutritive faculty" (*de
Anima*, 412a13, 414a32), and he also mentions reproduction (415a22).
What then distinguishes plants from animals? (Or to put it dangerously,
what is distinctive of the animal kind of soul?) Animals have the faculties of sense-perception, desire (412a33), and self-movement (414b18).
That is, animals, unlike plants, perceive through their sense organs and
move themselves around to fulfill their desires.

What then do human beings do or have that is extra to all this? Aristotle
says: the faculty of "thought and intellect" (414b19), but it may not be
immediately clear what he means: it must be a kind of thought that other
animals do not have, presumably thoughts that can be expressed in language, in claims that such-and-such is the case, and for which reasons for
and against can be given. The human soul or mind should thus be understood not as a thing, but as *a distinctive cluster of faculties, including
reasoning*, that are fundamental to the human way of living and functioning. Aristotle himself writes (*de Anima,* 408b15) "it is surely better
not to say that the soul pities, learns, or thinks, but that the man does
these with his soul," and we can suggest that it is better still to say that
the *man* pities, learns, and thinks (using his mental faculties or abilities).

So the soul of any living thing X is not a substance, an entity, an extra
(separable) thing; it is rather the way that X lives, operates, functions—
and that "way" may itself be analyzable as a set of faculties or ways of
functioning that normally go together. (But in special cases some can be
absent; e.g., somebody who loses their memory, or an infant who has not
yet learned to speak). On this conception, it makes no sense to talk of a
soul or mind existing without a body, for if there is no body (or, at least,
no *living* body), then there can be no *way* that the body is functioning,
for it is not functioning at all. Aristotle draws this conclusion at 414a19:
the soul cannot exist without a body (contrary to Plato), not because it is
itself a kind of body (contrary to the Greek materialists, who had suggested that the soul is a whiff of gas, composed of very fine particles or
atoms), but because the soul is not a thing of any kind, rather a complex
property of living bodies.

Aristotle makes a significant, but puzzling, qualification to this trenchant conclusion. He suggests that there is something especially different about the human intellect, namely our faculty for purely theoretical thought (which he calls "contemplation," though he has mathematics and physics in mind, rather than aesthetic contemplation, or meditation or prayer). And he seems to say that this faculty, or this kind of soul, can exist separately from the body, "as the everlasting can from the perishable" (*de Anima*, 413b26). But perhaps what Aristotle meant is that in gods, though not in us, there could be intellectual functioning without a body.

It looks as if Aristotle could not bring himself completely to reject his Platonic heritage, yet it is hard for us to see how he could consistently go back on the logic of his own general argument. How can we conceive of mathematical thought going on without there being a living, embodied mathematician? These days it will be suggested that a computer can do mathematics, but even if we allow that what it does can count as "thought," the fact remains that for it to happen there has to be a complex arrangement of wires and electrodes with currents pulsing through them—a material object, if not a *living* body. The notion of totally disembodied thought remains conceptually problematic. As we will see in the Historical Interlude, some of Aristotle's Islamic and Christian successors were happy to exploit this bit of apparent backtracking in his philosophy of mind.

In Chapter 4 we have examined Plato's tripartite theory of the soul. Aristotle must have been aware of this theory, but he reconceptualizes it. Insofar as he talks of "parts" or "elements" of the soul, Aristotle cannot mean this literally as spatial parts or bits, because for him the soul is not a body, but a set of capacities of the living body. A *part* of an Aristotelean soul obviously has to be understood as one such capacity, distinct from others in the set. One might expect Aristotle, then, to follow Plato's lead by distinguishing the capacities for reasoning, for emotion, and for bodily desire, but he does not exactly follow this tripartite division. He usually contrasts *two* elements, one possessing reason (the bit that does the thinking) and the other possessing reason only in the weaker sense that it can obey reason, though it can also be disobedient (NE1098a5). Elsewhere he talks of rational and nonrational aspects of the soul (NE1192a28 ff.). It seems that Aristotle sees the most important distinction as between Plato's Reason on one hand and Spirit and Appetite on the other: both emotion and desire being potentially obedient to reason, in the sense that how one feels and what one wants can be affected by one's considered judgment about what is best, although notoriously this does not always happen!

Later, Aristotle finds occasion to make a distinction *within* the rational part, between our capacity for reasoning about necessary propositions (in mathematics, and, in his view, in natural science), and our ability to deliberate about what to do (NE1139a5). This is the distinction between theoretical and practical reason, which is taken up by Kant (see Chapter 6).

Another crucial aspect of Aristotle's theory of human nature, like Plato's, is that we are ineradicably social beings. In the traditional translation, "man is a political animal" (NE1097b11, and *Politics*, I.2, 1252a24; his word *politikon* has also been rendered as "civic" or "social"). Elsewhere, he wrote that "social animals are those which have some single activity common to them all (which is not true of all gregarious animals); such are men, bees, wasps, ants, cranes" (*History of Animals*, I.1, 488a8). This is a striking anticipation of the sociobiological approach of E. O. Wilson, which we will examine in Chapter 10. But Aristotle recognized that what is distinctive of human social life is our awareness of justice and injustice (*Politics*, I.1, 1253a15). He believed that our human nature reaches its full development only when we live as members of an organized society, of which his paradigm was the *polis*, the Greek city-state, with a population of less than 100,000 or so.

But who exactly count as rational beings, qualified to take part in public life and politics? Aristotle's use of the masculine gender is no accident, for like most ancient Greeks he assumes without argument that women, although human, are innately different in mental capacity from men and less fitted for rational thought, so they should stick to their reproductive and domestic roles. He writes: "the relation of male to female is naturally that of the superior to the inferior—of the ruling to the ruled" (*Politics*, I.V.7), and "the male is naturally fitter to command than the female, except where there is some departure from nature" (I.XII.1). These appeals to "nature" do not seem to be based on any empirical study of the abilities of women; rather, like many other uses of the very slippery term "nature" through history, they are the "common sense" of the time, which may be nothing more than the expression of prejudice and perceived self-interest. With respect to women, Aristotle was conservative where Plato was ahead of his time.

Aristotle also assumed that there are innate differences between individuals in their ability to think and reason. He frequently talks of "good birth," and (like Plato) takes it for granted that there will be social classes based on the division of labor, with large numbers of workers (farmers, traders, craftsmen, and soldiers) who will not, for the most part, be capable of the higher forms of thought. He also displays some prejudice against the old and the young!

Moreover, like others of his time, Aristotle sees no general objection to slavery, for he believes that some people are slaves by nature:

> . . . all men who differ from others much as the body differs from the soul, or an animal from a man (and this is the case with all whose function is

bodily service, and who produce their best when they supply such service)—all such are by nature slaves, and it is better for them . . . to be ruled by a master. (*Politics*, I.V.8)

However, Aristotle admits that "the contrary of nature's intention often happens," so that slaves sometimes have the bodies (and upright carriage) of freemen (I.V.10); and if he were more open to an unprejudiced examination of the empirical facts, he would have to allow that some slaves have mental capacities at least equal to those of their masters. (Surely there are no humans, except perhaps the severely mentally disabled, who differ from other humans as much as a nonhuman animal from a human.) Aristotle's discussion of slavery is somewhat nuanced, for he makes a distinction between *just* slaveholding—in cases where (he claims!) there is a "natural" mental difference between master and slave, yet a community of interest and a relation of friendship between them—and unjust enslavement based only on legal sanction and superior power (I.VI.10).

Like other Greeks of his time, Aristotle also assumes, without argument, a "natural" distinction between Greeks and "barbarians." At *Politics*, I.II.4, he implies that all barbarians are slaves by nature, and quotes with approval the saying of a Greek poet that the barbarous people should be governed by the Greeks. At NE1154a30 he lets slip the racist remark that, although the "brutish" (animal-like) type of human being is rare, it is more common among non-Greeks.

Aristotle's assumptions of patriarchy, slavery, and imperialism are shocking to our contemporary sensibilities. One can imagine empire builders (especially the British colonial administrators of a century ago, with their classical education!) finding him sympathetic. But this should not prejudice us against the rest of his thinking: for there is nothing to prevent us from accepting an Aristotelian analysis of mind as a set of capacities of the living body and an Aristotelian idea of human fulfillment, while insisting that the distinctively human rational capacities are, on average, equally present in every person, irrespective of sex, class, race, and nationality, and that human needs and aspirations—and rights—are correspondingly universal.

IDEAL AND DIAGNOSIS: HUMAN FULFILLMENT, VIRTUES AND VICES, THEORETICAL AND PRACTICAL WISDOM

Aristotle accentuates the positive. Rather than diagnosing some fundamental fault in the human condition and prescribing a remedy for it—which is what many religions do—Aristotle first gives us an account of the end or purpose or meaning of human life, then suggests how it can be put into practice and how failures to live up to the ideal might be avoided or remedied. This is connected with the fact that where religions (and Plato, to some extent) tend to offer an otherworldly kind of salvation or solution, Aristotle offers a thoroughly this-worldly account of human fulfilment. In that respect his approach is more like Confucianism (Chapter 1) than the other theories we have considered so far.

(Whether one presents a theory in terms of its diagnosis and prescription—the framework we have chosen to use in this book—or in terms of ideal and realization—more in keeping with Aristotle's approach—is only a matter of emphasis and style of presentation. A diagnosis of what is wrong in human beings presupposes some value judgment about how we should ideally be; conversely, an ideal sets a standard that some human beings will be found not to achieve.)

Aristotle begins the *Nicomachean Ethics* by asking whether there is one end or aim that we seek, for its own sake, in all our actions and projects (NE1094a1–b12). He says that we can all agree that there is such an end, and that we call it "happiness," but we may disagree about what happiness actually is (NE1095a17). A word of caution is needed here about the use of "happiness" to translate Aristotle's *eudaimonia*. The etymology of the Greek word connects it with the notion of having a good guardian spirit or "genius" (*daimon*). In Aristotle's usage it does not carry any such supernatural connotation, but it does imply meeting an objective ethical standard, whereas "happiness" in contemporary English does not. We can say of a mentally disabled adult that he is happy with his toys, or of a drug-addict that she is happy when she has a source of supply and no side-effects, or of a rapist or pedophile that he is happy as long as he can find victims and not get caught out—but Aristotle would emphatically reject the notion that any of these people enjoy *eudaimonia*, for on his conception that is to imply that a person is leading an admirably fulfilled life. "Fulfillment" might indeed be a better translation; "flourishing" is another word that has been used to express the Aristotelian ideal; "felicity" or "perfection" also suggest it; "blessedness" might do, if divested of Christian connotations. (The latter has been used for the ideal recommended by Spinoza, which is a rationally contemplative state of mind, as Aristotle's own favored ideal turns out to be.)

Can we say anything more substantial about this state of ideal human fulfillment, which is the meaning or purpose of life? Aristotle applies his theory of human nature as having a uniquely rational capacity and comes up with a formula that puts a bit more content into his so far very abstract notion of *eudaimonia*:

... if all this is so, and a human being's function we posit as being a kind of life, and this life as being activity of soul and actions accompanied by reason, and it belongs to a good man to perform these well and finely, and each thing is completed well when it possesses its proper excellence; if all this is so, the human good turns out to be activity of soul in accordance with excellence (and if there are more excellences than one, in accordance with the best and most complete). But furthermore it will be this in a complete life. For a single swallow does not make spring, nor does a single day; in the same way, neither does a single day, or a short time, make a man blessed and happy. (NE1098a1 ff.)

The reader may be aghast to be told that this is one of the more eloquent passages in Aristotle! (He is a very sober and serious philosopher, always careful to put in all the qualifications that he sees as needed, however much they clog up his sentences.) The message that emerges is a valuable one, however: (a) that human fulfillment consists in *activity*, namely the exercise of our faculties, not in mere passive enjoyment; (b) that it must involve the use of our distinctively human *rational* capacity; (c) that this activity should be conducted "well and finely," displaying the best, most complete kind of "excellence" or *virtue*; and (d) that it should last over an extended *lifetime*.

This formula obviously invites further inquiry into the nature of human excellences (the Greek word *arete* has often been translated as "virtue," but it has to be realized that, for Aristotle, inanimate things can have *arete*; for example, an axe has it if it functions well in chopping (in English, we say it is a *good* axe, but not a *virtuous* one!). Corresponding to the reason giving and reason obeying parts of the soul, mentioned earlier, Aristotle distinguishes excellences of intellect and excellences of character (NE1103a15). The former divide into theoretical and practical. Two theoretical excellences are *sophia*, or intellectual accomplishment (what we would now call academic excellence), and *techne*, or technical expertise (Aristotle displays his prejudice by not valuing this so highly). Practical excellence is *phronesis*, practical wisdom; that is, being good at deliberating about what to do in real-life situations and reaching wise decisions about them.

Plato made no such distinction between *sophia* and *phronesis*, holding as he did that theoretical knowledge of the Forms was necessary for correct practice; Aristotle makes an important new contribution by emphasizing the independence of practical wisdom. As he puts it at 1139a21 ff.:

What affirmation and denial are in the case of thought, pursuit and avoidance are with desire; so that, since excellence of character is a disposition issuing in decisions, and decision is a desire informed by deliberation, in consequence both what issues from reason must be true and the desire must be correct for the decision to be a good one, and reason must assert and desire pursue the same things. This, then, is thought, and truth, of a practical sort.

Aristotle holds that practical wisdom does not consist in knowing and applying moral commandments and prohibitions, for he does not think it possible to formulate any set of general rules that can settle every particular choice that we meet in life: "the agents themselves have to consider the circumstances relating to the occasion" (1104a9). The wise person, the *phronemos*, learns from practical experience and will have to be trusted to make wise decisions in new cases.

Indeed, the whole of Aristotle's inquiry in the *Ethics* is undertaken not for the sake of theory, but to help people to become good (1103b27, 1179b1 ff.). His fundamental concern is not to display philosophical virtuosity and make an academic reputation, but to help promote virtue. It has to be admitted, though, that the demanding intellectual effort needed to understand Aristotle's intricately wrought philosophical prose is unlikely to make anyone virtuous who is not already well disposed. Aristotle is well aware that there is no substitute for a good upbringing, a training in virtuous habits from childhood. But the hope is that his laborious elucidation of the nature of human virtues may help social theorists and legislators ("political experts," as he calls them) in their thinking about how to organize society so as to promote human virtue and fulfillment (NE I.3).

The central books of the *Nicomachean Ethics* discuss particular practical excellences or virtues in considerable detail. As well as practical wisdom (often called "prudence"), there are the other three in the traditional list (deriving from Plato), namely moderation (or "temperance"), courage, and justice. But Aristotle extends this list considerably, and he offers a new analysis (which applies to many if not all of them) of virtue as a mean between two extremes. Courage is the right balance between cowardliness and rashness; temperance (with respect to bodily pleasures) is the mean between overindulgence and asceticism; "open-handedness" about money is the right balance between being spendthrift or miserly; "mildness" (in one's display of anger) is the mean between irascibility and meekness (NE III.6–V). To those who find Aristotle overly serious, it may be a relief to find him admitting that "life also includes relaxation, and relaxation includes amusement of a playful sort" (IV.8, 1127b35), though even here he does not relax his philosophical grip, but offers an analysis of wit as the appropriate mean between over-the-top buffoonery and humorless boorishness or stiffness!

Aristotle adds some virtues that seem more peculiar to the society of ancient Athens, such as "greatness of soul" (which consists in being worthy of great things and being conscious of it) and "munificence" (which consists in the appropriate and tasteful spending of money on public projects). The former, a suitable sense of one's own worth and honor, can be represented as a mean between conceitedness (thinking one is worthy when one is not) and "littleness of soul" (thinking one is less worthy than one is) (NE IV.3). But it is not universally agreed that greatness of soul is a virtue: the "beatitudes" in Jesus' sermon on the mount, "Blessed are the poor in spirit . . . " and "Blessed are the meek . . . " (*Matthew* 5:3–5), strongly suggest the contrary. Yet Nietzsche, in the late nineteenth century, fiercely rejected Christian humility and recommended something like Aristotelian great-souledness instead.

The virtue of justice (in something more like the modern, rather than the Platonic, sense) does not seem to fit into the pattern of a mean between two extremes. There is the corresponding vice of injustice or unfairness, of course, but there does not seem to be such a thing as being *too* just or *too* fair (although people can be overly scrupulous about exact equality in things that do not matter). Justice crucially involves other people, not just particular others to whom one is related by ties of family or friendship or contractual obligations, but potentially everyone in one's society (however the bounds of that society are delimited—for Aristotle it would be the *polis*). He is aware of the importance of equality before the law for commercial transactions and the solidarity of society. He writes: "it is reciprocal action governed by proportion that keeps the city together" (NE 1131b35).

All this examination of virtues has been outlining positive ideals for human life. Things go wrong when human actions, characters, and lives do not measure up to these ideals. Aristotle does not offer any all-embracing diagnosis of why, for although there is (he takes it) just one basic ideal of human fulfillment, he is aware that there are *many* different ways of falling short of it (1106b31). As we have seen, for most of the virtues there are two corresponding vices, which fail either by deficiency or by excess. The various possibilities arise from our mixed nature, as animals with bodily instincts but also with strong social susceptibilities and rational capacities. We can be tempted away from temperance by pleasure and from courage by fear. We can be moved to rashness by social ambition and to injustice by selfishness.

There is a further twist to Aristotle's diagnosis when he distinguishes three kinds of undesirable states: badness, lack of self-control, and brutishness (NE 1145a16). The first is the opposite of virtue, namely a settled disposition to do the wrong thing—not innately there from birth, but formed through some combination of bad training and wrong choices. The third is some innate, incurable disposition to act in ways that are "inhuman," whether harmful to others or just weird (e.g., psychopaths or congenital idiots). The second is the most interesting to Aristotle, and he gives a subtle philosophical analysis of self-control and the lack of it in Book VII.

As we saw in Chapter 4, Socrates held that nobody does what he knows to be wrong. But this conflicts with the fact of human experience that St. Paul reports: "For the good that I would I do not: but the evil which I would not, that I do" (Romans 7:19). Plato distinguished conflicting parts of the soul and posed the practical problem of how one can achieve inner harmony. One of Aristotle's important contributions is to point out that the person who lacks self-control is significantly different from he or she who is simply bad or vicious, for the latter typically has no awareness of how bad he or she is, whereas the former is painfully conscious—like St. Paul—of the gap between his or her aspirations and deeds (NE 1150b36). There is more hope of "curing" or improving the former (not that we should totally give up on the latter, for perhaps such people can be *made* aware of the wrongness of what they do).

On the positive side, there is a corresponding distinction between the person who does the right thing, but only after exercising self-control to master his or her inappropriate desires, and the person who is sufficiently advanced in virtue (or what others might call inner harmony, enlightenment, or the spiritual life) as not to feel inappropriate desires (or at least, not so strongly as to experience inner conflict), so that they do the right thing easily and gracefully. Aristotle's discussion is somewhat technical, but he puts this latter ideal of *sophrosune* before us (though "moderation" and "temperance" are rather pale words to express it in English).

REALIZATION OR PRESCRIPTION: POLITICAL EXPERTISE AND INTELLECTUAL CONTEMPLATION

How can human fulfillment be achieved? How can inner harmony be attained? Aristotle holds that virtue and vice are formed by "habituation"; that is, one's character is a result of one's past actions, so it seems that we can be held responsible for what we have made of ourselves, at least to some extent. Exhortation, praise, and blame can have some effect in promoting appropriate action in particular situations, but Aristotle ruefully acknowledges that "most people are not of the sort to be guided by a sense of shame but by fear" (NE 1179b11) and he is well aware that "it is not possible, or not easy, for words to dislodge what has long since been absorbed into one's character-traits" (1179b18).

So, because appropriate upbringing is the crucial ingredient in character formation, and upbringing and education presuppose a preexisting human society, Aristotle is led, like Plato, to inquire into how society should best be organized. The *Nicomachean Ethics* is mostly concerned with setting forth an ideal of human happiness or fulfillment, but as early as the second page Aristotle points out that putting it into practice is a matter of "political expertise":

> For even if the good is the same for a single person and for a city, the good of the city is a greater and more complete thing both to achieve and to preserve; for while to do so for one person on his own is satisfactory enough, to do it for a nation or for cities is finer and more godlike. So our inquiry seeks these things, being a political inquiry in a way. (1094b8)

And the *Ethics* ends by setting out a program for another inquiry into constitutions, legislation, and good government (1181b13).

Most of the detail of Aristotle's prescription is set out in this other work, the *Politics*, which (like Plato's *Republic*) covers a much wider range than its title suggests. In the *Politics*, Aristotle deals with such matters as marriage, parenthood, slavery, and household management (Book I); population, territory, town planning, nursery education, and the training of youth (Books VII–VIII); as well as citizenship and constitutions, revolution and reform (Books II–VI). Aristotle is more realistic than Plato in allowing for family life and private property, so he recognizes some limits to state power. But in other ways his ideal *polis* is still somewhat totalitarian, for he regards the upbringing of children and youth as so crucial for their moral development, and thus for the moral health of society, that "their upbringing and patterns of behavior must be ordered by the state" (NE1179b35). It seems that, from a very young age, the state must take a controlling power over the lives of children. It has been remarked that for Aristotle the ideal *polis* is like Calvin's Geneva in the sixteenth century in its power over the morals of its citizens. It is common these days to try to make a distinction between questions of politics and legislation on the one hand and "private" morality on the other, but Aristotle's view challenges us to consider whether any community or society or nation can survive and flourish without some measure of agreement on the most fundamental questions about how human life should best be lived.

Before leaving Aristotle, we should return to his notion of ideal happiness and consider the prescription that he himself favors in the last book (NE X.6–9). Here he argues that of the three conceptions of fulfilled life mentioned in I.5 (namely, lives devoted to pleasure, to political success and honor, or to intellectual inquiry and reflection) the third is best. He quickly dismisses the hedonistic life (X.6), he finds practical political activity second best (X.8, 1178a9 ff.), and awards the palm to the life of reflection (X.7–8). Aristotle's argument for this is that the best kind of happiness will be activity of the "highest" element within human nature, the ruling part, that which has "awareness of fine things and divine ones"—and that is, in his view, reflective activity (1177a13 ff.). This is the most self-sufficient kind of human activity, requiring only modest resources. Aristotle also claims, implausibly, that it is the only sort of activity that is done for its own sake (1177b1), thereby inviting the wrath of musicians, golfers, lovers, and anyone who enjoys a country walk!

At this point, comparison with "the gods" enters into Aristotle's argument (though one wonders how literally he takes them):

> If, then intelligence is something divine as compared to a human being, so too a life in accordance with this will be divine as compared to a human life. One should not follow the advice of those who say "Human you are, think human thoughts," and "Mortals you are, think mortal ones," but instead, so far as is possible, assimilate to the immortals and do everything with the aim of living in accordance with what is highest of the things in us; for even if it is small in bulk, the degree to which it surpasses everything in power and dignity is far greater. (1177b31 ff.)

Aristotle goes on to say that it is absurd to attribute practical doings to the gods, yet we believe they are blessed and happy in the highest degree and we conceive of them as alive and hence as active in *some* way—so that can only be the reflective way, which must be the highest kind of activity (1178b8 ff.). Moreover, if the gods care at all about humanity, he supposes they delight in what has the greatest affinity to themselves, namely our exercise of intelligence (1179a25).

All this argument is supposed to support Aristotle's rating of intellectual activity as the supreme kind of human happiness. But why need there be a first prize here, a picking out of one kind of fulfillment as the highest, all things considered? Obviously, Aristotle himself pursued the life of the mind, became a world leader in it, and must surely have derived immense satisfaction from it. But that need not commit him to rating other pursuits as inferior. Why can't they just be good in different ways? We might enlarge the scope of "intellectual activity" to include the creative arts. We can admire the successful politician, or at least he or she who does not pursue power for its own sake, but uses it to promote peace, prosperity, and social justice. We can also admire less exalted ways of life (e.g., craftsmen, farmers, engineers, athletes, teachers, and housewives or househusbands who devote much of their lives to their families). Indeed, many lives are devoted to multiple ideals (e.g., career, family, church, political commitment, music, sports) and there is no compulsion for everyone to have a single or permanent highest priority.

If we subtract from Aristotle that final overvaluation of the purely intellectual and replace it with a multiple set of human ideals (things worth doing for their own sake, none of which is compulsory), we have a more attractive conception of human flourishing or fulfillment that conforms to his formula (in I.7) of activity using our rational capacities, conducted "well and finely" over a lifetime—where "rational" includes practical as well as theoretical rationality. We have here the basis of a human-centered or humanist ethics.

But is there something missing? We may have qualms when we reflect that people in a fortunate class or nation might live very fulfilled lives by this sort of criterion—enjoying careers, family and friends, the arts and sciences, sports and hobbies, and so on, in whatever mixtures suit each individual—while many other people have little or no opportunity for such fulfillments. In Aristotle's own society, slaves or barbarians had few rights, if any; and it seems that even among male Greeks, only high-born aristocrats could aspire to intellectual or political careers. In our own time, in our so-called liberal, freedom-loving (and prosperous) democracies, it is painfully obvious that not everyone in our own society has the same opportunities for human fulfillment, let alone everyone in the wider world on which we depend for our resources.

It may be salutary, then, to compare the modified Aristotelian humanist ethic just outlined with Jesus' summary of the commandments: "Love the Lord thy God with all thy heart and all thy mind and all thy soul . . . and love thy neighbor as thyself" (Mark 12:30–31). Let us factor out the question of the *existence* of the Judeo-Christian God or the Aristotelian gods and just compare the ideals involved. The two conceptions of the divine, and the ideals thereby set up for human aspiration, are importantly different. Aristotle's gods are purely intellectual beings, and if they care at all about human affairs, he represents them as caring only that we (or the cleverest of us) should emulate their intellectual insight. But the Hebrew God was a God of love as well as knowledge, who is represented as caring about His people collectively and individually, and in particular as caring about social justice (e.g., about the fate of the poor and the orphaned) and as capable of forgiveness. All this carries over to the Christian conception of a God of Love (see Chapter 3).

Aristotle is far from ignorant of the importance of human love; indeed, he devotes two whole books (NE VIII and IX) to the topic of friendship. (These are some of the most readable sections and can be read almost independently of the rest.) And he notes that there is a sense in which one should love oneself, namely wishing for the very best for oneself (1168b30). But friendship (*philia*) is, on Aristotle's conception, only possible with a few people; moreover, it can only really exist between good people. In contrast, the New Testament conception of love (*agape*, formerly translated as "charity") is supposed to be universal and unconditional. It involves more, I take it, than Aristotle's "good will" (NE1166b30). The ideal it puts before us is first that we should be loving or compassionate to *all* our fellow human beings, regardless of sex, race, class, ethnicity, or nationality. And, second, that our love or compassion should not depend on good behavior or individual talents, so that a change of heart and forgiveness should always be seen as possible. This twin ideal is almost impossibly demanding on our frail human nature. But we may feel that there is something missing from an ethic that does not even set it before us.

FOR FURTHER READING

Basic text: Aristotle's *Nicomachean Ethics*. There are several English translations, of which the latest is *Aristotle, Nicomachean Ethics, Translation, Introduction, and Commentary* by Sarah Broadie and Christopher Rowe (Oxford University Press, 2002). Broadie provides an excellent introduction to the philosophical issues and presents a detailed argumentative commentary. J. O. Urmson gives a rather easier introduction in *Aristotle's Ethics* (Oxford: Blackwell, 1988).

Aristotle: Selections, edited by T. Irwin and G. Fine (Indianapolis: Hackett Publishing Company, 1995), is a good introductory selection from the whole of Aristotle's work.

There are several excellent introductions to the whole of Aristotle's philosophy: J. L. Ackrill, *Aristotle the Philosopher* (Oxford University Press, 1981), is good at relating Aristotle to contemporary philosophy; *The Philosophy of Aristotle*, 2nd ed., by D. J. Allan (Oxford University Press, 1970), goes into more detail about the texts and their historical background; Jonathan Barnes has a masterful "Very Short Introduction" in the Oxford University Press series.

There is a useful introduction to the *Politics* in *The Politics of Aristotle*, translated with an introduction, notes, and appendices, by Ernest Barker (Oxford University Press, 1946).

Historical Interlude

In our selection of "theories" of human nature, we are jumping over a long historical gap, from the ancient world to the late eighteenth century. Much happened in between, of course. It will help our understanding of Kant and his successors if I provide some thumbnail sketches of major intellectual developments in the intervening centuries. For each period, I have formulated a question to sum up its main concern.

> *Ancient thought after Plato and Aristotle: What guide to life does philosophy offer?*

In the Greek world after Aristotle, the small city-states like Athens were absorbed into the empire conquered by Alexander (and later into the Roman empire), so they became part of a more cosmopolitan society. Intellectual inquiry became institutionalized in Plato's Academy, Aristotle's Lyceum, and other "Schools." Sciences such as astronomy and medicine became more specialized, and philosophy took a more practical, quasi-religious direction: people expected "the love of wisdom" to issue not just in theoretical pronouncements but to give guidance as to how life can best be lived.

THE STOICS

The Stoics were one major school of thought that took up this theme. Their founder was Zeno, who flourished in the early third century B.C.E. The Stoics devoted some attention to logic and cosmology, but they are most famous for their prescription that life should be lived consistently "according to nature." Of course, everything depends on what is meant by "nature" here. The Stoic idea was that there is a rational principle or *logos* in the universe and in the human soul, and that we must submit to this rational or divinely appointed order. There is much in the world that we cannot change and must learn to live with; our only choice is how *well* to make the necessary adjustments (i.e., whether we use our rational powers to control our own emotions). Thus, the basic message is that we are free only to change ourselves. But we are capable of attaining virtue, and hence such happiness as is possible in human life, by the right adjustments of attitude.

The Stoical philosophy became influential in the early Roman Empire. It was one of the sources of the teaching of the Roman orator Cicero (first century B.C.E.). And it was reformulated by Seneca (first century C.E.), who was an adviser to the Emperor Nero, and by Epictetus (second century), a freed slave who insisted that *all* humans are "children of Zeus" and have the capacity for virtue (a universalist philosophy parallel to Christianity). The Stoical philosophy of life was also famously expressed in the *Meditations* of Marcus Aurelius, who was Roman Emperor from 161 to 180.

THE EPICUREANS

Another school of thought, sometimes represented as opposite to Stoicism, is Epicureanism. Epicurus (third century B.C.E.) sketched an empirical epistemology and an atomist cosmology, but his main interest was in ethics and his message is often summed up as saying that pleasure is the ultimate goal of life. However, this did not mean an unthinking hedonistic pursuit of the sensual pleasures of the moment. Epicurus prescribed a careful, prudent search for permanent "serenity of soul," with the minimum of pain and the kind of moderate pleasures that can be relied on to last. The practical results may thus not be very different from those of Stoicism. But there is a marked difference of emphasis. Epicureanism sounds ultimately selfish, in that virtue comes into the story only as a means to the end of happiness, whereas in Stoicism it seems that happiness comes in only as a by-product of virtue.

NEO-PLATONISM

In the later Roman Empire there was a remarkable growth of neo-Platonic thought. The most famous name here is Plotinus (third century C.E.), who developed Plato's notion of the preeminence of the Form of the Good into an elaborate doctrine of a transcendent God as the source of all being and knowledge. The implication for human life is that we are capable of an ethical ascent toward God, which can progress to a final state of mystical union. Plotinus's thought thus had much in common with Christianity, but though he must have been aware of this new religion he does not mention it. His disciple Porphyry wrote a biography of him and arranged his writings under the title *Enneads*. This school of thought was a major influence on St. Augustine.

The Middle Ages: What part does reason play in faith?

AUGUSTINE (354-430)

In the early fourth century C.E., the Roman Emperor Constantine adopted Christianity as the official religion of the Empire. Augustine was the most crucial connecting link between the ancient world and the Christian medieval worldview that dominated the next millennium in Europe. He came from North Africa, which was then part of the Roman Empire; he had a Christian mother, but Augustine was not at first a Christian. He was trained in the Roman tradition of rhetoric (public speaking) and he avidly studied the writings of the Manicheans (who held that there are twin Powers of Good and Evil), and the neo-Platonists. After contact with Christians and studying the Bible, Augustine eventually converted to Christianity in a prolonged intellectual and moral struggle vividly described in his famous *Confessions*. He was ordained as a priest, and soon became a bishop.

Augustine's voluminous writings achieved a synthesis of Christianity and neo-Platonic ideas (he had little knowledge of Aristotle). Plotinus's conceptions of God as the Source of everything and of the human potential for inner illumination were readily integrated with the Hebrew belief in God as Creator, and the Christian gospel of salvation. For Augustine, the intellect is subservient to faith: in a famous phrase, he said "I believe in order to understand," meaning that reason alone cannot reach the most important truths; he saw an act of will, or disposition of the whole person, as crucial.

Augustine thus had a strong sense of human free will, but he had an even stronger sense of human sinfulness. He held that nothing we can do by ourselves can reconcile us to God. Mired in original sin, we cannot free ourselves from it. Only God's free action, His "grace," can save us: if some get saved (and are predestined for it by God's choice or "election") while others do not, this is not because of any human merit. Augustine defended this view in a famous controversy with Pelagius (the first thinker from the British Isles to appear in history). He persuaded a Church Council to condemn Pelagius as a heretic, but the relation between human freedom and divine grace remains a crucial problem for theology.

Augustine's strong sense of human sin as manifest in our bodily desires also had a baneful influence on much subsequent Christianity, which tended to identify sin with sexuality—or at least to concentrate attention on sex as the primary exemplification of sin. And this was connected with a marked tendency in the Church to devalue women as supposedly more involved with unspiritual bodily matters and to regard marriage as second best to celibacy. (This ascetic tendency and the doctrine of predestination have roots in St. Paul.)

Augustine had a strong sense of history and Divine providence. In his book *The City of God*, he made a famous distinction between the City of Man (the temporal order of human politics and power, represented in his own time by Rome) and the City of God (the ideal human destiny in which God's will is eventually fulfilled). The Christian Church occupies an ambiguous position between the two: it is an imperfect human institution, changing and developing in time along with secular history and culture, yet it is supposed to embody and fulfill God's will. Augustine had a very strong belief in the authority of the Church and in the importance of its unity. When a division emerged between orthodox Catholicism and the "Donatist" Christians of North Africa, he used his position as bishop to get the civil powers to use force to make the Donatists conform.

THE ISLAMIC PHILOSOPHERS

Islam arose in the Arabian peninsula in the seventh century C.E., when the prophet Muhammed had a series of visions in which, he claimed, he was given direct revelations from God. When written down, these visions became the text of the Qu'ran. Islam thus resembles Judaism and Christianity in believing that a certain set of texts are the revealed Word of God. There was an early schism between Sunnis and Shi'ites, who disagreed about the nature of religious authority (Iranians and many Iraquis follow the Shi'ite tradition, whereas the majority of world Muslims are Sunnis). The supporters of this new religion spread rapidly from its Arabian home, conquering the East as far as India, North Africa, and half of Spain.

From the ninth to the thirteenth centuries, there was a great flowering of Islamic civilization in these regions. Islamic theology, philosophy, science, and medicine were more advanced than in medieval Europe. Baghdad was a great center of scholarship. Scholars had access to texts from the ancient world (including the works of Aristotle), and Islamic philosophers developed several intellectual systems that tried to combine Greek philosophy with Muslim faith. There was also an influential tradition of mysticism in the Sufi movement. For a while there was some fruitful contact between the rival civilizations; in fact, much of the thought of Aristotle that had been lost to the West was rediscovered via the Muslim scholars.

Islamic thought resembles medieval Christianity in assuming as an unquestionable premise the authority of a religious tradition based on a claimed divine revelation. But there emerged some hotly debated differences (comparable to those in the Christian world) about the relation of reason to faith and of individual religious experience to religious authority.

One such dispute resulted in the execution of al-Hallaj in the tenth century for proclaiming his Sufi belief in his attainment of mystical union with God, which was seen as heretical. Early in the eleventh century, ibn Sina (Latin name *Avicenna*) used Aristotle's subtle distinction between active and passive elements within the human mind to give a theory of "prophecy" or revelation: God is said to speak through the divine, active intellect working in the mind of Muhammed, whereas the human, imaginative side of the prophet's mind expresses religious truths in terms of vivid images. Such imagery is needed to persuade most human beings of religious truth and to impel them to action, but according to ibn Sina, philosophers can interpret the images in terms of higher spiritual truths. He also voiced doubts about the literal truth of bodily resurrection, so his Islamic orthodoxy was questioned.

Al-Ghazali (1058–1111) was a brilliant scholar who gave up his professorship in Baghdad for the life of a wandering ascetic and Sufi. In a book aggressively entitled *The Incoherence of the Philosophers*, he criticized previous Islamic philosophers for being overly influenced by Greek ideas and departing from Qu'ranic orthodoxy. He also made a striking anticipation of Hume's denial of the necessity of the cause-effect relation and used this to question metaphysical theories of God. He defended the Sufi appeal to religious experience rather than philosophical argument.

In Spain there was a redefense of philosophy by ibn Rushd (Latin name *Averroes*), who lived in Cordoba (1126–1198). He argued that because the text of the Qu'ran sometimes stands in need of rational interpretation, and because jurists tend to disagree on questions of law and ethics, Muslims cannot avoid the use of reason. Ibn Rushd wrote a reply to al-Ghazali entitled *The Incoherence of 'The Incoherence,'* arguing that it was inconsistent to use reason to subvert reliance on reason. He thus tended to subordinate theology to philosophy once again.

Ibn Sina and ibn Rushd had considerable influence on medieval Western thought. In the twelfth and thirteenth centuries, there was a fascinating *three*-way debate, involving also Jewish philosophers such as Maimonides (1135–1204), who wrote a famous work entitled *Guide for the Perplexed*. But this golden age of medieval multiculturalism in Spain was not to last: intolerance and conflict took over and, in the Reconquista of the Iberian peninsula by the Spanish Catholic monarchy, Jews and Muslims were forcibly expelled.

AQUINAS (1224–1274)

As we have seen, most of the works of Aristotle did not become available to the West until the twelfth century. This produced a revolution within late medieval thought, though some conservative Church authorities tried to ban the study of Aristotle! St. Thomas Aquinas's magnificent Christian systematization—expounded in his *Summa Theologica*—was based on Aristotle's philosophy, plus, of course, the Bible and the Church Fathers. The *Summa* is like a huge medieval cathedral—an enormous, impressive structure of high religious aspiration, full of intricate detail that makes one marvel at the faith and the workmanship that produced it. Though controversial in its time, the *Summa* has since become Catholic orthodoxy backed by Papal authority.

Aquinas allowed that the natural powers of human reason have a legitimate, if limited, place in the defense of Christian faith (something that Augustine and his late medieval followers like St. Bonaventure tended to deny). Aquinas held the Aristotelian (and empiricist) view that all human knowledge starts with perception through the senses, but he said that we have to use our intellect to recognize types or forms of things and to attain systematic scientific knowledge of the world. Crucially, he distinguished between rational theology and revealed theology: in the former, we can use unaided human reason to prove the existence of God (by the famous "Five Ways"); in the latter, we receive in faith the revelation of God through the Bible and the Church. Faith, it emerges, is not something under the control of our will, rather it is infused by the grace of God (*Summa Theologica*, II–II, Q.6, art.1).

On human nature, Aquinas follows a basically Aristotelian analysis of our "rational soul" as consisting in our capacities for perception, intellectual conception, theoretical reasoning, and practical deliberation resulting in exercise of our free will in action. He Christianizes Aristotle's conception of *eudaimonia* by identifying our ultimate fulfillment as consisting in the knowledge and love of God. And he supplements the four classical Greek virtues of courage, temperance, prudence, and justice with the three "theological virtues" of faith, hope, and divine love ("charity"), for which we need to receive divine illumination or grace.

On the question of immortality, Aquinas retained (with dubious consistency) an element of Platonism, saying that although the resurrection involves the re-creation of the human being as a living body, nevertheless the soul has a separate existence between death and resurrection. This tries to solve the problem of maintaining personal identity over the interim period, but at the cost of inviting the question how a disembodied soul can perceive or act.

Aquinas's appeal to reason was real, but limited. The authority of the Catholic Church remained paramount for him in all matters of faith. Like Augustine, Aquinas was prepared to sanction the use of force against disagreement: he wrote that those heretics who use their reason to produce perversions of the Christian faith may be "banished from the world by death" (*Summa Theologica*, II–II, Q.11, art. 3). His great intellectual cathedral was built for the glory of God, but also to buttress the authority of the Church, and in some of its darker corners a whiff of burning can still be smelled. Aquinas did not quite finish his great construction, for in the last year of his life he experienced a mystical vision and said that all he had written now "seemed to him as straw."

In the next century—the fourteenth—a new, stronger current of empiricist thought arose, especially in William of Ockham. Still within the orbit of medieval Christianity, but testing its limits, Ockham devoted much attention to questions of logic, language, and empirical knowledge of the material world; he doubted whether reason could prove the existence of God and left theology to the realm of faith.

The Reformation: Where lies the authority for faith?

Christianity was the dominant system of belief in Europe for some 1,500 years, from the fall of Rome, through the "dark ages" and the high medieval period, and into the modern age up to the nineteenth century (it is still influential in twenty-first-century America!). The Popes of the Catholic Church retained their center of power in Rome, although after the schism of 1054 the Eastern Orthodox version of Christianity became independent, centered in the Byzantine Empire in Constantinople, until the fall of that city to the Muslim Turks in 1453. (Orthodoxy continues to this day in Greece and Eastern Europe and is resurgent in Russia.)

Four successive movements of world historical importance developed in early modern Europe: the Renaissance, the Reformation, the Rise of Science, and the Enlightenment. In the Renaissance of the fifteenth and sixteenth centuries, new attention was devoted to the literature, arts, and philosophy of the ancient world, and these exerted a renewed influence on Western thought. The wisdom of the ancients was now seen directly, not through the prism of medieval Christianity. As a result there was a tendency to skepticism (e.g., in Montaigne) and to humanist philosophy concentrating on human nature rather than metaphysics or theology (e.g., in Pico della Mirandola and Erasmus).

The religious Reformation is generally recognized as starting in the early sixteenth century, led by Luther and Calvin, but it was presaged in the previous two centuries in the thought of Wycliffe in England and Huss in Bohemia (the latter was excommunicated and burned at the stake). Luther's main theme was the doctrine of justification or salvation by individual faith, without the mediation of Church authority (and without appeal to reason, either—Luther notoriously condemned reason as a "whore").

The unity of the Western Catholic Church was shattered and a number of different Protestant churches and movements developed, appealing to the Bible and to individual religious experience rather than the tradition of the Church. Translations of the Bible into the languages of the people became a crucial element in this new kind of spirituality; some of the early translators, such as Tyndale, were burned at the behest of those who felt the threat to their own ecclesiastical power. Appeal to Scripture became the fundamental source of authority for many, especially the Calvinists, who were dominant in Geneva and Scotland and later influenced America. In some circles, there developed a doctrine of the infallibility of the Bible. But the more radical sects, such as the Anabaptists on the Continent and the Quakers in England, appealed to "the inner Light" of God's revelation in the individual mind or heart.

The Rise of Science: How does scientific method apply to human beings?

Modern physical science arose in the seventeenth century. The combination of experimental method with systematic mathematical theory was exemplified in the work of Galileo and Newton. The explanatory success of the Newtonian system demonstrated how new knowledge about the world could be solidly established on the basis of carefully controlled (and measured) observation. Appeal could no longer be made to the traditional authorities of Aristotle, the Bible, and the Church on matters of fact about the workings of the physical world. The Catholic Church's attempt to preserve pre-Copernican, earth-centered astronomy against the discoveries of Galileo was a last-ditch defense of the indefensible.

The more difficult question (which still faces us today) was how far scientific method—now unrivalled in its authority over the world of inanimate matter—could be applied to human beings. To this, there seemed to be two starkly opposed answers associated with the rival metaphysics of materialism or dualism. Either we see ourselves as living bodies composed of the same kind of stuff that makes up the rest of the universe, and subject to the same physical laws (which were assumed to be deterministic until the advent of quantum mechanics in the twentieth century), or we see people as combinations of body and soul, where the latter is thought of as something immaterial, not subject to the laws of physical science, and therefore capable of rationality and free will.

HOBBES (1588-1679)

The Englishman Thomas Hobbes published his most famous work, *Leviathan*, in 1651, in the period of the English civil war. It is one of the classics of political philosophy, but his social conclusions are derived from premises about individual human nature. Hobbes vehemently rejected dualism (and medieval Aristotelianism) and claimed that the very notion of soul as incorporeal substance is self-contradictory. He espoused instead an uncompromising metaphysical materialism about human nature, treating life as a motion of the limbs, sensation as motion within the bodily organs, and desire as the states of the body that cause bodily movement.

This leads Hobbes to a bleak view of human nature as intrinsically selfish—each person's desires are for his or her own survival and reproduction. (He thus anticipates a crude version of Darwinism.) Human beings are in competition with each other for resources—for food, for land, for materials for shelter, clothing, and so on. If there is no social authority, no state, we live in fear of robbery and violence. There is thus a desperate need for an authority with effective monopoly of the use of force, to save people from the evils of "the state of nature." So it is in each person's self-interest to give up some individual freedom for the sake of security and acknowledge the authority of whatever power is strong enough to enforce the rule of law.

Hobbes's diagnosis and prescription is essentially materialist and atheist. He could not openly say so in the seventeenth century, so we still find talk of God in his writings. But, arguably, it is not essential to his main argument, in which there is no appeal to divine creation, purpose, or judgment. And in terms of actual power, Hobbes would subordinate all churches to the authority of the state.

DESCARTES (1596-1650)

The Frenchman Rene Descartes was a central figure in the scientific revolution of the seventeenth century. He contributed to the development of mathematics, physics, physiology, and philosophy. His scientific work has long been superseded, but his philosophical writings remain on the syllabus, because they express fundamental conceptions and arguments that any would-be philosopher must address.

What most concerns us here is Descartes's dualist account of human nature as consisting of body and soul—two distinct but interacting substances, each of which can exist without the other. In this Descartes followed a long tradition (including Plato), but he put a new gloss on the distinction and gave new arguments for it. According to Descartes, the body occupies space and is subject to the laws of nature that science studies, but it has no mental properties. It is the mind or soul that thinks, feels, perceives, and decides (thereby exercising free will). The soul is incorporeal; that is, it is not made of matter, it does not occupy space (although it is in time), it cannot be studied by the methods of physical science, and it can survive the death of the body, carrying the identity of a person into the afterlife. Descartes was thus led to sharply distinguish humans as possessing immaterial souls from animals, which in his view lack all consciousness.

In the *Discourse on Method*, Descartes wrote a preliminary exposition of his ideas in semiautobiographical form. Expressed more carefully in the *Meditations*, his main argument for dualism starts from the reflection that whatever else one can doubt, one cannot doubt one's own existence as a conscious being—although one can (he claimed) doubt whether one has a body. Descartes used pure reason in a reflective, introspective way to try to prove fundamental metaphysical truths about our souls and then argued from the ideas in our minds to the existence of God.

In Part V of the *Discourse,* however, Descartes presents a different, more empirical argument for dualism, as the hypothesis that best explains the observed behavior of people and animals. He argues that there is a distinction of kind rather than degree between the innate mental faculties of humans and animals, picking out language as a distinctive component of human rationality. It is this empirically based sort of rationalism (namely, the assertion of certain innate mental capacities as peculiar to the human species) that Chomsky has renewed in the twentieth century (see Chapter 10).

Having thus bifurcated human nature into two different metaphysical realms—the physical and the mental—Descartes (like many others) thought he could apply scientific method to the physical bit, studying our bodies in anatomy and physiology while remaining an orthodox Catholic believer in an infinite, immaterial God and an immaterial, immortal soul with free will.

SPINOZA (1632–1677)

The Dutch Jewish philosopher Benedict de Spinoza attempted a compromise between the stark alternatives of dualism and materialism. In his main work, the *Ethics* (which contains more metaphysics than ethics) he identifies God with the whole of nature. He thus retains some reverential talk of "God or Nature," but not the biblical conception of God as Creator of the whole of nature. Spinoza's view is pantheism, not orthodox theism.

On the question of human nature, Spinoza has an interesting theory that matter and mind are not two separate substances, but two attributes of one complex underlying reality. (This is often called "dualism of attribute," or "double-aspect theory.") His technical metaphysics of attributes is difficult to interpret, but it has an intellectual descendant in the twentieth century "identity-theory" of mind, which says that the mind is the brain, or less crudely (following Aristotle) that the mind is what the functioning brain *does*.

The Enlightenment: Can science be our guide to life?

From the mid-seventeenth century onward, as scientific method became widely accepted as the only way to gain knowledge of the material world, the question was raised of applying the methods of science to human beings. In the European movement of ideas called the "Enlightenment," centered in the eighteenth century, the hope emerged that scientific method would not only give us knowledge of human nature, but would enable us to improve the human condition. The Enlightenment can be briefly summed up as belief (or faith!) in the power of human reason to improve human life. It was thought that reason—in the form of scientific method applied to the benefit of human individuals (e.g., in medicine and education) and to the reform of human society (in economics and politics)—could lead to hitherto unimagined human progress. In its more extreme versions, this became the claim that science can replace *all* other guides to life, such as religion, morality, the authority of monarchs and aristocrats, and social tradition.

The Enlightenment took somewhat different forms in the rival nation-states of Britain and France. In Britain, which had been through the searing experience of civil war in the seventeenth century, there was a gradual evolution and piecemeal reform of society; in France, where absolute monarchy still prevailed, pressure built up until its violent release in the revolution of 1789.

Empiricism and materialism were already apparent in Hobbes. Locke gave a more thorough account of the origin of all our ideas in experience in his *Essay Concerning Human Understanding* (1690). Although he defended dualism and theism, Locke appealed to reason and experience rather than to revealed religion. His political thought derived the need for government (and for limitations on its power) from individual human needs and rights (especially property rights). This strongly influenced the drafting of the new American Constitution.

HUME (1711-1776)

The Scotsman David Hume was one of the seminal figures of the Enlightenment. His magnum opus is the three-volume *Treatise of Human Nature* (1739–40), written, miraculously, in his twenties; later he wrote more popular expositions of his main ideas in his two *Enquiries*. He went on to write on many other topics, including religion, politics, and history, as well as philosophy.

Hume applies empiricism more rigorously than ever before: he holds that all concepts are derived from experience and all knowledge about the world (including human nature) must be based on experience. Pure reason can prove results only about "relations of ideas" in logic and mathematics; it cannot yield any sort of metaphysical truth about the world. His *Treatise* is significantly subtitled "An Attempt to introduce the experimental Method of Reasoning into Moral Subjects" ("experimental" here means experiential or empirical). Hume's *Treatise* was one of the first attempts at a scientific theory of human nature, yet it does not consist entirely of empirical claims and remains more a work of philosophy than psychology.

Hume asserts as a fundamental empiricist premise that all ideas are derived from impressions, either of the senses or of "reflection" (i.e., introspective awareness of one's own states of mind). He argues that we have no idea of substance except as a bundle of perceptible qualities (in this Hume was anticipated by the Irish philosopher Berkeley, who denied that we can even *understand* the notion of material substance existing outside the mind). Hume goes further than Berkeley, however, when he argues that we have no coherent notion of soul or mental substance—we are only aware of a succession of mental states in ourselves, but have no notion of "self."

There is thus a skeptical, subversive tendency at the foundation of Hume's philosophy; but when it comes to practical matters, he is more common-sensical, humane, and cautious, even conservative. He gives an essentially humanist account of ethics and politics, appealing to the (alleged) facts about human nature, including our tendencies to benevolence as well as selfishness, our liability to emotions and our ability to moderate them by thought. He tends to support a gradual, progressive development and reform of human society. In his maturity, in the third quarter of the eighteenth century, Hume enjoyed fame as a central figure of the Scottish Enlightenment, along with Adam Smith and Thomas Reid.

In all this, Hume made no appeal to religion. He was one of the first to attempt a social scientific account of religious belief in his *Natural History of Religion*. He critically examined the traditional arguments for the existence of God, especially the argument from apparent design, in his *Dialogues concerning Natural Religion*, but these were too controversial to be published in his own lifetime! His reputation as an atheist excluded Hume from appointment to a Chair of Philosophy in Edinburgh, which he so richly deserved.

ROUSSEAU (1712-1778)

In eighteenth-century France there emerged a group of thinkers who put their faith in the application of reason to human affairs such as Voltaire, Diderot, d'Alembert, and Condorcet. Under the prevailing French system of absolute monarchy, aristocratic rights, and entrenched Catholicism, this was highly subversive. Some of these thinkers were deists (believers in a God who created the universe but does not intervene thereafter), while others were atheists. Some were explicit materialists, notably de la Mettrie, who published a book entitled *L'Homme Machine*. Most had a somewhat naive faith in the power of human reason to reform human affairs—a faith that was severely tested by the violent aftermath of the French Revolution.

Jean-Jacques Rousseau, born in the city-state of Geneva in Switzerland, was one of the most influential thinkers of the Enlightenment, but he was an eccentric, untypical figure in many ways, especially in his emphasis on feeling as well as reason. In his *Discourse on Inequality* (1755), he argued for the basic goodness of human nature. Rousseau offers a highly speculative history of the emergence of human society from primitive origins, claiming to show how the growth of what is called "civilization" has corrupted people's natural happiness, freedom, and morality, and allowed unnatural, unjust inequalities to develop.

In Rousseau's treatise on education entitled *Emile* (1762), he presents his idealistic vision of the essential goodness of human nature and his highly impractical ideal of how a boy could be brought up (from infancy to manhood and marriage) by a super-wise, all-controlling tutor. He displays considerable insight into child development, insisting that children are not miniature adults and should not be treated as such: their education should be tailored to their mental stage. His prescription is basically that each individual should be allowed to develop his own innately good nature, uncorrupted by society—especially by wealthy, urban, fashionable society, which Rousseau so strongly felt was thoroughly corrupt.

Rousseau writes with a sustained eloquence that many have found very persuasive—and his influence is still with us in the widespread assumption that what is "natural" must be good. (There is a parallel with the thought of Mencius in ancient China; see Chapter 1.) He does not seem to reckon, however, with the thought that selfishness, rivalry, aggression, and bullying also seem to be very natural. And for all his progressiveness, Rousseau is extremely retrogressive in his treatment of girls and women as subordinate to the male sex (see the last section of *Emile*).

In the section of *Emile* entitled "Profession of Faith of a Savoyard Priest," Rousseau expressed his attitude to religion. He defended belief in a deist conception of God and in an immaterial soul endowed with free will. But he expressed skepticism about all the claims of revealed religion put forward by religious authorities and expressed a naive faith in the infallibility of each person's conscience as a guide to good and evil. For this, Rousseau was condemned by both French Catholicism and Genevan Calvinism; he narrowly escaped arrest and had to live as an exile for much of the rest of his life. Though he may have hoped to find a middle way between the irreligious French *philosophes* and authoritarian Christianity (whether Catholic or Protestant), Rousseau did not satisfy either. But his insistence that "true worship is of the heart" was to influence many, including Kant. And his emphasis on the importance of human feeling was a precursor to the Romantic movement that was to take over from the Enlightenment, especially in Germany.

CONDORCET (1743–1794)

Condorcet was one of the most optimistic of the French Enlightenment thinkers. He was an enthusiastic supporter of the French Revolution, but in the unstable politics after 1789, Condorcet was of too independent a mind to survive in the factional fighting and he died in prison. Yet, while in hiding from his political enemies, he wrote a work on the progress of humanity, in which he set out his analysis of history as a series of stages from barbarism to civilization, and his belief in the perfectibility of human nature. Despite his own fate, Condorcet expected human progress to continue indefinitely. Compared with the thought of Kant, who had a strong sense of the radical evil in human nature, Condorcet's strain of Enlightenment optimism appears naive.

6

Kant: Reasons and Causes, History and Religion

KANT'S LIFE AND WORK

Immanuel Kant (1724–1804) is generally recognized, along with Plato and Aristotle, as one of the three greatest philosophers of all time. He spent all his life in the small Prussian city of Königsberg. Kant is typical of his age (and of much Western thought) in inheriting the twin influences of Christianity and science and in seeing the most fundamental problems of philosophy in how to combine the two.

The Christian inheritance includes the conceptions of God as omniscient, omnipotent, and benevolent, and of an immortal human soul endowed with free will. But there was a more specific influence on Kant from a radical form of Protestantism, the Pietism of his parents. Pietism was a movement within Lutheranism that emphasized personal devotion and right living above dogmas, creeds, and ritual.

Kant had a thorough knowledge of the science of his day. He understood the fundamentals of Newton's mathematical physics and respected it as a paradigm of natural science. He himself contributed to science when he developed the nebular hypothesis, the first account of the origin of the solar system. In the late eighteenth century the chemical revolution, the second main stage of modern scientific development, was under way, and Kant used examples from chemistry to illustrate his own philosophy. He predated the Darwinian revolution in biology, so what he says about "teleology" (purposiveness in nature) needs rethinking in light of the theory of evolution by natural selection.

Kant also had a well-grounded humanistic education, embracing classical philosophy and literature and European philosophy, theology, and political theory. He was brought up in the German rationalist tradition stemming mainly from Leibniz (1646–1716), who believed that pure reason could prove some striking metaphysical claims; for example, that God exists and orders everything for the best and that everything is made up of elementary minds called "monads." Kant's early writings wavered between the competing influences of metaphysical rationalism and empirical science; in his mature work he achieved a synthesis.

Kant was surely the deepest thinker of the Enlightenment. He believed in the potential for human reason to improve the human condition (here using the term "reason" in a wider sense than philosophical rationalism, to mean science and its social applications). One philosopher who made an especially deep impression on the development of Kant's thought was Rousseau, the maverick of the French Enlightenment. Rousseau's ideas on human nature, culture, education, and history, the importance of moral feeling and the unimportance of metaphysical theology, were eagerly absorbed by Kant into his own thinking.

The works of Kant's mature "critical" philosophy were published in the closing decades of the eighteenth century. His major writings are the *Critique of Pure Reason* (1781), *Groundwork* (or *Foundations*) *of the Metaphysics of Morals* (1785), *Critique of Practical Reason* (1788), *Critique of Judgment* (1790), *Religion within the Boundaries of Mere Reason* (1793), *The Metaphysics of Morals* (1797), and *Anthropology from a Pragmatic Point of View* (1798). (References to the first *Critique* use the A and B page numbering of its first and second editions; references to the rest are to the volume and page number of the Prussian Academy edition of Kant's works.) None of these is easy reading—Kant's thought and writing are formidably abstract and bristle with technical terms—but the *Groundwork* is a relatively short introduction to his moral philosophy. (Kant intended his *Prolegomena* to be a similar introduction to his theoretical philosophy.) The *Anthropology* is a compilation of Kant's popular lectures, but it does not take us to the heart of his thought. He also wrote some brief, stylish essays for the educated public on such topics as "What Is Enlightenment?," "Idea for a Universal History with Cosmopolitan Intent," and "On Perpetual Peace." He was not just an academic philosopher, but an influential progressive thinker.

Kant repeatedly expressed his faith in the free, democratic use of reason to examine everything, however traditional, authoritative, or sacred: such reasoning should appeal only to the uncompelled assent of anyone capable of rational judgment. He argued that the only limits on human reason are those that we discover when we scrutinize the pretensions and limitations of reason itself: thus human reason can provide its own self-discipline by philosophical reflection. His word "critique" means this self-conscious inquiry into the powers and limitations of the human mind. Kant applied this critical method to science and metaphysics, to decisions about what to do, to judgments of beauty and purpose, and to religion.

In his old age, when his international reputation was well assured, Kant got into trouble with his government. For most of his life he had benefited from the comparatively liberal rule of Frederick the Great, but after that monarch's death a more reactionary regime took over. Its censors detected an unorthodox tendency in Kant's *Religion* and forbade him to publish any more on the subject. There was no question of drinking hemlock, like Socrates, but it was their alleged subversion of state-approved religion that got both philosophers into conflict with those in power. (There are still places where such things can happen.) Kant's response was wily, if not conspicuously courageous: he gave a promise to obey, but worded it so that he felt bound only for the lifetime of Frederick William II, whom he managed to outlive.

METAPHYSICS AND THE LIMITS OF KNOWLEDGE

The impact of science on Kant is obvious and deep. One fundamental motive of his philosophy was to explain how scientific knowledge is possible. He developed a systematic theory of knowledge and human cognitive faculties that showed how the empirical methods of natural science depend on certain fundamental presuppositions; for example, that every event has a cause and that something is conserved through every change. He argued that these principles cannot be proved by observation (they are a priori rather than a posteriori), nor are they mere logical truths (they are synthetic rather than analytic). Such principles can, however, be shown by philosophical reflection (in "transcendental deductions") to be necessary conditions of any self-conscious, conceptualized perceptual experience of an objective world.

In the first half of the *Critique of Pure Reason* (the Aesthetic and the Analytic), Kant set out his detailed theory of the forms of intuition (i.e., our fundamental ways of perceiving everything in space and time) and the categories (the fundamental forms of thought, with their associated concepts such as substance and causation). These forms of intuition and categories are a priori in the sense that they are not derived from experience but presupposed by it.

Kant thus offers an account of how we have three kinds of knowledge. The vast majority of our knowledge is *empirical* (a posteriori; i.e., it is ultimately justifiable only by perceptual experience), including geography, history, and all the sciences; some knowledge (in logic) is *analytic* (provable by pure reasoning, involving only definitions); and some is *synthetic a priori* (the presuppositions of science—and Kant includes moral principles under this heading too). Kant argued that most of mathematics belongs in the third set, but many other philosophers would locate it in the second.

Kant had a strong sense of the reality of the material world and of the objectivity of the knowledge provided by the methods of science, including perception. He decisively rejected Berkeley's subjective idealism, according to which matter cannot exist unperceived. However, Kant felt it necessary to qualify his commitment to realism, offering a double-barreled thesis consisting in a combination of "empirical realism" (roughly as expressed in the first sentence of this paragraph) with "transcendental idealism," an elusive doctrine that has puzzled his interpreters ever since.

One persuasive insight behind Kant's transcendental idealism is his realization that, although material objects exist independently of our thought and perception (and much of the physical universe predates the existence of human beings), the *way* we perceive and think of things depends not only on what there is out there to affect our sense organs, but *also* on the way those inputs are processed through our minds. (We need not presuppose a dualist theory of minds here; we can think of mental processes as instantiated in the physical events in the brain.) There are some individual differences in processing; for example, someone with a defective retina may be color-blind, unable to discriminate colors that most people can; and a few individuals are unable to recognize people by their faces, due to a more deep-lying abnormality in their brain processing.

Kant was more concerned with what is common to all (normal) humans but may be peculiar to the human *species*: other creatures presumably perceive the world in rather different ways from us. He conceived of the possibility that our human ways of perceiving (our "forms of intuition") may systematically distort our representation of what is objectively out there, so that we can only know the world "as it appears" to us, not "as it is in itself." One way Kant expressed this thought is in his proposal for a "Copernican revolution" in philosophy, in which "objects must conform to our cognition" (Bxvi ff.). But that phrase is misleading, for it seems to imply that some properties of objects are produced by the nature of our human cognitive faculties, whereas all that seems justified is that *the ways in which we perceive and conceptualize* objects depend on our cognitive faculties.

Kant sometimes re-expresses his talk of things as they appear and as they are in themselves (two aspects of the same set of things) as a distinction between appearances and things in themselves (two sets of things). He also uses the terms "phenomena" and "noumena" for what may or may not be the same distinction. And, controversially, he applies these distinctions primarily to space and time, suggesting that space and time are merely *human* forms of perception. Kant thus opens up the possibility that, for all we know, the world as it is in itself may not be spatial or temporal (perhaps a divine being—endowed with "intellectual intuition"—can perceive it as such). Indeed, he slips into the even stronger assertion that the world in itself is definitely not in space or time. We do not need to evaluate these striking metaphysical theses here, but we will find Kant making a rather different use of the appearance/thing-in-itself distinction when he discusses human action.

In the "Second Analogy" in the first *Critique*, Kant argued that universal determinism—the principle that every event has a preceding cause; that is, a preceding state of affairs that makes that event necessarily happen—is a presupposition of science and, indeed, of any empirical knowledge of the world. Kant believed that sufficient causes for all material events can always be found among other material events, so he did not accept Descartes's interactionist dualism, according to which minds are nonmaterial entities that causally affect brains. In the "First Analogy," Kant argued that all events in the world (including mental processes) have to be seen as changes in persisting "substance," which means matter. And in the "Third Analogy," he said that everything in the world must be part of a single, interacting system of physical reality.

In the second half of the *Critique of Pure Reason* (the Dialectic), Kant diagnoses how and why human reason tries to go beyond the limits of its legitimate use. We tend to claim illusory metaphysical knowledge of things as they are in themselves (human souls, the universe as a whole, uncaused events, and God). Such claims have long been central to theology and to much philosophy, but they go beyond the bounds of human knowledge Kant set out in the Analytic. The Kantian view is that, although we can formulate and understand such metaphysical assertions (they are not meaningless, as the logical positivists of the twentieth century claimed), we can neither prove nor disprove them, we cannot even acquire probable evidence for or against them. Such assertions do not fall into the three forms of legitimate knowledge: empirical enquiry, logical reasoning, or synthetic a priori truths.

Kant's view makes a decisive break with the tradition of natural theology (by no means dead, even now), which tries to offer rational proofs (or empirical evidence) for the existence of God. But there has long been a "fideist" vein in religious thinking (exemplified in such different thinkers as Augustine, al-Ghazali, Pascal, and Kierkegaard), which says that faith goes beyond reason from the very beginning. At first sight, Kant would seem to fit into that tradition, retaining theological propositions in their traditional meanings, but saying that they are a matter for faith rather than knowledge. Whether this is the whole story, we shall see.

THEORY OF HUMAN NATURE: PERCEPTION AND CONCEPTS; REASONS, CAUSES, AND FREE WILL

The overarching problem of Kant's philosophy was to reconcile the claims of morality and religion with scientific knowledge. He hoped to paint one big, though complicated, picture, giving human nature its appropriate place within physical nature. In this, Kant is a central and characteristic figure of the modern era since the rise of science in the seventeenth century.

Let us start with Kant's account of human cognitive faculties. Early in the first *Critique*, he wrote:

> Our knowledge springs from two fundamental sources of the mind; the first is the capacity for receiving representations (receptivity for impressions), the second is the power of knowing an object through these representations (spontaneity in the production of concepts). Through the first an object is *given* to us, through the second the object is *thought*. . . . To neither of these powers may a preference be given over the other. Without sensibility no object would be given to us, without understanding no object would be thought. Thoughts without content are empty, intuitions without concepts are blind. (A50–51/B74–75)

Kant is here developing an epistemological theory that reconciles the one-sided views of his rationalist and empiricist predecessors. Perceptual knowledge depends on the interaction of two factors: (1) sensory states caused by objects outside the mind and (2) the mind's activity to organize these data under concepts and make judgments that are expressible in sentences. Animals have the first capacity ("sensibility"), but they lack the second ("understanding"), for they cannot express themselves in language. Animals perceive prey, predators, mates, and offspring, but they do not have concepts—they cannot *say* that anything is a predator, a mate, or a child—and there is no reason to credit them with such thoughts. Similarly, animals can feel pain and they can be in states of arousal such as lust or aggression, but they cannot say or think that they are in pain, randy, or afraid.

Kant thus builds on Aristotle's distinctions between plants, animals, and humans. But in the light of evidence about animal mentality that was not available in Kant's day, we may now have to allow that primates or dolphins can approximate to some kinds of human thought: the gulf may be less absolute than we used to think. (And human infants and mental defectives lack the mental powers of normal adults.) But the existence of shades of grey does not eliminate the difference between black and white: there remains a very clear distinction between the conceptual, linguistically expressible capacities of normal humans and anything that most other animals can do.

There is a further depth in Kant's account of our cognitive faculties, in his stress on "reason." Sometimes this seems to be just another name for the understanding, but a special role for reason emerges when Kant points out that we do not just make particular judgments about the world, we try to integrate all these bits of knowledge into a unified system. We often want to know why something happens: we try to explain one fact in terms of others. In the "Antinomies" section of the Dialectic (and in the Appendix on the regulative use of the ideas of pure reason) Kant gives an elaborate theory of how our faculty of "reason" leads us toward ever-increasing unification of our knowledge under general laws or principles.

There is also a vital *practical* dimension to Kant's conception of reason (echoing Aristotle). He points out that we are not merely perceiving, judging, and theorizing beings, we are *agents*—we do things, we affect the world by our actions. In this respect, too, we transcend the animals. Obviously, they do all manner of things and can act very effectively—in one sense of these words. But they cannot say what they are doing, they do not have *concepts* of what they are trying to achieve, so we cannot credit them with desires or intentions to make it the case that such-and-such a state of affairs obtains. (We say that the cat is trying to catch the mouse, but there is nothing in the cat's behavior to justify attributing to it the concept of mouse, rather than food, or prey, or rodent, or small animal.) There must be *causes* for behavior in internal desire and external perception, but because animals cannot say what they doing, they cannot give *reasons* for doing it.

Kant sketches a general conceptual framework for human actions in Chapter II of the *Groundwork* at 4:413, and in the opening sections of the *Critique of Practical Reason* at 5:19 ff. He makes a crucial distinction between hypothetical and categorical imperatives. Some of our reasons for action involve only our own desires (and factual beliefs), taking the general form: I want B, and I believe that A is the best way to achieve B, so I should do A. This is what Kant calls a "hypothetical imperative."

But Kant insists that not all reasons for action take this form, which involves only the rational selection of a means to satisfy one's own desires.

For we sometimes accept an obligation, a moral "ought," a reason for action that we conceive of as holding irrespective of our self-interested desires (and may go against them!). Examples include a situation where lying would be to your advantage but you think you ought to tell the truth nevertheless; a "Good Samaritan" situation where you encounter someone in manifest need of urgent help; a case in which you admit the claims of justice (e.g., fair shares in cutting the available cake). In such cases, Kant says that we recognize the validity of what he calls a "categorical imperative" taking the form: "I ought to do C, whatever my own desires may be."

This is what Kant calls "pure" or "a priori" practical reason; he means that morality is fundamentally a function of our reason, not just our feelings (as empiricist moral philosophers like Hume would have it). He gives some highly abstract formulations of this, but at bottom he appeals to the experience of moral obligation, our (often uncomfortable) awareness of the tension between our desires and what we accept as the valid demands of morality. Kant learned from Rousseau a deep respect for ordinary moral feeling, and even in the first *Critique*, which enters into some of the most abstruse philosophizing ever, he modestly added:

> . . . in regard to the essential ends of human nature even the highest philosophy cannot advance further than the guidance that nature has also conferred on the most common understanding. (A831/B859)

Kant's analysis of human cognitive faculties seems to me basically correct. But the large question that arises is what metaphysics of human nature makes these distinctive mental capacities possible. Here the going gets difficult and controversial. Kant's official line on the issue of dualism against materialism was that we *cannot know* what we are "in ourselves." In the "Paralogisms" section of the Dialectic, he argues that the traditional metaphysical arguments of "rational psychology" (e.g., in Plato and Descartes) cannot prove the existence of an incorporeal soul. We can only know ourselves as we appear to ourselves in introspection ("inner sense") and to each other as embodied human beings (perceived by "outer sense"). But Kant insisted that we cannot prove that we are merely material beings, either (A379, B420). In his characteristic fashion, he leaves the metaphysical question open. However, his own preference comes out when he rejects "a soulless materialism" (presumably he had in mind Hobbes or de la Mettrie) and suggests—though as a matter of faith, rather than knowledge—that we can survive death and live on into an infinite future (B424–26).

Kant was a rock solid believer in human freedom and moral responsibility. He sees us as free, rational beings who can make choices that are not predetermined; above all, we are capable of acting on moral reasons, not just on selfish desires. He dismissed the "compatibilist" account of free will offered by empiricists such as Hobbes and Hume (according to which a "free" action is one caused by the agent's own desires and beliefs) as "a wretched subterfuge" (second *Critique*, 5:96). Kant's view was that human actions cannot be entirely reduced to physical causation and that they involve choices that are not themselves caused.

His proffered solution to the Third "Antinomy" (the apparent contradiction between free will and determinism) is that insofar as we are appearances (perceptible human bodies in motion), everything about us is just as causally determined as everything else in the physical world, but insofar as we are rational beings who act for reasons, we can be free (A549/B577 ff.). Kant backs this up with a distinction between our "empirical" and "intelligible "characters:

> . . . for a subject of the world of sense we would have first an empirical character, through which its actions as appearances would stand through and through in connection with other appearances in accordance with constant natural laws . . . second, one would also have to allow this subject an intelligible character, through which it is indeed the cause of those actions as appearances, but which does not stand under any condition of sensibility and is not itself appearance. The first one could call the character of such a thing in appearance, the second its character as a thing in itself. (A539/B567)

It sounds as if Kant means that all the physical states and changes of our bodies—including the movements of our limbs and lips, the circulation of the blood, the excitation of neurons, the flow of hormones—would count as our empirical character. And presumably our beliefs, desires, hopes, fears, intentions, and emotions would count as our intelligible character. It is then tempting to say that all the former are subject to universal determinism through the causal mechanisms investigated by physiology, whereas talk about reasons for actions involves a rational, noncausal relation between beliefs, desires, and possible actions. For example, if someone wants a beer, and believes there's beer in the fridge, that gives the person a reason to go to the fridge. Anyone can see that elementary rational connection without knowing anything about brain functioning. And the relation is to a *possible* action, for that belief and desire still constitute *a reason* for making a move toward the fridge, even if the person has some *other* reason against doing so (e.g., laziness, asceticism, or morality—he or she knows it is someone else's beer).

The distinction between reasons and causes, rational explanation and causal explanation, is surely an essential part of any adequate account of human action, and we are in Kant's debt for opening up this topic (albeit somewhat obscurely!). If materialism (in the form sometimes called "physicalism") implies that there is only one valid kind of explanation— that of giving physical causes—then Kant persuades us to reject such a reductive thesis. But it remains open for us to say that human beings are *made* entirely of matter (and energy): that we have here a dualism of conceptual systems (reasons and causes) rather than a dualism of substances. Kant seems closer to Spinoza than to Descartes—though he might not welcome the comparison!

Making these distinctions does not entirely resolve the free will problem, however. At A534/B562, Kant declares that "freedom in the practical sense is the independence of the power of choice from necessitation by impulses of sensibility" (i.e., bodily based desires). He believes that human choice has this independence: although we feel the *influence* of our desires, our choices are not *determined* by them, we sometimes overcome them for prudential or for moral reasons. And just before that, Kant claims that this practical freedom is grounded in the "transcendental" idea of freedom; that is, an uncaused choice. But the absence of necessitation by *sensuous* impulses is not the same as the absence of *any* sort of cause. Can't we say, in the case of prudentially or morally motivated actions, that *nonbodily* desires or beliefs are among the causes? Could A's desire not to put on weight cause her refusal of the chocolate cake, or could B's recognition of A's right to say no cause his desistance from further sexual advances? Can't our choices have *rational* causes—in our combinations of beliefs and desires—while still being free? However, it is unclear whether Kant is prepared to accept this sort of compatibilty.

Here we surely need to distinguish two senses of reasons, connected with an ambiguity in the notion of beliefs and desires. In one sense, two people can have the same belief and desire—when they believe the same proposition and desire the same thing—and they can thus have the same reason for action. In another sense, only *my* belief and desire (i.e., my present state of believing and desiring) can motivate my action—how could someone else's mental states motivate *me*? The distinction is between the propositional contents of beliefs and desires, and individuals' mental states of believing or desiring (at particular times). Reasons in the sense of people's mental states can cause action, whereas reasons in the sense of propositions are not the sort of thing that can be causes at all.

Reasons in the latter, propositional sense are not states or events in time—which may help us interpret Kant's puzzling statement that "this acting subject, in its intelligible character, would not stand under any conditions of time" (A539/B567). This may also explain why he thought he could apply his distinction between (temporal) appearances and (nontemporal) things in themselves to the case of causes and reasons. However, the alleged "unknowability" of things in themselves hardly applies in this case, for we surely each know our own reasons for action in an immediate way—as Kant acknowledges when he says at A546/B575 that "the human being . . . knows himself through pure apperception, and indeed in actions and inner representations which cannot be accounted at all among impressions of sense." We have here a contrast not of the knowable and the unknowable, but of two different ways of knowing.

Does Kant solve the free will problem, then? I cannot follow up this question further here, except to note that in Chapter III of the *Groundwork* (4:450 ff.) he distinguishes "two points of view" by which we can regard ourselves as belonging to the sensible world of appearances or to the intelligible world of reasons and laws (he must mean moral rather than scientific laws here). Earlier in that chapter (4:446), Kant offers a distinctively practical defense of freedom. When one is making up one's mind what to do, reviewing reasons for and against various options, one cannot at the same time think of one's decision as already predetermined. However much one may be impressed by theoretical arguments for determinism, there is no escaping the necessity to arrive at a decision here and now, and one is sometimes painfully aware that the relevant reasons do not make the decision for one. As Kant puts it, we have to act "under the idea of freedom," so, from the practical point of view, we are already free.

DIAGNOSIS: SELFISHNESS AND SOCIALITY

We have seen how Kant emphasizes the distinction between self-interested inclinations and moral duty. He contrasts our human nature with the animals on one side and with the conception of a "holy will" on the other. Animals feel no tension between desires and duty, for they do not have the concept of duty. A rational being who had no self-interested desires (an angel?) would also not experience any such tension, but for the opposite reason: not being subject to temptation, the person would always do the right thing. But we human beings are mixed creatures, midway between animals and angels. We are finite beings with our individual needs—and these include not just physical desires, but emotional needs or drives for love, approval, status, and power. Yet, we are also rational beings: and for Kant that includes "pure practical reason," the recognition of moral obligations. The tension between these two sides of our nature is an inescapable feature of the human condition. We can never achieve moral perfection.

Some philosophers have asked how people can ever be motivated to do their duty, to fulfill a moral obligation when it goes against their own self-interested desires. "Why be moral?" the skeptic asks, and seems to expect some justification in self-interested terms. I think Kant does not see such skepticism as a real issue; he just presupposes what he takes to be the universal and necessary fact that we all accept the validity of some moral obligations or other (although we may disagree about what they are in particular cases).

It is relevant here to point out a distinction (which Kant recognizes) *within* the class of self-interested reasons, between desires for immediate satisfaction, and considerations of prudence, that is, longer-term self-interest. One can resist the allure of the third glass of wine, an item of designer clothing, or a seductive tempter, for the sake of one's health, wealth, or longer-term happiness. Our mixed nature is thus manifested in our ability to recognize prudential reasons and to act on them—at least sometimes! We all need to be able to postpone the satisfaction of immediate desires in the interest of other goals. To be unable to do this (e.g., in addiction), is to be reduced to an almost animal level. Any child needs to start learning at an early age to postpone gratification. But it is a difficult matter, which we each have to negotiate in our own way, what balance to strike between living for the moment and planning for the future.

In his works of ethical theory Kant tends to present his view in an apparently severe guise that suggests that the only motivation he really approves of is the grim determination to do one's duty irrespective of one's own inclinations. He may seem to imply that if one is naturally inclined to look after one's children, to tell the truth, or to help someone in distress, that does not make the actions admirable and might even *detract* from their moral value (*Groundwork* 4:398). Wider and more careful reading of Kant dispels this common misinterpretation. Of course he is concerned to encourage virtues as traits of human character: the more that people can develop the mental dispositions to do the right things, the better. Kant's point is that, as rational beings, we are not just bundles of innately given or socially trained inclinations; we have reasons for our actions, and the general principles presupposed by our reasons can be made explicit as "maxims" and can be rationally and morally assessed. It is not enough for us to bring about good results in the world (as utilitarian ethics suggests): virtue depends on inner motivation, we must act for the right reasons. As Kant puts it, the only thing that is unconditionally good is a good *will*.

In his late work *Religion within the Boundaries of Mere Reason,* Kant wrestles with the most profound problems of human nature and suggests some new insights, or new versions of old ones. He talks of the "radical evil" in human nature. He acknowledges our "frailty" (our difficulty in doing what we know we ought to do) and our "impurity" (our tendency to confuse or adulterate moral reasons with other motives). But for Kant, what is radically evil is not our naturally given desires, nor is it the tension between these and duty. It is rather the "depravity" of human nature—the freely chosen *subordination* of duty to inclination, the deliberate preference for one's own happiness (as one conceives of it) over one's obligations to other people (6:19 ff.).

This is another place where Kant, along with so many other thinkers, is pulled in two directions. On the one hand, he insists that the evil in us is a result of our own choice, our wrong use of our freedom. But on the other hand (in his version of the doctrine of original sin), Kant wants to say that evil is "radical" or innate in us, it is a universal and unavoidable feature of our condition as needy but rational beings:

> There is in the human being a natural propensity to evil; and this propensity itself is morally evil, since it must ultimately be sought in a free power of choice, and hence is imputable. This evil is *radical,* since it corrupts the ground of all maxims; as natural propensity, it is also not to be *extirpated* through human forces. . . . Yet it must equally be possible to *overcome* this evil, for it is found in the human being as acting freely. (*Religion* 6:37)

Kant's position is not that radical evil must attach to every rational but finite and needy creature: our needs as finite beings involve our animal nature, which Kant regards as innocent. Nor does he attribute a predisposition to evil to our rational nature, which would make us devilish beings. He thinks rather that radical evil attaches to our predisposition to rational self-love as a result of human development under social conditions.

This is the Rousseauian aspect of Kant's doctrine, what he calls the "unsocial sociability" of human beings: our need and inclination to be members of a human society, combined with our tendency to be selfish and competitive. Paradoxically, Kant's thesis that we are by nature evil amounts to much the same thing as Rousseau's assertion that we are by nature good (there was a related debate within the Confucian tradition; see the end of Chapter 1). The phrase "by nature" is used by the two philosophers in opposed ways: Rousseau means "prior to the social condition," and he argues that social development has corrupted original human nature, whereas Kant thinks that our truly human nature can be expressed only in society—he doesn't believe there is such a thing as a presocial, yet *human,* condition.

PRESCRIPTION: PURE RELIGION AND CULTURAL PROGRESS

How are right intentions and virtuous dispositions to be achieved and encouraged? It is not enough just to formulate a theory of what pure practical reason requires, universalizing the "maxims" behind our actions, applying them to all rational beings and treating each person as an end "in himself" (as Kant does in *Groundwork* Chapter II and in the second *Critique*). Nor is it enough to state more specific moral rules or their application in particular cases (as Kant does in his late work *The Metaphysics of Morals*). For, as Plato and St. Paul both saw, it is one thing to recognize an obligation, and another thing to do it. Philosophizing and moralizing notoriously have limited effects on human conduct!

There are very practical problems here for parents, teachers, social workers, legislators, and social reformers about how people can be taught and encouraged to develop the virtues. Kant has things to say about such questions (not all his writing is at the level of abstruse theory). One obvious response is to offer rewards or threaten punishment, but that does not produce Kantian virtue, for it amounts only to putting new self-interested reasons in place. That may induce outward conformity to rules, but it cannot create the truly virtuous inner attitude, the will to do the right action *just because it is right*.

Kant does not look on moral praise and blame as external incentives for people to comply with ethical duties: rather they are ways of "sharing in the reason of one another." Blame is not like a slap on the wrist; praise isn't like offering a sweet. Moral praise and blame are part of distinctively moral discourse, involved in moral education: they are intended to teach, to *convince* or *remind* someone about what is right or wrong. They are *not* meant to work only by appealing to people's motives to avoid social criticism and to gain the good opinion of others. For Kant, all punishments and rewards, even within social psychology nonmorally construed, concern only "the realm of law," not the realm of ethics.

Kant's answer to the problems of human nature shares the ambiguity of his diagnosis. The quotation from *Religion* presented earlier suggests that only a religious answer will suffice: if the evil in us cannot be "extirpated through human forces," yet needs to be "overcome," believers will be quick to say that only God's salvation (in their recommended version) can do the trick. Much of Kant's mature work, including the later sections of all three *Critiques*, touches on religious themes. A first glance might suggest that this is mere conventional piety, artificially tacked onto his serious philosophical work. But more careful reading shows Kant's understanding of religion to be far from Christian orthodoxy, which is why the Prussian censorship tried to hinder the publication of his thought.

In Chapter III of the Dialectic of the first *Critique*, Kant classifies all theoretical arguments for the existence of God into three—the ontological, cosmological, and "physico-theological" (design) arguments—and he examines each in turn. His arguments are clearly and vigorously expressed; they are classics of philosophical criticism of natural theology (along with

Hume's *Dialogues Concerning Natural Religion*). An original aspect in Kant is his claim that the argument from design presupposes that from cosmology, which in turn depends on the ontological argument. So if he is right, demolishing the latter brings down the whole house of cards.

But Kant destroys only to try to rebuild on a different, practical basis. Although propositions about God, immortality, and free will cannot be proved (or disproved) by the theoretical use of reason, he thinks they can be justified from a practical point of view. When we are thinking of how to *act*, different sorts of consideration are relevant. The idea of our own freedom is directly presupposed in our deliberations about what to do (as noted previously). But what about God and immortality? Where do they come in (if they have to come in at all)? Kant tries to explain in his various formulations of "moral theology": in the Method section of the first *Critique,* in the Dialectic of the second, in sections 86–91 of the third, and in *Religion.*

At A805/B833 Kant distinguishes three questions that sum up "all the interests of reason, speculative as well as practical":

1. What can I know?
2. What ought I to do?
3. What may I hope?

(In the *Jäsche Logic* 9:25, Kant adds a fourth question, which he says includes all the rest: "What is man?" But that seems to be only a verbal trick, for to answer that question properly, we have to answer the original three.) The first question is discussed in depth in the first *Critique.* The second is treated in the *Groundwork*, the second *Critique*, and other ethical works. The third (glossed as "If I do what I ought to do, what may I then hope?") introduces a new topic, somewhat neglected in philosophy, that is somehow both theoretical and practical. Kant's philosophy of history and of religion come under this heading of hope.

In the Dialectic of the second *Critique*, Kant gives his fullest exposition of his practical argument for belief in God and immortality. He is deeply concerned about the relation between virtue and happiness ("If I do what I ought to do, what may I then hope?"). Stoicism asserted virtue to be the highest good; whereas Epicureanism said that it is happiness. Kant's view is that we must not be concerned merely for our own happiness, yet he is unwilling totally to disconnect virtue from happiness, and so he argues that the "highest good," the final end of all moral striving, must be the *combination* of virtue and happiness (rather like Aristotelian *eudaimonia*).

But it is painfully obvious that virtue is not always rewarded with happiness in the world as we know it. All too often, evildoers seem to flourish. It is an obvious step—and one that millions of people have taken—to say that justice requires there to be a God, a "Supreme Reason" underlying nature, who knows the secrets of all human hearts and who will reward everyone appropriately in a future life beyond this world. It may seem that in invoking God and immortality Kant is doing no more than repeating this common human hope for justice and reward in a life after death. But it is fundamental to his moral philosophy that our motive for doing our duty should *not* be to reap benefit thereby, so it would be quite inconsistent for Kant to postulate rewards beyond death just to motivate right action.

And yet, Kant claims, we need to have ground to *hope* that virtue will eventually be rewarded. His case seems to be that our very motivation for moral action would be undermined unless we can at least believe that the highest good, the combination of virtue and happiness, is *possible.* One is not to aim directly at it for oneself, but one needs to have hope—we have to assume that doing the right thing here and now is not ultimately pointless.

But does such moral resolution really need belief in the metaphysical claims about God or immortality? In *Religion,* Kant tends to back off from such claims, at least in their traditional interpretations; for example, when he says of the conventional notions of heaven and hell that they are "representations powerful enough . . . without any necessity to presuppose dogmatically, as an item of doctrine, that an eternity of good or evil is the human lot also objectively" (6:69).

Later, Kant writes that "religion is (subjectively considered) the recognition of all our duties as divine commands"; and he adds in a footnote that in its theoretical aspect this needs "only a *problematic* assumption (hypothesis) concerning the supreme cause of things," and in its practical, moral aspect "this faith needs only the *idea of God* . . . without pretending to secure objective reality for it through theoretical cognition" (6:154, footnote). It seems, therefore, that we can take the "as" in "recognition of our duties as divine commands" just as the entertaining of a certain picture or hypothesis, not literal belief in the existence of a supernatural person.

Speaking of the struggle between "the good and the evil principles," by which Kant meant personifications of good and evil in Christ and Satan, he says:

> It is easy to see, once we divest of its mystical cover this vivid mode of representing things, apparently also the only at the time *suited to the common people* [Kant's emphasis], why it (its spirit and rational meaning) has been valid and binding practically, for the whole world and at all times:

because it lies near enough to every human being for each to recognize his duty in it. Its meaning is that there is absolutely no salvation for human beings except in the innermost adoption of genuine moral principles in their disposition. . . . (Religion 6:83)

Such "demythologizing" language worried the censors in Prussia and it unsettles Christian orthodoxy even today—perhaps especially now that we are less inclined (than Kant and Plato were) to distinguish what is believable by an elite and by "the common people."

Kant's overall tendency is to reinterpret theological claims in moral terms. He suggests that the Scriptures should be interpreted in terms of moral lessons for us, even if that is not their literal meaning. There is, in Kant's view, no need for belief in supernatural persons and powers, miracles or sacraments. But he saw a need for some sort of purified church, a human institution that will set forth ethical ideals and try to help its members aspire toward them. And he hoped that what is rationally and morally acceptable in the various "historical" or "ecclesiastical" faiths (Christian and non-Christian) could be gradually separated from what is morally unnecessary, and formed into a "pure religious faith" (*Religion* Parts III and IV).

Kant also entertained more this-worldly hopes, expressed in his essays on history (which paved the way for the historical philosophies of Hegel and Marx in the nineteenth century). He envisaged the possibility of continued progress in human culture and history through education, economic development, and political reform, with the gradual emancipation of people from poverty, war, ignorance, and deference to traditional authorities. He was a supporter of ideals of the French Revolution, though aware of its excesses. In his essay "On Perpetual Peace," Kant sketched a world order of peaceful cooperation between nations with democratic constitutions. (He would surely be delighted with the achievements of the European Economic Community, for all its faults.) At the end of his *Anthropology,* he explicitly expressed his hope for the gradual, if uneven, progress of humanity.

The status of Kant's historical hope is rather unclear, however. In his essay "Idea for a Universal History with Cosmopolitan Purpose" (1784), he repeatedly appeals to a conception of what "nature" intends or has willed for human progress. He thinks there is some sort of overall trend in history that we can, as theorists, at least dimly discern, although it goes way beyond all the specific intentions that people have in their particular actions: they are, Kant says, "unconsciously promoting an end which even if they knew what it was, would scarcely arouse their interest." Thus the "unsocial sociability" of humans (i.e., our social, yet competitive nature) is "the means employed by nature"—not here our human nature, but nature in some more cosmic sense—to produce in the long term a law-governed social order in which human talents and powers can be completely developed. By a law-governed order, Kant has in mind not only the existence of the state (as argued for by Hobbes) but also a law-governed international order (as detailed in his essay "On Perpetual Peace").

But this conception of nature's intentions, design, or will is unstably poised between the religious belief in God's will and providence—which, it seems, Kant does not mean to endorse here (otherwise why wouldn't he simply have used the traditional theological language?)—and belief in nature as having "designs" that are not the conscious intentions of any rational being, divine or human. Darwin made scientific sense of the latter sort of notion, to explain the marvelous adaptation of creatures to their environment in terms of natural selection (see Chapter 10). But there can be no similar Darwinian account of progress in human history, for our history has not been "selected" from a number of competing alternatives. It seems then that Kant's talk of nature's intentions for history cannot be justified (unless traditional theology can be justified!).

At the end of this essay on history, it emerges that Kant is less concerned with theoretical justification for his "cosmopolitan" view of history than with its practical usefulness as a guide to our social thought and action. The idea of progress toward an ever-greater fulfillment of human intellectual and moral and political potential can be set before us as an *ideal* toward which to aspire. It can encourage our *hopes*, and inspire what might be called a social *faith*. Its status for Kant thus seems to be like that of the concept of God.

Kant was in all this an Enlightenment thinker, but unlike many others of his time (such as, Condorcet), he had a vivid and realistic sense of the dark side of human nature, our potential for evil, which has been amply confirmed since his time. He saw the need not only for political and social reform through the power of the state, but also for an "ethical community"—his purified, rationalized form of church—that would work for the spiritual and ethical transformation of individuals. Kant's practical philosophy leaves us with this combination of hope for gradual social progress (with the resolution to contribute to it), and a religious viewpoint that puts our hope in something like divine grace to transform our fallen, selfish human nature (given individual acknowledgment of our faults and resolution to be better human beings).

FOR FURTHER READING

For a short introduction to Kant's thought, see Roger Scruton, *Kant* (Oxford University Press, 2001), a little gem of compressed insight. For a more comprehensive, but still digestible, introduction, see Otfried Hoeffe, *Kant* (Albany: State

University of New York Press, 1994). For a clear introduction to the ethics, see Roger J. Sullivan, *An Introduction to Kant's Ethics* (Cambridge: Cambridge University Press, 1994).

Allen Wood, in *Kant's Moral Religion* (Ithaca, N.Y.: Cornell University Press, 1970), defends Kant's theory of religion. Wood has also contributed a chapter on this topic to *The Cambridge Companion to Kant*, edited by Paul Guyer (Cambridge: Cambridge University Press, 1992).

For those brave enough to start reading Kant for themselves, the conventional starting points are his two formidably titled shorter works, *Groundwork for the Metaphysics of Morals* and *Prolegomena to Any Future Metaphysics*.

Easier reading for those more interested in the practical side of Kant's thought can be found in *Kant on History*, edited by L. W. Beck (Indianapolis: Bobbs-Merrill, 1963), or *Kant's Political Writings*, 2d ed., edited by H. Reiss (Cambridge: Cambridge University Press, 1991).

Some may like to look at Kant's *Religion within the Boundaries of Mere Reason*. There is a recent translation by George di Giovanni, with an introduction by R. M. Adams (Cambridge: Cambridge University Press, 1998).

7

Marx: The Economic Basis of Human Societies

Our contemporary view of Marxism is strongly colored by our knowledge of the rise and fall of Soviet rule in Russia and Eastern Europe in the twentieth century. To a lesser extent, we may be influenced by what we know of so-called communism in China (where Marx's influence has now dwindled to almost zero) or in Cuba and North Korea. However, this chapter will be about the mid-nineteenth century ideas of Karl Marx himself, not later versions of them in Leninist, Stalinist, or Maoist theory and practice. Of course, Marx's ideas were enormously influential on what happened in the twentieth century, but he cannot be held directly responsible for the failings and atrocities of the so-called Marxist or communist regimes.

If Kant was the deepest philosopher of the Enlightenment, Marx was the greatest theorist of the industrial revolution and the early phase of capitalism. Although hostile to religion, Marx inherited an ideal of human equality from Christianity, and he shared the Enlightenment hope that scientific method could diagnose and resolve the problems of human society. What was driving all his elaborate historical, social, and economic theorizing was a quasi-religious zeal to show the way toward a secular form of human salvation or redemption.

MARX'S LIFE AND WORK

Marx was born in 1818 in the German Rhineland, to a Jewish father who, under the discriminatory laws of the time, had to convert to Christianity to become a lawyer; the young Karl was brought up as a Protestant, but soon abandoned religion. He displayed his tremendous intellectual ability early, and in 1836 he entered the University of Berlin as a student in the Faculty of Law. There was a ferment of philosophical, aesthetic, and social ideas in the Romantic movement of that time, into which the young Marx eagerly plunged. He learned languages, wrote poetry, and worked on an academic dissertation on ancient Greek metaphysics, while also being deeply concerned with social reform. His early writing has a vigorous literary style, expressing the passionate intensity of his thought.

The dominant intellectual influence in Germany at that time was the philosophy of Hegel, and Marx became so immersed in Hegel's ideas that he abandoned his legal studies and devoted himself to philosophy. The leading inspiration in Hegel's thought was the idea of progress in human history through various stages of mental and cultural development. Hegel conceptualized historical progress in terms of his peculiar conception of *Geist*; that is, Mind or Spirit. He seemed to be reinterpreting theological language with a meaning closer to humanism or pantheism than to the biblical conception. Hegel interpreted the whole sweep of human history as the progressive self-realization of *Geist,* with increasing consciousness or self-awareness. Successive eras of human social life express increasingly adequate ideas of reality and display greater degrees of freedom; each stage is subject to conflicting tendencies, but its demise lays the basis for a fuller development of freedom at the next stage.

Hegel developed a conception of "alienation" in which the knowing subject is confronted with an object other than and unknown to ("alien to") himself. The distinction between subject and object is supposed to be overcome in the process of getting to know the object, thus (supposedly) coming to realize that it does not, after all, exist in total independence of the subject. (There is an echo here of Kant's transcendental idealism, mentioned in Chapter 6.) According to Hegel, the processes of mental and cultural development come to an end at a stage in which there is "absolute" knowledge—and he seems to have thought, immodestly, that he himself had achieved it! In that he differed from Kant, who insisted that we can never have knowledge of things as they are in themselves and cannot achieve moral perfection either.

The followers of Hegel split into two camps over how his ideas applied to society, politics, and religion. The "Right" Hegelians (who seem to have included Hegel himself, in his later years) held that the processes of history had already led to the full development of human potential. They tended to see the contemporary Prussian state as ideal, and thus were conservative in politics, and also tended to favor a theological interpretation of Hegel's thought. But the "Left" or "Young" Hegelians held that the highest form of human freedom had yet to be realized, that European society of the time was far from ideal, and that it was up to people to help change the old order and bring about the next stage of human development. Accordingly, they looked for radical reform or revolution.

One of the most important thinkers in the latter group was Ludwig Feuerbach, whose *Essence of Christianity* was published in 1841. Feuerbach held that Hegel had got everything upside down, that far from God progressively realizing Himself in history, religious ideas and beliefs are produced by human beings as a pale reflection of human life in this world, which is the fundamental reality. People become "alienated" in that they project their own higher potential into theological fantasies and undervalue their actual lives. Feuerbach diagnosed metaphysics (and with it, the whole of theology) as "esoteric psychology"; that is, the expression of our own feelings in the disguised form of obscure claims about the universe. Religion is a symptom of alienation, from which we must free ourselves by realizing our human destiny in this world. Feuerbach was a forerunner of the sociological or psychological explanations of religion offered by Marx, Durkheim, and Freud.

This was the intellectual atmosphere of Marx's formative years. His reading of Feuerbach broke the spell that Hegel had cast on him, but he retained the assumption that Hegel's philosophy of historical development and his vision of the overcoming of alienation contained truths about human nature and society in an inverted form. Marx wrote a critique of Hegel's *Philosophy of Right* in 1842–43, and became editor of a radical journal called the *Rheinische Zeitung*. This was soon suppressed by the Prussian government, and Marx escaped to Paris. In 1845 he was expelled from Paris and moved to Brussels. In these formative years, Marx encountered the other great intellectual influences of his life: his wide reading included the British economist Adam Smith and the French socialist Saint-Simon. He met other socialist and communist thinkers, such as Proudhon and Bakunin, and began his lifelong collaboration with Friedrich Engels.

In the 1840s Marx and Engels began to formulate their "materialist conception of history." By inverting Hegel's view as Feuerbach had suggested, Marx came to see the driving force of social change as material rather than spiritual. Not in mere *ideas,* and certainly not in any cosmic Spirit, but in the *economic* conditions of life lay the key to history.

Alienation is at root neither metaphysical nor religious, but social and economic. Under the capitalist system labor is something alien to the laborer in that he does not work for himself but for someone else—the capitalist—who directs the process and owns the product as private property, and is therefore in a position to exploit his employees. This conception of alienation is expressed in the "Economic and Philosophical Manuscripts," which Marx wrote in Paris in 1844, but which remained unpublished for a century. The materialist conception of history was, however, published in other works of this period, notably the *German Ideology* of 1846 (written with Engels) and the *Poverty of Philosophy* of 1847.

Marx became involved with the practical organization of the communist movement, for he saw the purpose of his work as "not just to interpret the world, but to change it" (as he famously put it in his *Theses on Feuerbach* in 1845). Convinced that history was moving toward the revolution by which capitalism would give way to communism, Marx tried to educate and organize the "proletariat," the class of industrial workers who had to sell their labor in order to survive, and to whom he thought victory in the class struggle must eventually go. He was asked to write a definitive statement of the aims of the international communist movement, so (with Engels) he produced the famous *Manifesto of the Communist Party* in 1848. Later in that year (although hardly as a result of the *Manifesto*) there were abortive revolutions in many European countries. After the failures Marx found exile in Britain, where he remained for the rest of his life.

In London Marx lived a life of comparative poverty, existing on journalism and gifts from Engels. He did systematic research in the Reading Room of the British Museum, where he found extensive documentation on social conditions. In 1857–58 he wrote another set of manuscripts, the *Grundrisse*, sketching a plan of his total theory of history and society (the complete text was not available in English until the 1970s). In 1859 he published the *Critique of Political Economy*, and in 1867 the first volume of his magnum opus, *Capital*. These last two works contain much detailed economic and social history. Although not now making overt use of Hegelian philosophy, Marx was still trying to apply his materialist interpretation of history to show the inevitability and desirability of surpassing capitalism by communism.

It is these later works, from the *Communist Manifesto* onward, that have become best known, and they have formed the basis of most subsequent communist theory and practice. In them we find German philosophy, French socialism, and British political economy, the three main influences on Marx, welded into an all-embracing theory of history, economics, sociology, and politics. This is what Engels came to call "scientific socialism": Marx and

Engels claimed to have discovered the correct *scientific* method for the study of human society, and thus to be able to establish the objective truth about its present workings and future development.

However, the publication in the twentieth century of Marx's earlier works, particularly the *German Ideology* and the *Economic and Philosophical Manuscripts* of 1844, has shown us much about the origin of his thinking in Hegelian ideas. So the question has been raised whether there were two distinct periods in his thought: an early phase that has been called humanist or existentialist, giving way to the later "scientific socialism." The consensus of opinion is, however, that there is a continuity between the two phases—that the theme of human alienation and the hope for salvation from it is still there in the later work. My discussion of Marx will be based on the assumption that his thought is basically a unity.

THE MATERIALIST THEORY OF HISTORY

Marx was an atheist, and the general trend of his thought was materialist and determinist. In his later period especially, he tended to present himself as a social scientist, treating all human phenomena by the methods of science (as he understood them). But this is not peculiar to Marx: the same applies to many thinkers of the eighteenth-century Enlightenment (e.g., Voltaire, de la Mettrie, and Hume).

What is distinctive of Marx is his claim to have found the truly scientific method for studying the *economic history* of human societies. In his early philosophizing, he looked forward to the day when there would be a single science, including the science of man along with natural science. But that single science would have to include many levels, such as physics, chemistry, biology, psychology, and sociology. Admittedly, Marx compared his method to that of physics when he said (in the preface to the first edition of *Capital)* that "the ultimate aim of this work is to lay bare the economic law of motion of modern society"; and he wrote elsewhere of the natural laws of capitalist production "working with iron necessity towards inevitable results." But these are verbal flourishes (Marx was a great rhetorician!); the detail of his theorizing does not show that he was a *reductionist* materialist (or a strict determinist). He did not expect every fact about human individuals or human societies to be explained in terms of the vocabulary of physics (or of brain science). Rather, he looked for distinctively *sociological* laws: he held that there are general socioeconomic laws applying to human history.

This is the most fundamental feature of Marx's worldview: his "materialist" theory of history. Influenced by Hegel's historical mode of philosophizing, but interpreting it in economic rather than mental terms, Marx believed that there are laws of history by which each stage of economic development gives rise to the next. He applied this materialist conception both synchronically and diachronically. At any one time, the economic base is supposed to determine the ideological superstructure (for instance, Marx would dismiss what well-off people say in defense of capitalism as mere "ideology," consciously or unconsciously motivated by their own economic interests).

Over time, there are processes of technological and economic development that eventually result in large-scale social and ideological change. Marx divided history into epochs identified by their different economic bases—primitive tribes, the Asiatic system of absolute monarchy, the ancient world of Greece and Rome (with slavery), the feudal system of the Middle Ages (with peasants tied by obligations to their feudal lord), and the bourgeois or capitalist phase (with industrial workers selling their labor)—and he held that each stage had to give way to the next when the technological and economic conditions were ripe.

The best-known summary of the materialist theory of history is in Marx's Preface to the *Critique of Political Economy* (1859), which begins as follows:

> In the social production of their life, men enter into definite relations that are indispensable and independent of their will, relations of production which correspond to a definite stage of development of their material productive forces. The sum total of these relations of production constitutes the economic structure of society—the real basis, on which rises a legal and political superstructure, and to which correspond definite forms of social consciousness. The mode of production of material life conditions the social, political, and intellectual life process in general. It is not the consciousness of men that determines their being, but, on the contrary, their social being that determines their consciousness. . . .

In some popular expositions of Marxism, this has been taken as saying that the economic basis of a society determines *everything* else about it. But Marx's own considered statements are weaker than that—he talks here only of the foundation "conditioning" (or, as another translation puts it: "determining the *general* character") of social life, not of determining its every detail. He can admit the influences of nationalism, religion, wars, and of particular charismatic characters (Caesar, Napoleon, Lenin, etc.) who attain positions of power. There is no realistic prospect of treating history as an exact, quantitative science like physics, and Marx was under no illusion about that.

Everyone now recognizes that economic factors are hugely important in human history and society, and no serious study of history or social science can ignore them. Marx can take much of the credit for the fact that we now acknowledge this. But what did he mean by saying that the economic basis of a society "conditions" its superstructure and that social consciousness "corresponds to" economic structure? The quotation from Marx's Preface is difficult to interpret, for there is an ambiguity about where he intends to make the dividing line between foundation and superstructure.

Careful attention to the whole passage shows that Marx distinguishes *three* levels rather than two: (a) material powers of production, (b) relations of production, and (c) the ideological superstructure of a society (i.e., its concepts, beliefs, morality, laws, politics, religion, and philosophy). He talks of "the material powers of production," which presumably would include natural resources (land, climate, plants, animals, minerals), technology (tools, machinery, communication systems, etc.), and human resources (the labor power, skills, and knowledge embodied in human beings). He talks of the "economic structure" as including "relations of production," which presumably means the way in which work is organized (e.g., the division of labor, hierarchies of authority in the workplace, the legal rights and powers of ownership, the systems of rewards and payments). The description of these relations of production, at least in modern societies, involves legal concepts, like ownership and property, and economic concepts, like money, capital, and wages.

What then did Marx mean by "the real basis" or "foundation"? Is it (a) alone, or (a) plus (b)? Is he saying that (a) determines (b), and thereby (c)? That (b) alone determines (c)? Or that (a) plus (b) together determine (c)? If he means that the basis includes only (a), the strictly material powers of production, Marx is committed to a thesis of "technological determinism," but this may seem implausible because similar natural resources and technologies can surely be used in societies with different ideologies or legal systems (e.g., Christian, Islamic, or secular; capitalist, socialist, or communist). If the basis is (a) plus (b), and is said to determine (c), there is the difficulty that the legal concept of property seems to belong in (c), yet it also seems to be part of (b).

An answer to the latter objection may be that Marx could, if he were more careful, give an account of level (b), the social relationships involved in economic production, in terms of actual relations of power and effective control without (yet) using legal concepts of property, contracts, and so on. After all, he wants to apply his theory to primitive societies that lack the formalities of law, but where it may be very clear who has control over various natural resources—and over other people! Even in our own society there are times and places where personal power, asserted with force or the threat of it, is stronger in practice than legal niceties! And where the law's writ does run, Marx can still express his thesis in terms of power rather than legality.

It is also open to Marx to maintain a double-barreled determining or "conditioning" thesis: first, that (a), the material powers of production, condition or limit (b), the relations of production (e.g., the handmill allows a feudal structure, the steam mill requires capitalism); second, that (a) and (b) together ("the economic structure") condition or limit (c), the ideological superstructure. If talk of "conditioning" or "limiting" does not mean full-scale determining of every last detail, then Marx can avoid the objection that the same technology can be used in different societies, he can just say that those societies must have some relevant features in common (a modern example might be that widespread use of computer technology requires a certain standard of education for most members of society).

But that just raises the question what Marx's talk of "conditioning" or "corresponding to" really amounts to? How much determinism did he wish to assert (synchronically or diachronically)? Obviously, any society has to produce the necessities of life, to provide for individual survival and reproduction. We have to eat if we are to do anything or think anything, but it does not follow that how we produce what we eat determines everything that we do or think. The plausible thing to say—and it seems to be what Marx did say, when he was careful—is that the economic basis has a very significant influence on everything else: it sets limits within which the other factors play their part. The way in which a society produces the necessities of life may even have an influence on how people in that kind of society characteristically think. But the trouble is that this is *vague*—it is left open what counts as "very significant" or "important." In the end, we have only a recommendation to seek the economic factors in each particular case and examine how far they influence the rest. However, that has proved an immensely fruitful methodology in historiography, anthropology, and sociology.

It might also be the case that Marx's theory of economic "conditioning" is more plausible when applied diachronically as an explanation of historical change, than synchronically as an explanation of social structure—or vice versa. The issues here are surely empirical.

History is an empirical study in that its propositions must be tested by evidence of what actually happened. But it does not follow that it is a *science,* in the sense of involving *laws of nature* (i.e., generalizations of unrestricted universality). For history is, after all, the study of what has happened in human societies on this planet, in a finite period of time. The subject matter is one *particular* series of events; we know of no similar histories elsewhere in the universe—nor can we experiment on reruns of historical events!

Now for any particular series of events—even the fall of an apple from a tree—there is no limit to the number of different laws and contingent facts that may be involved in its causation (e.g., the laws of gravity and mechanics, the weather and gusts of wind pressure, the decay of wood and the elasticity of twigs, or tweaking by human fingers). If there is no closed system of influences (and hence no determinism) governing even the fall of a single apple, how much more implausible it is to say that the course of human history is predetermined. There may be some long-term and large-scale *trends* to be found (e.g., the increase of human population). But a trend is not a law; its continuation is not inevitable, but may depend on conditions that can change. (Population growth may be reversed by war, disease, famine, or environmental catastrophe.)

However, from his general theory of history, Marx predicted that capitalism would become more and more unstable, that the class struggle between the owners of capital and the proletariat who have to sell their labor would increase, with the latter getting both poorer and larger in number, until in a major social revolution they would take power. However, Marx did not confidently predict that the revolution would start in the countries where nineteenth-century capitalism was most developed, namely Britain, France, and the United States. In the *Communist Manifesto,* he pointed to Germany, which was still semifeudal at the time, as the place where he expected a bourgeois revolution to be shortly followed by a proletarian one. In some of his journalistic writing, Marx suggested that communism might be first achieved in China. And he saw that communist ideas could be imported into countries where a relatively small proletariat, allied with impoverished peasantry, could seize power from the traditional ruling class, as Bolsheviks under the leadership of Lenin did in Russia in October 1917.

About Russia and China, Marx may have been roughly right in predicting revolution, if not its subsequent vicissitudes (we can hardly count the imposition of Soviet rule in Eastern Europe by the Red Army after 1945 as a proletarian revolution in Marx's sense). But in the advanced capitalist countries the economic system has on the whole become more stable (with notable exceptions, such as the great depression of the 1930s, and we have yet to see what the twenty-first century holds in store!). Conditions of life for most people have improved vastly on what they were in Marx's time, and class divisions have seemingly been blurred rather than intensified (consider the large numbers of white-collar workers—office and managerial staff, civil servants, teachers, etc.—who are neither manual laborers nor industrial owners).

The nonoccurrence of communist revolution in the West would seem to be a major falsification of Marx's theory. It cannot be explained away by saying that the proletariat have been bought off by concessions of higher wages—for Marx predicted their lot would get *worse*. Unrestrained nineteenth-century capitalism as Marx knew it (with its dreadful conditions for the working class, including child labor) has ceased to exist in the West: gradual reforms have greatly ameliorated our economic system. Through direct or indirect investment, many people have some small share in the ownership of capital (though not in its control).

It may be suggested, however, that colonies and underdeveloped countries have formed the proletariat vis-à-vis the industrialized countries, and that even now we are benefiting from the exploited agricultural labor and sweatshops of the third world. Admittedly, some countries, such as Scandinavia, have not had colonies, but their economies must have benefited from the overall patterns of world trade. In Britain and America, it was not just those who owned slaves who profited from them; the system of slavery contributed to our general economic development.

THEORY OF HUMAN NATURE: ECONOMICS, SOCIETY, AND CONSCIOUSNESS

Except in his study of Hegel and the Greeks as a young man, Marx was not interested in questions of "pure" or academic philosophy, which he would later dismiss as idle speculation compared to the vital task of changing the world. So when he is labeled a materialist, this refers to his materialist theory of history rather than to a position in the philosophy of mind about the relation of mental states to the brain. Even if we take a strict interpretation of Marx as saying that all states of consciousness are determined by the material foundations of society, this could still be an "epiphenomenalist" position: that consciousness, although ontologically nonphysical, has its *contents* determined by material events. Marx diagnosed many people's ideas as "false consciousness," not properly supported by the reasons or rationalizations they offer for them, but caused rather by their socioeconomic role, through an unconscious mental process of which the subjects are not aware. He was not interested in a metaphysically materialist view that consciousness is to be literally identified with brain processes.

What is more distinctive of Marx's concept of humanity is his view of our essentially *social* nature: in one place he even wrote that "the real nature of man is the totality of social relations." Apart from obvious biological facts, such as our bodily makeup and the need to eat and reproduce, Marx would say that there is no such thing as a fixed, individual human nature—for what is true of people in one society or period may not be true in another place or time. Indeed, he remarked that "all history is nothing but a continuous transformation of human nature." Whatever a person does is an essentially social act, which presupposes the existence of other people standing in certain relations. Even the ways in which we produce our food and bring up our children are socially learned. Economic production typically requires cooperation. We do not need to conceive of society as an abstract entity that mysteriously affects individuals: rather, what kind of individual one is and what kind of things one does are affected by all one's interactions in the society one lives in. What seems "instinctive" or "natural" in one society or epoch (e.g., a certain role for women) may be quite different in another.

We can summarize this crucial point by saying that sociology is not reducible to psychology. Not everything about human beings can be explained in terms of facts about individuals; the kind of society they live in must be considered too. This methodological point is one of Marx's most distinctive contributions, and one of the most widely accepted. For this reason, he is recognized as one of the founding fathers of sociology. And this method can be accepted whether or not one agrees with Marx's particular conclusions.

But there is at least one universal generalization that Marx makes about human nature: we are *active*, productive beings, we are different by nature from the other animals because we *produce* our means of subsistence—and not just like bees producing honey, for we make conscious plans how to produce our livelihood in new situations. It is natural for human beings to plan and work for their living. No doubt there is a factual truth here, but (as with so many assertions about what is "natural" for human beings) Marx also associates a value judgment with it, namely that the kind of life that is *appropriate* for us involves purposive productive activity. As we shall see, this is implicit in his diagnosis of alienation as a lack of fulfillment in industrial labor and in his prescription for future communist society in which everyone can be free to cultivate his or her own talents in every direction. Because of this point, which is clearest in his early writings, Marx has been called a humanist.

What does Marx's theory imply about women? If there is a point in his concentration on processes of production, there is surely also a truth about the necessity for *reproduction*. But we must think of the latter as including not just sexual intercourse, pregnancy, and childbirth ("labor" in that sense of the word!), but the longer process of childcare, education, and socialization—which is laborious in its own way, and can involve men! Obviously no society can survive unless it can produce new members to carry it on. Marx acknowledged this in the German *Ideology*, and, in *The Origin of the Family, Private Property and the State*, Engels argued that economic factors determine both kinds of production: labor and the family. But, on the whole, Marx was a man of his time in his assumption that the traditional sexual division of labor in the family, with women being almost totally responsible for childcare, has a "purely physiological foundation." It seems he did not realize that even what he thought of as biologically determined differences between the sexes are affected by socioeconomic factors. Technical developments, like reliable contraception and infant formula, and economic developments that require mental skills more than heavy manual labor have transformed the question of male and female "nature" in ways that Marx himself did not foresee, but that his theory has the resources to deal with.

DIAGNOSIS: ALIENATION, CAPITALISM, AND EXPLOITATION

Marx's diagnosis of what is wrong with people and society under capitalism was expressed in his early writings in terms of his concept of alienation or estrangement (derived from Hegel and Feuerbach). For Marx, alienation involved both a description of certain features of capitalist society and a value judgment that they are fundamentally wrong. But it is difficult to decide exactly *which* features he is criticizing. He was not, after all, totally condemnatory of capitalism: he acknowledged that it leads to a great increase in productivity (and would thus make communism economically possible). Marx believed that capitalism is a necessary stage through which society has to go, but he thought that it will be (and ought to be) surpassed.

Logically, alienation is a relation, it must be *from* somebody or something; one cannot be just "alienated," any more than one can be married without being married *to* someone. Marx wrote in one place that alienation is "from man himself and from Nature." For him, "Nature" seems to mean the *humanly made* world (the opposite of its usual meaning!), so presumably he thought that people are not what they should be because they are alienated from the products they create and from the social relations involved in production. People without capital have to sell their labor in order to survive and are therefore in a position to be exploited by the owners of industrial capital, who can dictate the terms of their employment.

Sometimes it sounds as if it is private property that Marx primarily condemns: in one place he asserts that "the abolition of private property is the abolition of alienation." But elsewhere he says, "although private property appears to be the basis and cause of alienated labor, it is rather a consequence of the latter." Marx describes this alienation of labor as consisting in the fact that the work is not part of the worker's nature, he does not fulfill himself in his work, but feels miserable, physically exhausted, and mentally debased. His work is forced on him as a means for satisfying other needs, and at work he does not "belong to himself," he is under the control of other people. Even the materials he uses and the objects he produces are alien to him because they are owned by someone else.

Sometimes Marx seems to be blaming alienation on the use of money as a means of exchange that reduces all social relationships to a common commercial denominator ("callous 'cash payment'" as he put in the *Manifesto*—and one wonders why cash payment should always be "callous"). In that context, Marx was making a contrast with feudal society, in which there were nonmonetary economic relationships—though no doubt they could be callous in their own way! Elsewhere he suggests that it is the division of labor that makes work into an alien power, preventing people from switching from one activity to another at will (as we may look forward to doing in retirement, and as Marx once implausibly suggested everyone will be able to do in future society).

What then *is* Marx diagnosing as alienation? It is hard to believe that anyone can seriously advocate the abolition of money (and a return to a system of barter?), the end of all specialization in work, or the communal control of everything whatever (even toothbrushes, clothes, books, etc.?). It is the private ownership of *industry*—the means of production and exchange—that is usually taken as the defining feature of capitalism. The practical program of the *Communist Manifesto* includes the nationalization of land, factories, transport, and banks. But it seems unlikely that state control of these can cure the alienation of labor that Marx describes in such psychological terms in his early works. (Were not people just as alienated in communist Russia or China?) If it is the *state* that is the basis of social evils (or one main cause of them), nationalization might make things worse by increasing the power of the state.

The competitiveness of life under capitalism conflicts with the ideal of solidarity with other human beings. Perhaps we should understand Marx as saying that alienation consists in a lack of *community,* so that people cannot see their work as contributing to a group of which they are members because the state is too large to be a real community. Such a diagnosis would suggest a prescription not for nationalization but for decentralization into "communes" (in which the abolition of money, specialization, and private property might look more realistic). But the feasibility and desirability of this is obviously contentious on Marxist economic grounds: how can the kind of high-technology worldwide production and distribution on which we have now come to depend be organized in a society of independent communes? And the communes that have been tried have not had a good track record of stability.

In his later work, Marx made a more direct diagnosis of the evil of capitalism (though the notion of alienation did not entirely disappear from his writing). He condemned the exploitation of labor by capital—more precisely, this is exploitation of the class of people who have to sell their labor by the much smaller class of people who own capital. He developed a detailed theory of this, involving his "labor theory of value" and his concept of the "surplus-value" that industry generates and that is appropriated by the owners of industry rather than the workers. These have been much discussed and disputed in economic theory, and I will not attempt to go into them here. Marx's main claim is clearly a moral one, about the (alleged) *injustice* of the economic structure of capitalism.

There is a more general diagnosis implicit in Marx that would perhaps command universal assent: that it is wrong to treat any human being as only a means to an economic end (cf. Kant's moral law always to treat rational beings as ends in themselves). Human beings were treated as mere means of production in the unrestrained capitalism of the early nineteenth century, when adults and children worked long hours in filthy conditions and died early deaths after miserably unfulfilled lives. This still happens in some countries; and even in the advanced nations where capitalism is trumpeted as a stunning success, there is a constant tendency for managers to try to extract the greatest possible profit from the labor of their employees, driving down wages, cutting the workforce, or extending working hours. The state may put legal restrictions on this, but as soon as they are relaxed, each corporation or business makes the most of its opportunities. The latest trend is to relocate in a country where labor is much cheaper and legal regulations weaker.

The general idea that emerges is that capitalist society does not enable the full development of the potential of human nature, but does allow the exploitation of many people by those who own capital. The average worker for small businesses, large corporations, or for government agencies (whether manual laborer, pen-pusher, keyboard-clicker, computer-programmer, salesperson, or middle manager striving to meet targets imposed from above) may be "alienated" from his or her human potential by the conditions of the workplace, and is liable to exploitation by those who are in control of the system. In this sense, the "proletariat" does not have to be restricted to manual industrial laborers, but includes all those who have to find employment in order to survive.

Perhaps we can express Marx's main point in a paraphrase of Jesus' saying about the Sabbath: human beings do not exist for the purpose of production, rather production is supposed to be for human benefit. And this should apply to *all* the people involved—employers, employees, consumers, and anyone affected by side-effects such as pollution. The practical difficulty is, of course, how to give social effect to this ideal.

PRESCRIPTION: REVOLUTION AND UTOPIA

"If man is formed by circumstances, these circumstances must be humanly formed." If alienation and exploitation are social problems caused by the nature of the capitalist economic system, then the solution is to abolish that system and replace it by a better one. Marx thought that this was bound to happen anyway: capitalism will burst asunder because of its inner contradictions, and the communist revolution will usher in the new social order. Rather in the way that Christianity claims that God's salvation has been enacted for us, so Marx claimed that the resolution of the problems of capitalism is already on the way in the movement of history, and our responsibility is to align ourselves with it.

Marx's view on the metaphysical question of free will is rather ambiguous. His overall view obviously sounds determinist, yet there seems to be an irreducible element of human freedom left, since Marx and his followers appealed to people to realize the direction in which history is moving, and to *act* accordingly, to help bring about the communist revolution. Within the Marxist movement, there were controversies between those who emphasized the need to wait for the appropriate stage of economic development before expecting the revolution, and those (like Lenin) who proposed to act decisively to bring it about. But perhaps there is no contradiction here, for Marx can say that while the revolution is bound to occur sooner or later, it is possible for prescient individuals and organized groups to hasten its coming and "ease its birth pangs."

Marx held that only a complete revolution of the capitalist economic system will properly solve its problems. Limited reforms such as higher wages, shorter hours, pension schemes, and so on, may be welcome ameliorations of the harshness of capitalism, but they do not alter its basic nature. Hence the radical difference between the Communist Party and most trade unions and democratic socialist parties. But again, followers of Marx have disagreed about practical political strategy. Some thought that working to reform the system may distract attention from the reality of the class struggle and the need to overthrow the existing order. Others said the very process of arousing workers to combine together to work for reform will "raise their consciousness," create class solidarity, and thus hasten revolutionary change.

Piecemeal reforms *have* modified capitalism considerably, beginning with the British Factory Acts, which limited the worst exploitation of workers and children, continuing with national insurance schemes, unemployment benefits, and national health services (in Europe, though not in the United States). Trade unions have made steady progress in increasing real wages and improving working conditions. In fact, many of the specific measures proposed in the *Communist Manifesto* have long since come into effect in the so-called capitalist countries; namely, graduated income tax, free education in state schools, centralization of considerable economic control in the hands of the state, nationalization of some major industries in some countries. The unrestrained capitalist system as Marx knew it in the mid-nineteenth century has ceased to exist in the developed countries—and not by revolution. This is not to say that what we have now is perfect, but it does suggest that the rejection of gradualist reform is mistaken; and reflection on the violence and suffering involved in revolutions elsewhere may confirm this.

Like Christians, Marx envisaged a total regeneration of humanity, but he expected it within this secular world. He described communism as "the solution to the riddle of history," for the abolition of private property is supposed to ensure the disappearance of alienation and exploitation and the coming of a genuinely classless society. Marx was extremely vague on how all this would be achieved, but he was realistic enough to see the need for an intermediate period before the transition to true communism can take place, and that this will require what he called "the dictatorship of the proletariat." Alienation cannot be overcome on the day after the revolution. In a phrase that sounds ominous in the light of twentieth-century history, he wrote that "the alteration of men on a mass scale is necessary"—but in Marx's defense it may be said that he had in mind an alteration of consciousness, not the forcible methods of Soviet Russia. In the higher phase of communist society, the state is supposed to wither away and the realm of freedom will begin. Then human potentiality can develop for its own sake, and the guiding principle can be: "From each according to his ability, to each according to his needs."

Much of this utopian vision must surely be judged unrealistic. Marx gives us no good reason to believe that communist society will be genuinely classless, that those who exercise the dictatorship of the proletariat will not form a new governing class with many opportunities to abuse their power and develop new forms of exploitation. There is no ground for expecting any set of economic changes to eliminate *all* conflicts of interest and all feelings of boredom or alienation at work. States have not in fact withered away; they have tended to become more powerful; although these days we must also recognize the enormous power of the big corporations and the increasingly global nature of the market, which restricts the power of any one government.

Yet, with other elements in Marx's vision, we can surely agree. The application of science and technology to produce the necessities of life for everybody, the shortening of the working day, and the provision of universal education so that all human beings can develop their potential, the vision of a decentralized society in which people cooperate in communities for the common good, and of a society in balance with nature— these are ideals that almost everyone will share, though it is no easy matter how they can be compatibly realized. No doubt, it is because Marxism has offered this kind of hopeful vision of a human future that it has been able to win the allegiance of so many people. Like religions, Marxism is more than a theory, it has, for many, been a secular faith, a prophetic vision of social salvation.

Even now, despite the disputability of some of Marx's theoretical assertions in their more extreme formulations, and the failures of the communist regimes of the twentieth century, his ideas are far from dead. His diagnosis is more convincing than his prescription, it has to be admitted. Although social reforms and technical developments have altered the face of the economic system in many ways, many people see the need for a further transformation of global capitalism, and look to Marx for inspiration for such a change.

However, the Marxist emphasis on *economic* factors directs our attention to only one of the obstacles in the way of human fulfilment. Sexuality and family relationships are surely vital, too, as are our existential attitudes to the noneconomic limitations of life, such as moral failures, illness, and mortality. And human conflict—from tribalism to nationalism, nuclear confrontation and terrorism—seems to involve something in human nature other than economic competition. We must look elsewhere—to psychology, existentialism, evolutionary theory, and perhaps to religious conceptions—for deeper insights into the nature and problems of human individuals and human societies.

FOR FURTHER READING

There is no one main text by Marx that one can recommend as basic. The *Communist Manifesto* is an obvious starting point, but it is more polemical than theoretical, and its third section is dated; the *German Ideology* is deeper and longer, but fairly readable.

There are various useful selections, such as *Karl Marx: Selected Writings in Sociology and Social Philosophy*, translated by T. B. Bottomore, edited by T. B. Bottomore and M. Rubel (London: Penguin, 1963; New York: McGraw-Hill, 1964), which is helpfully organized under themes; *Marx and Engels: Basic Writings on Politics and Philosophy,* edited by L. S. Feuer (New York: Anchor Books, 1959), and most recently *Karl Marx: Selected Writings*, 2d ed., edited by David McLellan (Oxford University Press, 2000).

There are biographies of Marx by Isaiah Berlin, *Karl Marx: His Life and Environment*, 3d ed. (Oxford University Press, 1963), and Francis Wheen, *Karl Marx* (London: Fourth Estate, 1999).

A classic criticism of Marxism was presented by Karl Popper, in *The Open Society and Its Enemies*, Vol. I, 5th ed. (London: Routledge, 1966).

The religious dimension of Marx's thought is brought out by Robert Tucker, in *Philosophy and Myth in Karl Marx* (New York: Transaction Publishers, 2000). There is a discussion of Marx on human nature in J. Plamenatz, *Karl Marx's Theory of Man* (Oxford University Press, 1975).

For a sophisticated defense of Marx's materialist theory of history using the methods of analytical philosophy, see G. A. Cohen, *Karl Marx's Theory of History: A Defence* (Oxford University Press, 1978).

On the relation of Marxist theory to feminism, see F. Engels, *Origin of the Family, Private Property and the State* (New York: Lawrence & Wishart, 1987), and A. Jaggar, *Feminist Politics and Human Nature* (Totowa: Rowman & Littlefield, 1983), Chapter 4.

A post-communist defense of Marx's ideas is given by Keith Graham in *Karl Marx Our Contemporary: Social Theory for a Post-Leninist World* (University of Toronto Press, 1992).

There is a very readable recent reevaluation by Jonathan Wolff, *Why Read Marx Today?* (Oxford University Press, 2002); he addresses the labor theory of value, which was not discussed in Chapter 7.

C   H   A   P   T   E   R

8

Freud: The Unconscious Basis of Mind

Freud's psychoanalytic approach revolutionized the understanding of human nature in the first half of the twentieth century. He spent the whole of his long career developing and modifying his theories, touching on a vast range of subjects, including neurology, psychiatry, child development, sexology, anthropology, sociology, art, and religion. He also led the development of the worldwide psychoanalytic movement, trying to keep it under his own control. I concentrate here on Freud himself, not the many later developments in psychoanalytic theory and practice. In this chapter, I have found it convenient to keep my critical points for two sections at the end.

FREUD'S LIFE AND WORK

Sigmund Freud was born in Moravia in 1856, but in 1860 his family moved to Vienna, where he lived and worked until the last year of his life. Even in his school days, Freud's precocious interests ranged over the whole of human life, and when he entered the University of Vienna as a medical student he attended lectures on other subjects, such as those of the philosopher of mind Franz Brentano. Freud became deeply interested in biology and spent six years doing research in the laboratory of the famous physiologist Brücke, writing papers on technical topics such as the nervous systems of fishes. (And he almost made a controversial reputation for himself in pioneering the medical use of cocaine.) In order to marry his fiancée, Martha Bernays, Freud needed more secure employment, so he reluctantly began work as a physician in the Vienna General Hospital. In 1886, he set up a private practice in "nervous diseases"; that is, psychological problems, which he continued for the rest of his life.

Freud's subsequent intellectual career can be divided into three main phases. In the first of these he arrived at his original hypotheses about the nature of neurotic problems and developed his distinctive theory and method of treatment, both of which have come to be known as "psychoanalysis." His interest in human psychology had been fired by a visit to Paris in 1885–86 to study under Charcot, a French neurologist who was using hypnotism to treat "nervous" problems. Many of Freud's early patients were middle-class Viennese women suffering from what was then called "hysteria." Typically, they had mysterious paralyses, loss of speech, or loss of sensation in bodily regions that bore no relation to neurology but only to the ordinary concepts of body parts such as hand or arm. Etymologically, the word "hysteria" comes from ancient explanations of such symptoms as due to disturbances of the womb, and nowadays the word tends to mean a state of extreme emotion, but in Freud's time it referred to a puzzling syndrome that orthodox medicine found almost impossible to treat. (One wonders, of course, if its prevalence in late nineteenth-century bourgeois women had something to do with their repressed social situation.) Freud was impressed by how Charcot's purely psychological method of hypnotism seemed to induce dramatic cures.

Faced with similar symptoms in his own patients, Freud used electrotherapy or hypnotic suggestion, but finding them unsatisfactory, he began to try another method derived from Breuer, a senior Viennese consultant. Breuer's approach was based on the assumption that hysteria was caused by some intense emotional experience (a "trauma") that the patient had apparently forgotten; his treatment was to induce the recall of the experience and a "discharge" of the corresponding emotion. This hypothesis that people could suffer from an "idea," an emotion-charged memory that they were not aware of, but from which they could be relieved by bringing it into consciousness, is the basis from which Freud's psychoanalysis developed.

Freud found that the traumatic ideas in his patients typically had some sexual content and (ever ready to make a generalization) he suggested that neuroses *always* have a sexual origin. In many cases, his patients came up with reports of "infantile seduction"—what we now call child sexual abuse. At first he believed them, but then—in a dramatic change of theoretical tack that he regarded as a crucial discovery—he came to think that in many cases the reports were based on fantasy; that is, on unconscious desires rather than memories of anything that actually happened. (In view of recent controversies, we have to wonder whether Freud's first thoughts on this matter may not have been somewhat nearer the truth.) In 1895, he published *Studies on Hysteria* jointly with Breuer, but the latter was unable to agree about the universal importance of sexuality, the collaboration broke up, and Freud went on his own theoretical way. (For Freud, this was the first of many disputes with colleagues.)

In the closing years of the nineteenth century, Freud began to formulate his theories about infantile sexuality and the interpretation of dreams, both of which are central to psychoanalytic theory. He introduced his distinctive theoretical concepts of resistance, repression, and transference. He also attempted to psychoanalyze himself! At this time he wrote (in correspondence with Fliess, a medical friend given to unorthodox speculations, who influenced him strongly in this period) the *Project for a Scientific Psychology*. Freud was ambitiously trying to relate his developing psychological theory to a physical basis in the nerve cells in the brain, which he had studied in his physiological work. Although excited by this interdisciplinary project, he came to think it too much ahead of its time and did not publish these thoughts (the rediscovered manuscript was eventually published in 1950). But its ghost haunts all Freud's later works in the form of a background assumption that the mental processes postulated in psychoanalytic theory would eventually be identified with movements of electrical energy in the neurons in the brain.

The second phase of Freud's work, in which the works expounding his mature theory appeared, can conveniently be dated from the publication in 1900 of *The Interpretation of Dreams*. There followed in 1901 *The Psychopathology of Everyday Life*, in which he analyzed the unconscious causation of everyday errors such as slips of the tongue, and in 1905 his *Three Essays on the Theory of Sexuality*. These works applied psychoanalytic theory to normal mental life, not just neurotic patients. International recognition followed, and the spread of psychoanalysis began: in 1909 Freud was invited to America, where he gave the *Five Lectures on Psycho-Analysis,* a brief, popular exposition of his ideas. In 1915–17 he delivered the much longer *Introductory Lectures on Psycho-Analysis* at the University of Vienna, in which he expounded the complete theory as it had developed up to then.

From after the end of the First World War until his death in 1939, the third phase of Freud's work saw some important changes in his theories, together with wide-ranging speculative attempts to apply his ideas to social questions. In 1920 came *Beyond the Pleasure Principle,* in which he first introduced the concept of the "death instinct" (to try to explain aggression and self-destruction) as well as the "life instincts" (self-preservation and sexuality), which he had postulated up to then. Another late development was the tripartite structure of the mind—id, ego, and superego—which was presented in *The Ego and the Id* (1923). In a second popular exposition, *The Question of Lay Analysis* (1926), Freud expounded his theory in terms of this new three-part structure.

Most of Freud's last years were devoted to social theorizing. (Already, in 1913, he had speculatively tried to relate his theories to anthropology and human prehistory in *Totem and Taboo*.) In *The Future of an Illusion* (1927), he treated religion as a system of false beliefs whose deep root in our minds can be explained psychoanalytically. In *Civilization and Its Discontents* (1930), he discussed the conflict between the demands of human instincts and of civilized society, and in *Moses and Monotheism* (1939), he offered a controversial psychoanalytic interpretation of Jewish history. In 1938 Hitler annexed Austria, and Jews were in danger. Freud was ethnically Jewish (and had already been the victim of Austrian anti-Semitism). Because of his huge international fame, the Nazis allowed him to flee to London, where he spent the last year of his life writing a brief final *Outline of Psycho-Analysis*.

METAPHYSICAL BACKGROUND: NEUROLOGY, DETERMINISM, AND MATERIALISM

What is distinctive in Freud's thought is, of course, his theory of the human mind, but we first should take note of his metaphysical and methodological assumptions. He started his research career as a physiologist and claimed to remain a scientist throughout: his constant hope was to explain all the phenomena of human life scientifically. (How far he lived up to this self-description, we shall see!) Freud rejected all theology or transcendent metaphysics. He was not a Marxist, but he did share the nineteenth-century belief in processes of historical development as explanatory of the present state of things.

Given Freud's wide knowledge of biological science as it had developed up to his day, and his thorough training in physiological research, he assumed that everything that happens is determined by the laws of physics, chemistry, and biology, and that human beings are subject to these too. He was steeped in the confidence of late nineteenth-century biology, after the advent of Darwin's theory of evolution, accepting that human beings are one species of animal (albeit of a special sort). Freud has been described as a "biologist of the mind," but we shall see how far he moved away from purely physiological methods of explanation and treatment. He applied nineteenth-century historicism in biology, psychology, and anthropology, assuming that so-called primitive races have mental processes like those of childhood.

Freud was a philosophical materialist as well as a determinist. He acknowledged a distinction of some sort between mental states and physiological states, but this was for him only a dualism of concepts or aspects, not of two substances or two different sets of events. Materialist philosophers agree that in talking of states of consciousness such as sensations, thoughts, wishes, and emotions we are not committed to metaphysical dualism, and Freud says the same about the *unconscious* mental states that he postulates. After his bold early attempt to relate psychology and physiology in his *Project*, he was content to leave the material basis of psychology to be discovered in the future development of brain science. Enormous progress has been made in this area in recent years, but it has not vindicated Freud's specific neurological theories.

THEORY OF HUMAN NATURE: MENTAL DETERMINISM, THE UNCONSCIOUS, INSTINCTS, AND CHILD DEVELOPMENT

I shall expound Freud's approach in four main areas. The first is his strict application of determinism—the principle that every event has preceding causes—to the realm of the mental. Thoughts and behavior that had formerly been assumed to be of no significance for understanding a person, such as slips of the tongue, faulty actions, dreams, and neurotic symptoms, Freud assumed must be determined by hidden causes. He thought that such errors could be highly significant, revealing in disguised form what would otherwise remain unknown. Nothing a person thinks or does or says is really haphazard or accidental; everything can in principle be traced to some cause or other, presumably in the mind (hence the concept of the "Freudian slip").

This would seem to imply a denial of free will, for even when we think we are choosing perfectly freely, Freud would claim that there are unknown causes determining our choice. There is an interesting parallel with Marx here, in that he and Freud both say that the contents of our consciousness, far from being uniquely "free" and "rational," are determined by causes of which we are not normally aware. But whereas Marx says that the causes are social and economic, Freud claims they are individual and psychological, rooted in our biological drives.

The second and most distinctive feature of Freud's theorizing—the postulation of *unconscious* mental states—thus arises out of the first. But we must be careful to understand his concept of the unconscious correctly.

There are lots of mental states, for instance memories of particular experiences or facts, of which we are not continually conscious but that can be recalled to mind whenever they become relevant. These Freud calls "preconscious"; he reserves the term "unconscious" for states that *cannot* become conscious under normal circumstances. His crucial assertion is that our minds are not coextensive with what is available to conscious attention, but include items of which we can have no ordinary awareness. To extend a well-known analogy, the mind is like an iceberg, with some of it visible above the surface of the sea, some of it occasionally visible as the waves rise and fall, but with a vast hidden bulk exerting its influence on the rest. Freud would happily accept the findings of recent cognitive science that there is unconscious information processing involved in perceptual recognition of objects; the perceiver is unaware of these processes in his or her own mind, but psychologists can infer them as the best explanation of the facts of perception (and misperception).

So far, this gives us a *descriptive* account of the unconscious, but Freud's concept is also *dynamic*. To explain puzzling human phenomena such as hysterical paralyses, neurotic behavior, obsessional thoughts, and dreams, Freud postulated the existence of emotionally charged ideas in the unconscious part of the mind that actively yet mysteriously exert causal influences on what a person thinks, feels, and does. Unconscious desires or emotions can make people do things that they cannot explain rationally, even to themselves. Some unconscious states have previously been conscious (e.g., traumatic emotional experiences) but were repressed because they became just too painful to acknowledge. "Repression" is thus postulated as a mental process of pushing ideas into the unconscious and keeping them there. But the rest of the unconscious consists of the driving forces of our mental life (the "instincts"), which operate from infancy.

Freud introduced a new *structural* concept of the mind into his theory in the 1920s, which does not coincide with the distinction between conscious, preconscious, and unconscious. In this later phase, he distinguished three systems within the mental apparatus. The *id* contains the instinctual drives that seek immediate satisfaction like a small child (they operate according to "the pleasure principle"). The *ego* has the conscious mental states and its function is to perceive the real world and to decide how to act, mediating between the world and the id (the ego is governed by "the reality principle"). Whatever can become conscious is in the ego (though Freud says it also contains elements that remain unconscious), whereas everything in the id is unconscious. The *superego* is a special part of the mind containing the conscience (i.e., the moral norms learned in early childhood); it can confront the ego with rules and prohibitions like a strict parent. The forces of repression are located in the ego and superego, and they typically operate unconsciously. The poor old ego has the difficult job of trying to reconcile the conflicting demands of id and superego, given the often unhelpful facts of the real world. This is Freud's dramatic picture of the human condition, beset by external problems and internal conflict.

There are interesting, if partial, parallels with Plato in this theory of tripartite mental structure. The id obviously corresponds closely to Appetite or desire, but it is not so clear how ego and superego correspond to Plato's Reason and Spirit. In its reality-knowing function, the ego would seem to be akin to Reason, but Reason for Plato has also a moral function that Freud assigns to the superego. And Plato's spirited element seems to be performing a moralistic function in the example of feeling disgusted at one's own desires by which he introduced it (see Chapter 4).

The instincts or drives are a third main feature of Freud's theory. In postulating the existence of motivating factors of which the person may not be aware, he was following up on the ideas of Schopenhauer and Nietzsche, two nineteenth-century philosophers who theorized about the will as an unconscious instinctual force. Freud's word was *Trieb,* and though this is often translated as "instinct," the term "drive" is perhaps better because it is part of Freud's theory that the same underlying *Trieb* can be the motivating force or energy behind a variety of different behaviors. These drives are the only motive forces within the mental apparatus, they generate the energy that seeks discharge.

Freud used this mechanical or electrical language in an almost literal way, influenced by his scientific training and the psychophysical theory of his early *Project,* in which he presciently wrote about flows of electrical charge through the neurons in the brain. His conception of mental drives is of electrical charges or hydraulic pressures that have to be discharged in one way or another. His psychological classification of instincts is, however, one of the most speculative and variable parts of his theory. He admitted that we can distinguish an indeterminate number of "instincts," but he suggested that they can all be derived from a few basic drives that combine or even replace each other in multifarious ways.

Of course, Freud held that one main kind of drive is sexual, and he notoriously traced much human behavior back to sexual thoughts and desires (sometimes repressed into the unconscious). It is, however, a common misinterpretation to say that he tried to explain *all* human phenomena in terms of sex. What is true is that Freud gave sexuality a much wider scope in human life than had formerly been recognized, claiming that it is manifest in much more than "normal," adult heterosexual intercourse. He claimed that the beginnings of sexuality exist in children from birth, that sexual factors play a crucial role in adult neuroses, and that sexual energy ("libido") can be "sublimated" in other activity, such as art.

But Freud always held that there was at least one *other* basic drive. In his early period he distinguished what he called the "self-preservative" instincts for eating and self-protection from the sexual drive. He first treated sadism as a perversely aggressive manifestation of sexuality. But in later works he radically changed his classification, putting libido and hunger together into one "life" drive or instinct (*Eros*), and referring sadism, aggression, self-destruction, and so on, to a biologically implausible "death" instinct (*Thanatos*). In popular language, the duality of love and hunger was replaced by love and hate.

The fourth main point in Freud's theory is his developmental account of individual human character. This is more than the obvious truism that personality depends on experience as well as on hereditary endowment. Freud started from Breuer's discovery that particular traumatic experiences could, although apparently forgotten, exercise a baneful influence on a person's mental health. The full-fledged theory of psychoanalysis generalizes from this and asserts the crucial importance for adult character of the experiences of infancy and early childhood. The first five years are the time in which the basis of each individual personality is laid down. So one cannot fully understand a person until one comes to know the psychologically crucial facts about his or her early childhood.

Freud produced detailed theories of the psychosexual stages of development through which every child is supposed to grow. He extended the concept of sexuality to include any kind of pleasure involving parts of the body. He claimed that infants first obtain a sexual kind of pleasure from the mouth (the oral stage), and then from the other end of the alimentary tract (the anal stage). Both boys and girls then become interested in the male sexual organ (the phallic stage). The little boy is alleged to feel sexual desire for his mother and to fear castration by his father (the "Oedipus complex"). Desire for mother and hostility to father are then normally repressed. From age five until puberty (the "latency" period), sexuality is much less apparent. It then reappears, and if all goes well it attains its full genital expression in adulthood.

Freud suggested that at the time of the Oedipus complex in boys, little girls develop "penis envy"; but he never treated female psychology and sexuality so thoroughly. In *The Question of Lay Analysis*, he made a statement that is astonishing (coming from someone whose professional practice consisted so largely in treating the psychological problems of women), that "the sexual life of adult women is a dark continent for psychology"! Dark continent or not, Freud was not inhibited from making some dogmatic, unsupported assertions about female psychology. In

Civilization and Its Discontents (Ch. IV), he said that women "represent the interests of the family and of sexual life." Don't men do the same, one wonders?! And in the next sentence he asserted, without any appeal to evidence, that women are little capable of the instinctual sublimations that men can manage in doing "the work of civilization." It seems that on this topic Freud was firmly imbued with the prejudices of his time.

DIAGNOSIS: MENTAL DISHARMONY, REPRESSION, AND NEUROSIS

Like Plato, Freud says that individual well-being or mental health depends on a harmonious relationship between the various parts of the mind and between the whole person and society. The ego has to reconcile id, superego, and external world, seeking opportunities for satisfying the instinctual demands of the id without transgressing the moral standards required by the superego, the internal representative of society. If the world does not supply enough opportunities for fulfillment, the result will be pain or frustration; but even when the environment is more favorable, there will be mental disturbance if there is too much inner conflict between the parts of the mind. In Freud's view, neurotic illnesses result from the frustration of the sexual instinct, either because of external obstacles or because of internal mental imbalance.

There is one particular mental process that Freud thought was crucial in the causation of neurotic illnesses; namely repression. In a situation of mental conflict, where someone experiences an instinctual impulse that is sharply incompatible with the standards they feel they must adhere to, it will be repressed out of consciousness, so that as far as subsequent awareness is concerned, it does not exist. Repression is the basic "defense mechanism" by which people attempt to avoid inner conflict. But it is essentially a pretense, a withdrawal from reality, and is doomed to failure. For what is repressed does not go out of existence, but remains in the unconscious portion of the mind. It retains all its emotional energy and exerts its influence by sending into consciousness a disguised substitute for itself in the form of a neurotic symptom. Thus, people can find themselves behaving in ways that they may admit are irrational, yet they feel compelled to continue. By repressing an idea, they have given up effective control over it; they can neither get rid of the symptoms it causes, nor lift the repression and recall it to consciousness.

Freud located the decisive repressions in early childhood and held that they are basically sexual. It is essential for future mental health that the child successfully pass through the normal stages of development of sexuality. But this does not always proceed smoothly, and any hitch leaves a predisposition to future problems; the various forms of sexual perversion can be traced to such a cause. One typical kind of neurosis consists in what Freud called "regression," the return to one of the stages at which childish satisfaction was obtained. He even identified certain adult character types as "oral" and "anal," by reference to the childhood stages from which he thought they originated.

There is much more detail in Freud's theories of the neuroses into which we cannot enter here, but he attributes part of the blame for them on the external world, and we should note this social aspect of his diagnosis. The standards to which a person feels obliged to conform are one of the crucial factors in mental problems, but they are a product of the social environment—primarily the parents, plus anyone else who has exerted emotional influence over the growing child. The instilling of such standards is an essential part of education, making children into members of society; for as Freud sees it civilization requires self-control, some sacrifice of instinctual satisfaction, in order to make work and human society possible.

However, the standards imposed by any particular family or society may not be the most conducive to happiness. Maladjusted parents are notoriously likely to produce maladjusted children. Freud entertained wider speculations that the relationship between society and individual has gotten out of balance, so that our whole civilized life might be described as neurotic. This theme came to the fore in his late work *Civilization and Its Discontents*, but as early as the *Five Lectures* of 1909 he had suggested that our civilized standards tend to make life too difficult for most people and that we should not deny a certain amount of satisfaction to our instinctual impulses. So there is a basis for those neo-Freudians, such as Erich Fromm, who diagnose our troubles as lying as much in society as in individuals.

PRESCRIPTION: PSYCHOANALYTIC THERAPY

Freud proposed that our human problems can be diagnosed and ameliorated by the methods of science. His hope was to restore a harmonious balance between the parts of the mind, and (if possible) to suggest a better adjustment between the individual and the world. The latter would involve programs of social reform, but Freud did not try to specify any such thing; his own professional practice consisted in the treatment of neurotic patients. And he was realistic about the limits of his therapeutic influence, famously describing the aim of psychoanalytic therapy as only to replace neurotic unhappiness by ordinary unhappiness. It is this therapy that we must now examine.

Freud's method developed gradually out of Breuer's discovery that a hysterical patient could be helped by being encouraged to *talk* about the thoughts and fantasies that had been filling her mind, and seemed to be cured when she was able to remember the traumatic experiences that had induced her problems in the first place. Freud tried using this "talking cure," assuming that the pathogenic memories were still in his patients' unconscious minds; he asked them to talk to him quite uninhibitedly, hoping that he could interpret the unconscious forces behind what was said. He required them to say whatever came into their mind, however absurd or embarrassing it might be (the method of "free association"). But he often found that the flow would dry up, the patient would have nothing more to say and might even object to further inquiry. When such "resistance" happened, Freud took it as a sign that the conversation was getting near the repressed complex. He assumed that the patient's unconscious mind was trying to prevent the painful truth becoming conscious, just as someone with a painful part of their body may flinch from examination. If the repressed material could only be brought back into consciousness despite the resistance, the conscious, rational mind could be given back power over the noxious ideas, and the neurosis would be cured.

But to achieve this happy result could take a long process, involving weekly sessions over a period of years. The analyst must try to arrive at the correct interpretations of the patient's unconscious mental states and to present them at such a time and in such a way that the patient can accept them. Dreams can provide very fruitful material for interpretation, for according to Freud's theory the "manifest" content of a dream is the disguised fulfillment of unconscious wishes that are its real or "latent" content. Errors and faulty actions can also be interpreted to reveal their unconscious causation. There will typically be discussion of the patient's sexual life, childhood experiences, infantile sexuality, and relationship with parents.

Clearly, all this demands a relationship of peculiar confidence between patient and analyst, but Freud found that much more than this happened; in fact, his patients often manifested a degree of emotion toward him that could amount to love or hatred. He called this "transference," on the assumption that the emotion was projected onto the analyst from the life situations in which it was once present, or from the unconscious fantasies of the patient. The handling of such transference is of crucial importance for the success of the therapy, for it itself needs to be analyzed and traced back to its sources in the patient's unconscious.

The goal of psychoanalytic treatment can be summarized as self-knowledge (echoing Socrates!). What the cured neurotic does with the new self-understanding is up to him or her, and various different outcomes are possible. The person may replace the unhealthy repression of instincts by a rational, conscious control of them (suppression rather than repression); or may be able to divert the instincts into acceptable channels ("sublimation"); or the person may decide to satisfy them after all. But, according to Freud, there is no need to fear that primitive instincts will "take over" the person, for their power is *reduced* by being brought into consciousness.

Freud never thought of psychoanalysis as the answer to *every* human problem. When thinking about the problems of "civilized" modern society, he was realistic enough to accept their extreme complexity and to abstain from offering any social program. But he did suggest that psychoanalysis had wider applications than just the treatment of neurotics. He said that "our civilization imposes an almost intolerable pressure on us": he had primarily in mind the conventional (but, of course, frequently flouted) restriction of sex to marriage, and he speculated that psychoanalysis might help prepare a corrective—presumably some loosening of the moral rules. Much of the restriction on sexual expression that was characteristic of Freud's era has been lifted (making some of his remarks about "civilization" sound old-fashioned), but it is not obvious that we are any happier, overall.

CRITICAL DISCUSSION: FREUD AS WOULD-BE SCIENTIST

The validity of psychoanalysis has been a matter of dispute ever since its inception. An enormous variety of psychoanalytic (and more generally, psychotherapeutic) theories and methods have developed, starting from the early "heretics" from the Freudian fold—Adler and Jung. However, most academic psychologists have tended to condemn Freud's theories as unscientific, either too vague to be testable or not supported by the evidence where the claims are testable. Psychoanalytic therapy has been criticized for working by the power of suggestion, like brainwashing or witchcraft. Some critics have fastened on the orthodoxy that has often been imposed by institutes of psychoanalysis and the "indoctrination" imposed on all aspiring analysts by the requirement to be analyzed themselves. Psychoanalysis has thus been likened to a religious cult.

Freudian theory obviously has a readily available method of disparagingly analyzing the motivations of its critics. Any questioning of its truth can be alleged by its defenders to be based on the unconscious resistance of the critic. So, if it also has a built-in method of explaining away any evidence that appears to falsify it, it will be a closed system in the sense defined in the introduction to this book. And because belief in the theory is a requirement of membership of psychoanalytic societies, it can even be said to be the ideology of those groups. However, we should look more closely before we pass judgment.

We can distinguish two areas to question: the truth of Freud's theories and the effectiveness of treatment based on them. Any doubts about psychoanalytic theory will naturally extend to the therapy based on it. Because psychoanalysis has been widely applied, surely we can make some estimate of its success. This might in principle give an empirical test of the theory: if the theoretical claims were true, one might expect the therapy based on them to be effective.

But these matters are not straightforward. First, understanding the causes of an unwanted condition does not necessarily give us the power to change it (climate change may be one example, another might be the effects of a traumatic childhood, which might be impossible to undo, however well understood). Second, a true theory might be inadequately applied in clinical practice—all sorts of things can go wrong in medicine, in psychiatry, and in psychotherapy. Third, there is considerable vagueness about what constitutes cure from neurosis, for who is to make such a judgment—the patient, the therapist, or society generally? Should we require the complete disappearance of any symptoms labeled neurotic, or just a reduction of them? A recovery rate of two thirds has been claimed as the approximate success rate for patients who persist with psychoanalysis. This may sound favorable, but it must be compared with control groups of similarly neurotic people who have not been treated (or who have been treated by other methods). The rate of spontaneous recovery from neurosis has also been estimated as two thirds, so on those sorts of figures there is no clear evidence of any therapeutic effectiveness of psychoanalysis.

On the question of the truth of the theories, the fundamental issue is whether they are empirically testable at all. We have seen that Freud put forward his theories as scientific hypotheses to explain the observable evidence, and testability by observation is a necessary condition for scientific status. But, for some of the central propositions of Freudian theory, it is not clear whether or how they are testable. I will illustrate this from different levels of Freud's theorizing.

By applying his postulate of psychic determinism, Freud arrived at some very specific claims, such as that all dreams are wish-fulfillments, often in disguised form. But even if we accept that the content of every dream must have a cause of some sort, it does not follow that the cause must be *mental* rather than physical. Couldn't the cause be something one has eaten or a neurophysiological need for some sort of "cleaning-out" process of information in the brain? And even if the cause is mental, it does not follow that it is unconscious or deeply significant—why couldn't it involve only quite banal experiences of the day or ordinary concerns about the morrow?

Can Freud's generalization that the cause of every dream is a wish (often unconscious and often disguised) be tested? Where an interpretation in terms of an independently established wish of the dreamer is made plausible, well and good. But what if no such interpretation is found? A convinced Freudian may say there *must* be a wish whose disguise has not yet been seen through. But how then could we ever show that a given dream is *not* a disguised wish-fulfillment? It is notoriously difficult to prove such a negative statement. This threatens to evacuate any empirical content from Freud's general claim, leaving only the practical suggestion that we should always look for a disguised wish. (Similar doubts arise about the postulation of unconscious causes for *every* slip of the tongue or mistaken action.)

Consider next the basic postulate of unconscious mental states. Freud rightly dismissed the a priori view held by some philosophers that being mental entails being conscious; there are no such strict rules governing all use of the term "mental." Although Descartes may have thought in this way, and the behaviorists rejected any conceptions of mental state that were not definable in terms of observable behavior, psychologists these days go in for all sorts of theorizing about mental states of various levels or kinds. The relevant constraint is only that any such claim needs to be explanatory of the observable evidence to be accepted as true. So we must ask ourselves whether Freud's postulation of unconscious mental states offers any good explanation of what we can know in ordinary ways about human beings and their behavior.

After all, in explaining human action and behavior in everyday terms, we appeal to *conscious* perceptions, sensations, desires, and intentions— and none of these are literally observable states in other people, although people are introspectively aware of them. Some of Freud's theorizing goes only a little way beyond this everyday sort of mental explanation. Under hypnotic suggestion, a subject may deliberately perform unusual, even silly actions that the hypnotist has told him or her to do (e.g., opening an umbrella indoors); if asked why he or she is doing these things, the person does not seem to remember the hypnotist's instructions but offers rather lame rationalizations for the actions (e.g., there might be drips from the ceiling). In this case, it seems plausible to explain the subject's behavior (and rationalizations) in terms of an unconscious memory of the hypnotist's instructions. Some of the symptoms of Freud's hysterical patients invited very similar explanations. And sometimes such explanations can be confirmed by independent evidence about what the person has previously experienced or done, or does or says in new situations.

It has sometimes been suggested that psychoanalytic theory is not so much a set of scientific hypotheses to be tested empirically as a "hermeneutic" method; that is, a way of understanding people, of seeing a *meaning* in their actions, mishaps and errors, jokes, dreams, and neurotic symptoms. Because human beings, as conscious and rational beings, are so different from the entities studied by physics and chemistry, why—it is asked—should we criticize psychoanalysis for failing to meet criteria for scientific status taken from the *physical* sciences? Perhaps the psychoanalytic account of a dream or a symptom is more akin to the interpretation of a poem or painting, in which there may be reasons (of an inconclusive kind) for a variety of interpretations.

Many of Freud's theoretical conceptions can be seen as extensions of our ordinary ways of understanding each other in terms of concepts such as love, hate, fear, anxiety, rivalry, and so on. And perhaps the experienced psychoanalyst can be described as someone who has acquired a deep intuitive understanding of the springs of human motivation and a skill in interpreting the complexities of how they work out in particular situations, regardless of how well the analyst can articulate the reasons for his or her interpretations. However, there is still a perfectly reasonable demand (on both everyday and psychoanalytic interpretations) that any particular interpretation should be backed up with independent evidence about the relevant person and their life-context before it is accepted as *correct*.

The hermeneutic view of psychoanalysis has been given philosophical backing by the distinction between *reasons* and *causes*. The typical form of scientific explanation in terms of causes has been contrasted with the explanation of human actions in terms of the beliefs and desires that made it rational for the agent to do what they did. (See Chapters 6 and 9 for what Kant and Sartre have to say on this topic.) It has even been suggested that Freud misunderstood the nature of his own theories by presenting them as *scientific* discoveries about the causes of human behavior. However, the sharpness of this dichotomy has been questioned by those who argue that beliefs and desires are both reasons *and* causes, and that *unconscious* beliefs and desires can play this dual role too. There are deep philosophical issues here about how far the methods of investigation and explanation that are characteristic of the physical sciences are applicable to human beliefs and actions.

Even if we accept that unconscious mental states can explain behavior under hypnosis, some dreams and errors, and certain kinds of neurotic behavior, success in these special cases is far from proving the whole of Freud's theories. The trouble with many of the Freudian unconscious states is the lack of clarity of the criteria for inferring their presence or absence in any particular person. If stamp collecting is asserted to be a sign of unconscious "anal retentiveness," how could one show that such an unconscious trait is *not* present in someone?

The developmental approach to individual character and the theory of the stages of infantile sexual development are rather more easily tested by observation. In this area, some of Freud's propositions seem confirmed by the evidence, others are not supported, while some are difficult to test. The *existence* of what Freud called the oral and anal characters has been confirmed by the discovery that certain traits of character (for instance, parsimony, orderliness, and obstinacy) do tend to go together. But the claim that these types of character *arise* from certain kinds of infant-rearing procedures is not so well supported. There are practical difficulties in establishing correlations between infantile experience and adult character, so the theory is hard to refute. For some other parts of Freud's psychosexual theories, there are conceptual difficulties about testing. How, for example, could one test whether infants get distinctively *erotic* pleasure from sucking?

Freud formulated some very speculative theories that go a long way beyond our everyday explanations in terms of reasons. In particular, he appealed to the concept of repression as a postulated process of pushing mental ideas into the unconscious and keeping them there by force. Here he is in danger of talking of persons within the person, internal "homunculi" with knowledge and purposes of their own. What exactly is it that does the repressing, and how does it know which items to select for repression? As we shall see in Chapter 9, Sartre asks a critical question at just this point.

One can describe as instinctive any form of behavior that is not learned in the lifetime of the individual (although it may be difficult to *show* that it has not been learned in some way). But is anything added by referring instinctive behavior to *an* instinct? And when Freud claims that there are only a certain *number* of basic instincts or drives, how can we decide which are basic, and how they are to be distinguished and counted? If the sexual drive is alleged to be behind behavior that we do not ordinarily recognize as sexual (such as artistic creation); how are we to decide whether this is right? A similar question arises when, in his late work, Freud suggested a "death" instinct to explain destructive behavior and explained aggression in terms of this. Could any evidence settle whether either of Freud's main instinct theories is right, as against, say, an Adlerian theory of a basic instinct of self-assertion or a Jungian theory of an instinctual need for God?

This treatment of a few examples suggests why there is serious doubt about the scientific status of Freud's key theoretical assertions. Some seem untestable because of conceptual unclarities, and among those that *can* be tested only a few have received definite empirical support. He seems to have been overly confident about his own ability to synthesize ideas from a large number of sources into a single interdisciplinary science of mind.

CRITICAL DISCUSSION: FREUD AS MORALIST

Freud's theory of instincts or drives got out of empirical control, as is suggested by his vacillations on the subject. Often, his account seems unduly reductionist and physiological. In *The Question of Lay Analysis*, he wrote: "What, then, do these instincts want? Satisfaction—that is, the establishment of situations in which the bodily needs can be extinguished." Obviously, Freud had sexual intercourse in mind, plus eating and drinking. But is it plausible to say that *all* human behavior is driven, directly or indirectly, by short-term bodily needs? This is not true even of many animals. Consider parental behavior: many creatures expend tremendous energy on the feeding and defense of their young, and it seems that such behavior is instinctual, but with a different drive from that for copulation. Humans also show (however imperfectly) parental behavior that surely has an instinctive, biological component.

In *Civilization and Its Discontents* (Ch. II), Freud wrote that the question of the purpose of human life has never received a satisfactory answer; but what men show by their behavior to be the purpose of their lives seems to be merely the operation of "the pleasure principle" (i.e., the seeking of immediate satisfaction for their instinctual impulses). He also said that "in the last analysis, all suffering is nothing else than sensation." Both of these assertions express a very reductionist concept of human life, assimilating us far too closely to the animals, from which Plato, Aristotle, and Kant distinguished us. Are we not manifestly capable of *mental* forms of happiness and unhappiness?

Freud conceded that there is what we call a "finer and higher" joy for artists in creating and for scientists in discovering, but he remarked (a) that such satisfactions are mild compared with "the sating of crude and primary instinctual impulses," for they do not "convulse our physical being"; and (b) that such higher satisfactions are accessible only to a few people, with rare gifts. But he did not mention other less bodily forms of satisfactions or sources of happiness that do not depend on special talents, such as friendship, pleasure in the growth and successes of one's children or grandchildren, or the appreciation of nature, art, or music. These quiet joys may not convulse our physical being (like orgasm or drug-induced "highs"), but they are more reliable, long-lasting, relatively independent of the body, and free of side-effects—and they can even be enjoyed in old age!

Freud no doubt had his reasons (or causes!) for the gloomy account of the human condition that he offered toward the end of his life. He was in continued pain from cancer of the jaw, and several operations could not cure it. He had lived through the First World War, knew all about its horrors, and had seen the aggressive and extremely nationalistic feelings that were aroused by it. And in the 1920s and 1930s he was witnessing the rise of Nazism and anti-Semitism, which eventually came literally home to him, forcing him to emigrate from Vienna in the last year of his life.

Freud refused to offer consolation where he thought none was to be had: his own morality sternly requires us all to face up to unvarnished reality! In *The Future of an Illusion*, Freud firmly rejects religious belief as an illusory projection onto the universe of our childhood attitudes to our parents. We would like to believe that our heavenly father, who brought us into being, is also in beneficent control of our lives, and we see ourselves as having a duty to live up to the standards he has set (see also the final lecture "The Question of a *Weltanschauung*" of Freud's *New Introductory Lectures*). Thus, Freud explains the immense power of religion, as compared with science and philosophy, as due to its having "the strongest emotions of human beings at its service."

In *Civilization and Its Discontents* (Ch. IV), Freud asserted, on the authority of his lifetime's study of the human mind, that those few saintly people who seem able to live up to the biblical injunction to "love thy neighbor as thyself" really derive the relevant mental energy from the sexual instinct. He wrote: "What they bring about in themselves in this way is a state of evenly suspended, steadfast, affectionate feeling, which has little external resemblance any more to the stormy agitations of genital love, from which it is nevertheless derived." One has to say that this is mere assertion without argument. It would seem more intuitively plausible to say that if Christian *agape* is derived from any natural tendency, the instinctual love of parents for their children (and the protective and affectionate feelings that many people have for most children) would be a stronger candidate.

Similarly, Freud's assertion that the energy that some people devote to art or to science must also be "aim-inhibited libido," a sublimation of the sexual drive, seems unproven. (Presumably, he would have to say the same about athletic and sporting achievement and many other human activities that do not involve food or sex.) Freud wanted a biological theory of human motivation, but he seems to have assumed that it must all reduce to nutrition and copulation, which is an oversimplified account of much animal behavior (see the discussion of ethology in Chapter 10). As

Sartre realized (see the end of Chapter 9), we have a need for meaning and purpose. We need to work, or at least to try to do something that serves some meaningful end; if our desires for food, drink, and sex are plentifully fulfilled (as in some gross conceptions of paradise) but there is nothing else to do, we soon get bored!

Freud remarked that, in his view, not everybody is worthy of love. He had little respect for the vast mass of humanity who, he thought, behave in accordance with "the pleasure principle," and he had little hope that human nature could be fundamentally changed, for instance, by the radical social experiments in Soviet Russia. In *Why War?* (an exchange of open letters with Einstein), Freud suggested a need for Platonic guardians of the state when he wrote that "more care should be taken than hitherto to educate an upper stratum of men with independent minds, not open to intimidation and eager in the pursuit of truth, whose business it would be to give direction to the dependent masses." At the end of his letter, Freud expressed a modicum of hope for the long-term future of humanity without war, if the evolution of culture will allow a strengthening of reason and an internalization of aggressive impulses.

No unambiguous verdict can be passed on Freud's work as a whole. His imaginative power in suggesting new psychological hypotheses is obvious. But his theorizing was overly ambitious and too distant from its empirical roots. And he was prone to dogmatism, refusing to learn from the progress of other disciplines and other approaches within psychology and psychiatry. He was blessed with a considerable literary gift, and many readers have been carried along by the stylishness of his prose. But, however influential and persuasive someone's writing may be, we should never excuse ourselves the task of critical evaluation.

FOR FURTHER READING

A good starting point for reading Freud is his *Five Lectures on Psycho-Analysis*, reprinted in *Two Short Accounts of Psycho-Analysis* (London: Penguin, 1962), and in *A General Selection from the Works of Sigmund Freud*, edited by J. Rickman (New York: Bantam Doubleday Dell, 1989). There is also Freud's second "short account," "The Question of Lay-Analysis," which introduces the later theory of id, ego, and superego. Exploration of his fundamental theory could continue with the *Introductory Lectures on Psycho-Analysis* of 1915–17. Much of his social thought is reprinted in Volume 12 of the Pelican Freud library, entitled *Civilization, Society and Religion*.

For relatively brief, reliable introductions to Freud's thought, see Anthony Storr, *Freud* (Oxford University Press, 1989), and Richard Wollheim, *Freud* (London: Fontana, 1971).

Biographies started with the classic, if somewhat hero-worshipping, three-volume work by Ernest Jones, *The Life and Work of Sigmund Freud*, abridged version, by L. Trilling and S. Marcus (London: Penguin, 1964; New York: Basic Books, 1961). More recently, there has been Frank J. Sulloway, *Freud: Biologist of the Mind* (New York: Basic Books, 1979; London: Fontana, 1980). Jeffrey Masson, in *The Assault on Truth: Freud's Suppression of the Seduction Theory* (New York: Farrar, Strauss & Giroux, 1987), controversially questioned Freud's integrity over the issue of childhood sexual abuse.

Among many general evaluations of Freud's theories, B. A. Farrell, *The Standing of Psycho-Analysis* (Oxford University Press, 1981) gives a clear, balanced survey. Patricia Kitcher, *Freud's Dream: A Complete Interdisciplinary Science of Mind* (Cambridge, Mass.: MIT Press, 1992), shows how his interdisciplinary theorizing rapidly became outdated, and draws lessons for our own day.

For a survey of post-Freudian psychoanalytical theory, see Morris N. Eagle, *Recent Developments in Psychoanalysis: A Critical Evaluation* (New York: McGraw-Hill, 1984).

For discussion of philosophical issues arising from Freud's work, see R. Wollheim and J. Hopkins, eds., *Philosophical Essays on Freud* (Cambridge: Cambridge University Press, 1982), and Jerome Neu, ed., *The Cambridge Companion to Freud* (Cambridge: Cambridge University Press, 1991).

9

Sartre: Radical Freedom

Jean-Paul Sartre (1905–1980) was a philosopher in two senses. He had a brilliant student career, in his thirties he wrote some strikingly original books, and after the publication of *Being and Nothingness* he was widely recognized as France's leading philosopher. But he was also a very public intellectual who expressed his ideas in novels, plays, and biographical studies, and applied them to the great social and political issues of his time, taking controversially radical stances against the conventional wisdom of the day.

Let me first put Sartre in the context of the historical development of existentialist thought. Three main concerns are central to existentialism. The first is with *individual* human beings: existentialists tend to think that general theories about human nature leave out precisely what is most important—the uniqueness of each individual and his or her life situation. Second, there is a concern with the *meaning* or purpose of human lives rather than with scientific or metaphysical truths, even if the latter are about human beings. Inner or "subjective" experience is at the center of existentialist attention, rather than "objective" truth. Third, there is a strong emphasis on *freedom,* on the ability of each individual to choose not just particular actions, but his or her attitudes, projects, purposes, values, or lifestyles. And the typical existentialist concern is not just to assert this, but to persuade people to *act* on it, to exercise their freedom.

These themes can be found in a wide variety of contexts, in descriptions of the concrete detail of particular characters and situations in biography or fiction. But to be an existentialist *philosopher* involves some general analysis of the human condition; and the most obvious division is between theist and atheist accounts.

The Danish Christian thinker Søren Kierkegaard (1813–1855) is generally recognized as the first modern existentialist, though there is, of course, an existential dimension to all religions—notably in Paul, Augustine, Luther, and Pascal in the Christian tradition. Like his contemporary Karl Marx, Kierkegaard reacted against Hegel's philosophy, but in a very different direction. He rejected the abstract Hegelian system, likening it to a vast mansion in which the owner does not actually live; Kierkegaard concentrated instead on what he thought supremely important; namely, the individual person and his or her life choices. He distinguished three basic attitudes to life: the aesthetic (essentially the search for pleasure), the ethical (commitment to marriage, family, work, and social responsibility), and the religious (seeing everything in terms of the eternal, the transcendent, the divine). He held that the religious (more specifically, the Christian) way is the "highest," although it can be reached only by a free, nonrational "leap into the arms of God."

The other great nineteenth-century existentialist was a crusading atheist. The German writer Friedrich Nietzsche (1844–1900) argued that since "God is dead" (i.e., the illusions of religious belief have now been seen through), we will have to rethink the whole foundations of our lives and find our meaning and purpose in human terms alone. In this, he had much in common with his earlier compatriot Feuerbach. What is most distinctive of Nietzsche is his emphasis on our radical, unsettling freedom to change the basis of our values. As in other existentialist thinkers, there is a tension between a "relativist" tendency to say that there is absolutely no objective basis for choosing or valuing one way of life more than another, and a recommendation of a particular choice. In Nietzsche's case, the latter is expressed in his vision of the "Superman," who will reject our conventional, meek, religiously based values and replace them by the "will to power" (a phrase that has acquired sinister connotations in the light of subsequent history).

In the twentieth century also, existentialism included both religious believers and atheists. There were existentialist theologians such as Marcel in France, Bultmann in Germany, and the Jewish thinker Martin Buber. Existentialist philosophy developed mainly in continental Europe. Though influenced by the unsystematic thinkers Kierkegaard and

Nietzsche, it became in the hands of Heidegger and Sartre a more academic, jargon-ridden, and system-building style of philosophy. Another source of this was "phenomenology": the philosophical movement started by Edmund Husserl (1859–1938), who hoped to find a new method for doing philosophy, namely to describe the "phenomena" as they appear to human consciousness. This concern with human experience rather than scientific truth is characteristic of existentialist philosophers (but a less dramatic version of it was also a feature of "ordinary language" philosophy in the English-speaking world, stemming from Wittgenstein's later thought).

The most original and influential of twentieth-century existentialists was Martin Heidegger (1889–1976), whose *Being and Time* was published in 1927. Heidegger's language is strange and difficult: in his attempt to question the fundamental concepts of Western philosophy since Plato, he invents hyphenated neologisms in the German language to try to express his distinctive insights. Although he often seems to be doing abstract metaphysics (like Aristotle), it emerges that he has a central existential concern with the meaning of human existence, our relation to "Being"; and he points to the possibility of "authentic" life through facing up to one's real situation in the world, especially to the inevitability of one's own death. "Being" in Heidegger's writing sounds like an impersonal substitute for God—the ultimate reality of which we can become aware if we attend in the right sort of way. In his later philosophy, there is an emphasis on quasi-mystical kinds of experience that may be expressed in poetry or music but cannot be formulated in literal scientific or philosophical statements.

SARTRE'S LIFE AND WORK

Sartre's philosophy is indebted to Heidegger, but his writing (some of it, at least!) is rather more accessible. He had absorbed the thought of the great European philosophers, especially the three German Hs: Hegel, Husserl, and Heidegger. Many of the obscurities of Sartre's writing can be traced to the influence of those purveyors of ponderous abstractions. Themes from Husserl's phenomenology are prominent in Sartre's first books, the remarkable philosophical novel *Nausea* of 1938 and his studies in the philosophy of mind, *Imagination* (1936) and *Sketch for a Theory of the Emotions* (1940). The centerpiece of his early philosophy is the lengthy and difficult *Being and Nothingness* (1943), strongly influenced by Heidegger's *Being and Time,* but written with Sartre's own flair.

At the beginning of the Second World War Sartre served as a meteorologist in the French army and became a prisoner of war (who spent the time reading Heidegger!). After release he was sympathetic to the French Resistance to Nazi occupation, but devoted himself to writing *Being and Nothingness*. Something of the atmosphere of that time can perhaps be detected in the pessimistic conception of the human condition that he presents in that work. The choice that confronted each French citizen of collaboration, risky resistance, or quiet self-preservation was a very obvious example of what Sartre saw as the ever-present necessity for individual choice. Similar themes are expressed in his trilogy of novels *Roads to Freedom* and in the plays *No Exit* and *Flies*. After the liberation, he gave a stylish account of his atheistic existentialism in *Existentialism and Humanism,* a lecture delivered in 1945 to much public acclaim—but his treatment there is brief and popular, and does not express the depth of his thought.

Sartre rejected the academic career that was then open to him and became a freelance writer and a leading French intellectual for the rest of his life. As time went on, he began to modify the very individualist approach of his early writings and devoted more attention to social, economic, and political realities. He asserted the need for a classless democratic society if genuine human freedom was to be possible for everyone, and he came to espouse a form of Marxism that he described as "the inescapable philosophy of our time," though needing refertilization by an existentialist account of individual human freedom. He joined the French Communist Party at the time of the Korean war, but left it a few years later when the Soviets invaded Hungary.

The works of the later phase of Sartre's philosophy started with *Search for a Method* (1957) and continued with his second magnum opus, the *Critique of Dialectical Reason*, the first volume of which (concentrating on the French Revolution as a historical case study) appeared in 1960; the second volume (about the Russian Revolution) was published posthumously in 1985. Sartre developed a strong sympathy for the oppressed, both the workers under capitalism and the population of third world countries suffering from colonialism or imperialism. He supported Algeria's violent struggle for liberation from French rule and he campaigned against the American war in Vietnam. He gave a notable lecture on his new approach to ethics in Rome in 1964, and toward the end of his life, unable to write because of his blindness after a stroke, Sartre gave interviews that have since been published. His funeral was attended by some 50,000 people.

Like that of any other serious philosopher, Sartre's thought was never at rest and cannot be captured in a single system. There is a fairly clear distinction between his early philosophy, which focuses almost obsessively on individual freedom, and the second main phase, which explores the social and economic limitations on human freedom. The former is that for which Sartre became most famous, but now that so much of the latter has been published, we can begin to appreciate him as a more rounded whole. This presents a problem for writing an introduction. I propose to concentrate on *Being and Nothingness* (making page references to the English translation), but I will add a final section giving an outline of Sartre's second phase.

It is only fair to warn the reader that *Being and Nothingness* is far from easy reading. This is a matter not just of length and repetitiousness, but of a word-spinning delight in the technical term, the abstract noun, and the unresolved paradox. Sartre seems to enjoy teasing his readers with obscure, apparently contradictory, or grossly exaggerated statements! The influence of Hegel, Husserl, and Heidegger may explain this, but can hardly excuse it. One does wonder whether he could not have said what he had to say more clearly—and a lot more briefly. Sartre had an extraordinarily self-confident facility to pour out philosophical verbiage onto pages (in Parisian cafés, at the dead of night, so the story goes), but he does not seem to have been so good at self-criticism or editorial revision (legend has it that his manuscripts were delivered straight to the printers from the café tables). There are passages of relative lucidity and insight, however, and the effort to understand his system reveals a view of human nature that has a certain compelling fascination. (At the end of this chapter, I suggest some sections of *Being and Nothingness* to excerpt for a first—or only!—reading.)

METAPHYSICS: CONSCIOUSNESS AND OBJECTS, ATHEISM

The most basic feature of Sartre's system is his radical distinction between consciousness or "human reality" *(etre-pour-soi,* being-for-itself) and inanimate, nonconscious reality *(etre-en-soi,* being-in-itself). These terms are derived from Hegel, but are given new definitions by Sartre in the introduction to *Being and Nothingness.* This distinction may sound like the dualism of mind and body of Sartre's French predecessor Descartes, but it is important to see how different it is. Sartre affirms that a human being is a unified reality ("the concrete is man within the world," p. 3); what he is distinguishing are not two substances or beings, but two modes of being—the way that conscious beings exist is different from the way that inanimate things exist. Sartre understands consciousness as "intentional" in the sense made famous by Brentano: states of consciousness are *of* something conceived as distinct from the subject (p. xxvii), though they also involve an implicit awareness of self (pp. xxviii–xxx). In contrast, being-in-itself (e.g., the mode of existence of rocks, mountains, and tables) involves no awareness *of* anything, and no conception of itself (pp. xxxix–xlii). (What Sartre would say about animal perception and intention is not clear!)

Sartre also distinguishes between reflective (positional, thetic) consciousness and prereflective (nonpositional, nonthetic) consciousness. All consciousness is "positional" consciousness of something taken to be distinct from the subject. But "every positional consciousness of an object is at the same time a non-positional consciousness of itself" (p. xxix). If I am counting the cigarettes in my case, I am conscious of the cigarettes, and that there are a dozen of them; and I am *prereflectively* conscious that I am counting them (as is shown by the answer I can immediately give when asked what I am doing); but I am not *reflectively* conscious of my activity of counting until someone asks such a question.

Sartre's second most important metaphysical assertion is his denial of the existence of God. (He does not take over the mystical or quasi-religious dimension of Heidegger's concept of "Being," though a posthumously published work called *Truth and Existence* remains closer to the spirit of Heidegger.) Sartre says that we all fundamentally desire to be God in the sense that we want to "be our own foundation"; that is, we would like to be perfectly complete and self-justifying: as he puts it, we aspire to become "in-itself-for-itself" (p. 566). But this ideal, which he identifies with the idea of God, is self-contradictory (pp. 90, 615).

Like Nietzsche, Sartre holds the absence of God to be of the utmost significance for human life; the atheist does not merely differ from the theist on a point of metaphysics, he holds a profoundly different view of human life. In the worldview of *Being and Nothingness*, there are no transcendent objective values set for us—neither commandments of God, nor a Platonic Form of the Good. Nor is there any intrinsic meaning or purpose in human existence (no Aristotelean *telos*). In this sense, our life can be described as "absurd": we are "forlorn" or "abandoned" in this world. There is no heavenly Father to tell us what to do or help us do it; as grown-up people, we have to decide for ourselves and look after ourselves. Sartre repeatedly insists that the only foundation for values lies in our own choices; there can be no external or objective justification for the values, projects, and way of life that anyone chooses to adopt (pp. 38, 443, 626–27).

THEORY OF HUMAN NATURE: EXISTENCE AND ESSENCE, NEGATION AND FREEDOM

In one sense, Sartre would deny that there is any such thing as human nature for there to be theories about. This is a typical existentialist rejection of generalizations about human beings and human lives. Sartre expresses it in his formula "man's existence precedes his essence" (pp. 438–39). He means that we have no "essential" nature, we have not been created for any particular purpose, either by God or evolution or anything else, we simply find ourselves existing by no choice of our own and have to *decide* what to make of ourselves, so each of us must create his or her own nature or "essence." Of course, Sartre cannot deny that there are some true generalizations about our bodily nature, for instance; the necessity to eat, our metabolism, and our sexual impulses. But as we noticed when discussing Marx, there is room for dispute about what count as *purely* biological facts. Sartre thinks there are no general truths about what human beings *want* to be: the project of becoming God is only the abstract form of our particular desires, which are many and various (pp. 566–67). Certainly, he holds that there are no general truths about what we *ought* to be.

An existentialist *philosopher*, however, has to make *some* general statements about the human condition. Sartre's central assertion is human freedom. We are "condemned to be free"; there is no limit to our freedom except that we cannot cease being free (p. 439). He derives this conclusion from his understanding of consciousness as *of* something conceived of as distinct from oneself. (Even if one is mistaken in a particular case, as Macbeth was about the illusory dagger, one is thinking of something that one *believes* to exist objectively at a particular position in space.) Sartre sees a connection between consciousness and the mysterious concept of "nothingness" that appears in the title of his book. The subject is aware in a *non*reflective ("nonthetic") way that the object is *not* the subject (pp. xxvii–xxix, 74–75). That is one way in which negation enters into the nature of conscious awareness.

Another way is that many of our judgments about the world are negative in their content; we can recognize and assert what is *not* the case, as when I look unsuccessfully for my friend in the café where we arranged to meet and say "Pierre is not here" (pp. 9–10). If we ask a question, we understand the possibility of the reply being "No" (p. 5). A related point is that we perceive the world as full of *possibilities* for our actions, and this involves our conceiving of states of affairs that are *not* already the case (they are "nothingnesses," in Sartre's rebarbative language!), but that we might decide to make real. Desire also involves recognition of the *lack* of something (p. 87), as does intentional action (p. 433 ff.). Thus, conscious beings who can think and say what *is* the case can also conceive of, and act to bring about, what is *not* the case.

Sartre indulges in verbal play with his concept of nothingness, in paradoxical phrases such as "the objective existence of a non-being" (p. 5)—which presumably means that there are true negative statements—

sometimes in dark metaphorical sayings like "Nothingness lies coiled in the heart of being—like a worm" (p. 21). The concept of nothingness makes a conceptual connection for him between consciousness and freedom. For the ability to conceive of what is not the case involves the freedom to imagine other possibilities (pp. 24–25) and to try to bring them about (p. 433 ff.). As long as one is alive and conscious, one can always conceive of something being otherwise than it is, and one may desire it to be otherwise (we can never become "in-itself-for-itself"). The mental power of negation thus involves both freedom of mind (to imagine new possibilities) and freedom of action (to try to actualize them). To be conscious is to be continually faced with choices about what to think and what to do.

Sartre contradicts two fundamental Freudian claims. His view is plainly incompatible with complete psychic determinism (p. 458 ff.). He also rejects the postulate of unconscious mental states, for he holds that consciousness is necessarily transparent to itself (p. 49 ff.). But the latter point sounds like mere verbal legislation: of course *consciousness* cannot be unconscious, but Sartre has not shown that it is illegitimate to talk of unconscious states that are *mental* in some wider sense.

Every aspect of our mental lives is, in Sartre's view, in some sense chosen and ultimately our own responsibility. Emotions are usually thought to be outside the control of the will, but Sartre maintains that if I am sad it is only because I choose to make myself sad (p. 61). His view, explained more fully in his *Sketch for a Theory of the Emotions,* is that emotions are not just moods that "come over us," but ways in which we apprehend the world: emotions typically have objects—one is fearful of some possible event, angry with someone about something. But what distinguishes emotions from other ways of being aware of things is, in Sartre's view, that they involve an attempt to transform the world by magic—when one cannot reach the bunch of grapes, one dismisses them as "too green," attributing this quality to them even though one knows quite well that their ripeness does not depend on their reachability. We are *responsible* for our emotions, for they are ways in which we choose to react to the world (p. 445).

There is something right about this, in that emotions presuppose both beliefs and evaluations; for example, anger with someone involves belief that they have done something wrong. If one ceases to believe that they did it, or to see it as wrong, one's anger disappears. (Thus, the Stoics tried to cure us of emotion by persuading us to stop caring about anything other than our own virtue.) But much of what we care about, whether our own health and freedom from pain, the sexual attractiveness of some people, or the well-being of our children, does not seem a matter of choice but

more like a biological given. On emotion and care, Sartre seems to over-
state his case.

Sartre holds us responsible for longer-lasting features of our personality or character. He argues that one cannot just assert "I am shy" (or a
great lover, or unfit for work) as if these were unchangeable facts about
oneself like "I am male, or black, or six feet tall," for the former descriptions depend on the way we behave in certain situations—and we
can always try to behave differently. To say "I am ugly" (or attractive,
persevering, or easily discouraged) is not to assert a determinate fact already in existence, but to anticipate how people will react to what one
does in the future, and one has choices about that (p. 459). But, again,
we need to integrate what truth there is in this with the increasing evidence of genetic influences on personality and sexuality.

Sartre tries to extend our freedom and our responsibility to everything
we think, feel, and do. He suggests there are times when this radical freedom is clearly manifested to us. In moments of temptation or indecision
(e.g., when the man who has resolved not to gamble any more is confronted with the gaming tables once again), one realizes, painfully, that
no motive and no past resolution, however strong, determines what one
does *next* (p. 33). Every moment requires a new or renewed choice.
Following Kierkegaard and Heidegger, Sartre uses the term "anguish" to
describe this consciousness of one's own freedom (pp. 29, 464). Anguish
is not fear of an external object, but the uneasy awareness of the ultimate
unpredictability of one's own behavior. The soldier fears injury, pain, or
death, but he feels anguish when he wonders whether he is going to be
able to "hold up" courageously in the coming battle. The person walking
on a cliff top fears falling, but feels anguish when she realizes that there
is nothing to stop her from throwing herself over (pp. 29–32). Fear is
common, but anguish is more rare because it is "the *reflective* apprehen-
sion of freedom by itself" (p. 39).

DIAGNOSIS: ANGUISH AND BAD FAITH, CONFLICT WITH OTHERS

Anguish, the consciousness of our freedom, is mentally painful, and we
typically try to avoid it (pp. 40, 556). Sartre thinks we would all like to
achieve a state in which there are no choices left open for us, so that we
would "coincide with ourselves" like inanimate objects and would not be
subject to anguish. But such escape from responsibility is illusory, for
conscious beings are necessarily free, and without justifications for our
choices. Such is Sartre's metaphysical diagnosis of the human condition.
Hence his gloomy description of our life as "an unhappy consciousness

with no possibility of surpassing its unhappy state" (p. 90), "a useless passion" (p. 615).

A crucial concept in Sartre's diagnosis is that of "bad faith" (*mauvaise foi*, sometimes translated as "self-deception"). Bad faith is the attempt to escape anguish by trying to represent one's attitudes and actions as determined by one's situation, or one's character, one's relationship to others, employment or social role—anything other than one's own choices. Sartre believes bad faith is the characteristic mode of most human life (p. 556).

He gives two famous examples of bad faith, both of them scenes from the Parisian cafés that were his favorite haunts (pp. 55–60). He pictures a young girl sitting with a man who, she has every reason to suspect, would like to seduce her. But when he takes her hand, she tries to avoid a decision to accept or reject his advances by seeming not to notice: she carries on their intellectual conversation while leaving her hand in his as if she were not aware of his holding it. In Sartre's interpretation, the girl is in bad faith because she somehow pretends—not just to her companion, but *to herself*—that she can be distinguished from her body, that her hand is a passive object, a mere thing; whereas she is, of course, a conscious embodied person who knows perfectly well what is going on and is responsible for her actions—or lack of reaction, in this case.

The second example is of the café waiter who is doing his job a little too keenly; his movements with the trays and cups are flourished and overly dramatic, he is "acting the part" of being a waiter. If there is bad faith here at all (and there need not be), it would lie in his identifying himself completely with the role, thinking that it determines his every action and attitude, whereas the truth is, of course, that he has chosen to take on the job and is free to give it up at any time, even though he might face unemployment. He is not *essentially* a waiter, for nobody is essentially anything. Sartre writes: "the waiter cannot be immediately a café waiter in the sense that this inkwell *is* an inkwell"; "it is necessary that we *make ourselves* what we are" (p. 59). An employee's actions are not literally *determined* by company policy, for he or she can always decide to object or to resign. Even a soldier can refuse to fight, at the cost of court martial or execution. Anything we do, any role we play, and (Sartre wants to add) any value we respect (pp. 38, 627) is sustained only by our own constantly remade decision.

Sartre rejects any explanation of bad faith in terms of unconscious mental states (pp. 50–54). A Freudian might try to describe Sartre's café cases as examples of repression into the unconscious: the girl might be said to be repressing the knowledge that her companion has made a sexual advance to her. But Sartre points out an apparent self-contradiction in the

very idea of repression. We must attribute the act or process of repressing to some element within the mind ("the censor"); yet this censor must
be able to make distinctions between what to repress and what to retain
in consciousness, so it must be aware of the repressed idea, but supposedly in order *not* to be aware of it. Sartre concludes that the censor itself
is in bad faith and that we have not gained any explanation of how bad
faith is possible by localizing it in one part of the mind rather than in the
person as a whole (pp. 52–53).

He goes on to argue that "good faith," or "sincerity," presents just as
much of a conceptual problem. For as soon as one describes one's role
or character in some way (e.g., "I am a waiter," "I am shy," "I am gay"),
a distinction is involved between the self doing the describing and the
self described. The ideal of complete sincerity seems doomed to failure
(p. 62), for we can never be mere objects to be observed and described
like any external matter of fact. An example Sartre offers here is of someone with a clear record of homosexual activity, but who resists description of himself as gay (p. 63). He is in bad faith because he refuses to
admit his inclinations and tries to offer some other explanation of his homosexual encounters. His friend, "a champion of sincerity," demands that
he acknowledge that he is gay. But in Sartre's view nobody just *is* gay
in the way that a table is made of wood or a person is red-haired. If the
person were to admit that he is gay, and thereby imply that he *cannot*
cease his homosexual activity, he would also be in bad faith—and so
would any "champion of sincerity" who demanded such an admission
(p. 63).

Sartre is touching here on the deep difficulties of self-knowledge. But
his account threatens to make these matters even more perplexing, for he
displays an inordinate fondness for the paradoxical formula that "human
reality must be what it is not, and not be what it is" (pp. xli, 67, 90). This
is, of course, a self-contradiction, so we cannot literally believe it. Did
Sartre enjoy provoking his philosophical readers? Did he deceive himself
into thinking that by its incantation he had achieved insight? Or did he
just present the paradox, while shirking the difficult task of explaining in
clear, consistent terms what it is about the concept of consciousness that
generates the possibility of bad faith? He leaves us some hints about how
to resolve the paradox, however. I suggest that we take it as misleading
shorthand for "people are not *necessarily* what they are, but must be *able*
to become what they are not yet" (which is my variation on something
he says on p. 58). The crucial point is that we are always free to *try* to
become different from what we are.

In Part Three of *Being and Nothingness,* entitled "Being-for-Others,"
Sartre gives his philosophical analysis of interpersonal relations and

comes to a very pessimistic conclusion. He throws some new light on the philosophical problem of other minds, arguing by appeal to common experience that we often have an immediate, noninferential awareness of other people's mental states. When one sees a human (or even an animal) face with two eyes directed at oneself, one immediately knows one is being observed, and one knows it with as much certainty as anything about physical events in the world. The "look" of another human can have a special power over us. If we are engrossed in doing something not normally approved of, such as spying on someone through a keyhole—or picking our nose—and we hear (or think we hear) a footstep of someone approaching, we suddenly feel *ashamed,* for we become aware of someone else who might be critical of our actions. Conversely, when witnessed doing something admirable, we can feel pride. Many of our emotions involve in their conceptual structure the existence of other people and their reactions to oneself.

Sartre goes on to argue for the more disputable thesis that the relationship between any two conscious beings is necessarily one of conflict. Supposedly, another person represents a threat to one's freedom by his or her very existence, in that the person's perception of one "objectifies" oneself as a mere object in the world. According to Sartre, one has only two strategies to ward off this threat: one can treat the other as a mere object without freedom, or one can try to "possess" the person's freedom and utilize it for one's own purposes (p. 363). He gives a persuasive version of Hegel's famous discussion of the relation between master and slave in which, paradoxically, the slave ends up with more psychological power because the master needs the slave to *recognize* him as master. Sartre applies this analysis to some forms of sexual desire, especially sadism and masochism (p. 364 ff.). He demonstrates that human sexual relations raise deep philosophical issues about human nature. But he goes on to allege that genuine respect for the freedom of other people, in friendship or in erotic love, is an impossible ideal (p. 394 ff.). At this stage of Sartre's writing, the outlook seems bleak indeed.

But is there not a contradiction between Sartre's insistence on our freedom and his analysis of the human condition as determined in these respects? He asserts that we all aspire to fill the "nothingness" that is the essence of our existence as conscious beings; that is, we aspire to become a Godlike being that would be the foundation of its own being, an "in-itself-for-itself" (pp. 90, 566, 615). And as we have just seen, Sartre also claims that any relationship between two people always involves conflict, in the form of an attempt to deny or to possess the freedom of the other (pp. 363, 394, 429). In these two ways, he represents human life as a perpetual striving for the logically impossible. But *must* it be like that? Can't someone choose *not* to aspire to become an object or to make other people into objects?

PRESCRIPTION: REFLECTIVE CHOICE

In view of his rejection of objective values, Sartre's prescription has to be a somewhat empty one. There is no *particular* project or way of life that he can recommend. What he condemns is bad faith, the attempt to think of oneself as not free. Bad faith may be the usual attitude of most people, but Sartre implies that it is possible reflectively to *affirm* one's own freedom. It looks as if all he can praise is the making of our individual choices with fully self-conscious, "anguished" awareness that nothing determines them. We must accept our responsibility for everything about ourselves—not just our actions, but our attitudes, emotions, and characters. The "spirit of seriousness," namely the illusion that values are objectively in the world rather than sustained by human choice—which Sartre ascribes especially to "the bourgeois" who are comfortable with their situation—must be decisively repudiated (pp. 580, 626).

In *Existentialism and Humanism*, Sartre illustrated the impossibility of prescription by the case of a young Frenchman at the time of the Nazi occupation who was faced with the choice of joining the free French forces in England or staying at home to be with his mother, who lived only for him. The former course would be directed to the nation, though it would make little difference to the total war effort. The latter would be of immediate practical effect, but directed to the good of only one person. Sartre holds that no ethical doctrine can arbitrate between such incommensurable claims. Nor can strength of feeling settle the matter, for there is no measure of such feeling except in terms of what the subject actually does—which is precisely what is at stake. To choose an advisor or moral authority is only another sort of choice. So when Sartre was consulted by this young man, he could only say: "You are free, therefore choose."

It has to be admitted, however, that no system of objective ethical values (whether Platonic, Aristotelian, Christian, or Kantian) can claim to offer a single, determinate answer to *every* individual human dilemma in each concrete situation. Often, there are difficult dilemmas, in which more than one course of action may be morally permissible; but this is not to say that *anything* is permissible, that *no* moral question ever has a right answer, which seems to be what Sartre implies.

Sartre does commit himself to the intrinsic value of "authentic," self-conscious choice. His descriptions of particular cases of bad faith are not morally neutral, but implicitly condemn any refusal to face the reality of one's freedom and affirm one's own choices. He thus offers another perspective on the ancient virtue of self-knowledge put before us by Socrates, Spinoza, Freud, and many others. For all its obscurities and exaggerations, there is something important to learn from Sartre's analysis of how the very notion of consciousness involves freedom. His view is not a mere misuse of language. For we commonly reproach each other not just for our actions, but for our attitudes, reactions, and emotions: "How *could* you feel like that, when you know that p?" "I don't like your attitude to X" "*Must* you be so selfish? So impatient?" Such reproaches—and more neutral psychotherapeutic interventions—are not without effect, for to make someone *aware* that they are feeling or behaving in a certain way can make a difference. The more they are aware of their own anger or pride or self-centeredness, the more they may become capable of change.

Sartre's understanding of the nature and possibility of self-knowledge differs from Freud's, however. Sartre rejects the very idea of unconscious causes of mental events; for him everything is supposed to be already available to consciousness (p. 571). But in view of how much has been discovered about the operation of the brain, we have to see this as assertion rather than argument. There is now an overwhelming empirical case for the existence of unconscious processes that deserve to be called mental.

In what Sartre calls "existential psychoanalysis" we have an interpretative, hermeneutic program rather than a scientific one. We are to look not for the *causes* of a person's behavior, but for the *meaning* of it; that is, for intelligible *reasons*, which will involve the person's beliefs and desires. For Sartre, desires are based on fundamental value choices rather than biological drives or instincts (pp. 568–75). (Some psychiatrists have adopted this methodology, seeking to understand how patients see their world, rather than looking for unconscious drives, or brain states, behind their behavior.)

Sartre holds that because a person is a unity, not just a bundle of unrelated desires or habits, there must be for each person a fundamental choice (the "original project") that gives the ultimate meaning or purpose behind every aspect of his or her life (pp. 561–65). The biographies he wrote of Baudelaire, Genet, and Flaubert are exercises in "existential psychoanalysis," applied to the whole of a life. But it is not at all obvious that for each person there must be a *single* fundamental choice. Sartre allows that people can sometimes make a sudden "conversion" of their original project (pp. 475–76). And need there be just one such project in each period of someone's life? Can't someone have two or more projects that are not derived from any common formula (e.g., family and career, plus perhaps sport, or art, or politics)?

If no reasons can be given for fundamental choices, they would seem to be unjustified and arbitrary. It looks as if on his own premises Sartre would have to commend the man who "authentically" chooses to devote himself to exterminating Jews, seducing women, abusing children, or playing computer games, provided that he makes such choices with full reflective awareness. Could Sartre find within his own philosophy any reason to criticize a Nietzschian *Ubermensch* who resolutely and reflectively developed his own freedom at the cost of other less-than-super human beings? Conversely, if someone devotes himself or herself to bringing up his or her children, helping the poor, or playing music, but deceives himself or herself (in Sartre's view) into thinking that these are objective values, would Sartre condemn the person as living in bad faith?

In some intriguing footnotes to *Being and Nothingness*, Sartre uses quasi-religious language to suggest that it is *possible* to "radically escape bad faith" in "a self-recovery of being which was previously corrupted." He calls this redemption "authenticity" (in the footnote on p. 70), and he talks of "an ethics of deliverance and salvation" and of "a radical conversion" (p. 412). And in the middle of some of his most obscure theorizing in Part Two, Sartre identifies what he calls "pure" or "purifying" reflection as opposed to "impure" or "accessory reflection" (pp. 155, 159 ff.). He seems to attribute a peculiarly moral power to the former, which can, he says, only be attained as the result of a "katharsis" or cleansing. But he says that these suggestions cannot be developed in a work of ontology, and he ends with a promise to write another book on the ethical plane (p. 628). Sartre never published any such work, presumably because as he worked toward it his view began to change. His conception of human nature moved on into his second phase, which was less abstract and individualistic, more concrete and social.

THE "FIRST ETHICS": AUTHENTICITY AND FREEDOM FOR EVERYONE

Sartre's *War Diaries* and *Notebooks for an Ethics* have been published posthumously, so we can now see in what direction his ethical thought was heading. Here I will rely on the useful summary in Chapters 4 and 5 of Thomas C. Anderson's book *Sartre's Two Ethics* (which saves us wading through hundreds of pages of notes, which are, Anderson says, "of uneven clarity and significance"!).

Sartre came to recognize more explicitly how human freedom is situated in the midst of what he calls "facticity," the facts about oneself and one's situation that constrain the ways in which one can express one's freedom. One kind of facticity depends on the vulnerability of the human body; for example, one's freedom is importantly limited or "contaminated" if one contracts a serious illness such as tuberculosis. Another kind of facticity is one's situation in a given society at a certain stage in history. A slave, a manual laborer, a worker on an assembly line, a sales assistant, a cleaning lady, or a "sex-worker," may have some limited choices about how to act in his or her socioeconomic situation, but it would be a cruel deception to assure the person that he or she really is as free as every other human being. In the abstract terms of *Being and Nothingness*, perhaps they are, but in concrete, realistic terms they are not. Sartre now begins to acknowledge the obvious—that socioeconomic factors limit human freedom, even if they do not determine every individual choice. And he rejects "abstract morality" in favor of an ethics that takes account of bodily, economic, and social factors, and places its hopes in social (perhaps revolutionary) change, at least as much as in individual psychological transformation.

In the *Notebooks*, Sartre says some interesting things about pure reflection and the authentic human existence it is supposed to give rise to. Pure reflection enables us to give up the project of becoming Godlike beings, which *Being and Nothingness* represented as our inevitable but useless passion. We can, after all, come to accept the contingency of our existence, and in a creative, generous spirit we can give meaning and purpose to our lives, and thereby to the world:

> . . . authentic man never loses sight of the absolute goals of the human condition . . . to save the world (in making there be being), to make freedom the foundation of the world, to take responsibility for creation, and to make the origin of the world absolute through freedom taking hold of itself. (Notebooks, p. 448)

It seems we are to give up the project of becoming Godlike in one sense by becoming Godlike in another sense; namely, recognizing ourselves as the only sources of meaning and purpose in the world!

In authentic existence, relations with other people can also be transformed. Another person's perception of me, although "objectifying" in that they perceive my body as one object among others, is not necessarily a threat:

> . . . It only becomes so if the Other refuses to see a freedom in me *too*. But if, on the contrary, he makes me exist as an existing freedom as well as a *Being/object* . . . he enriches the world and me, he *gives a meaning* to my existence *in addition to* the subjective meaning that I myself give it. (*Notebooks*, p. 500)

Sartre thus allows that sympathetic comprehension of another person, and assistance in pursuing his or her goals, is possible after all. He even talks of "authentic love" (reminiscent of Christian *agape*) that "rejoices in the Other's being-in-the-world, without appropriating it" (*Notebooks,* p. 508).

The freedom of the individual thus becomes Sartre's basic value. But this has to be understood as asserting not merely the necessary truth that every conscious being is free in the abstract sense, but the value judgment that every person ought to be able to *exercise* his or her freedom in concrete ways, and thus that human society should be changed in the direction of making this a reality for everyone. Authenticity, the lucid assuming of responsibility for one's own free choices, must involve respecting and valuing the freedom of all other conscious, rational beings.

Sartre had made a suggestion in this Kantian direction in *Existentialism and Humanism* (p. 29), where he said that in choosing for oneself one chooses for all men and thereby creates an image of man as one believes he ought to be. In the *Notebooks,* he uses the phrase "a city of ends" to express this goal, which he now sees as "absolute" or objectively valid. This choice of words carries echoes of two previous ideals, namely Augustine's "City of God" (the heavenly ideal, distinct from all earthly societies), and Kant's formula of the "Kingdom of Ends" (that we should treat every rational being never merely as a means, but always as an end). Sartre tends, however, to interpret the goal in more down-to-earth terms as a socialist, classless society—invoking the same sort of utopian ideal as Marx's envisioned "truly communist" state of future society in which all human beings will be able to express their freedom.

THE "SECOND ETHICS": SOCIETY AND HUMAN NEEDS

In Sartre's later period, from about 1950 onward, he acknowledged the power that social circumstances have over individuals and he began to analyze the social conditions that restrict freedom. In his *Critique of Dialectical Reason,* he presented a frankly materialist view of human nature, in both the ontological and the Marxist senses. He now defines man, not as a free consciousness, but as a material organism, an embodied animal—though endowed with the power of rational thought and action. And he adopts an explicitly Marxist standpoint on the processes of history, accepting that the material, economic foundations of any stage of human society place definite limits on the possibilities for individuals in that culture. There is "a dialectical relationship"; that is, a mutual interaction between human beings, the natural world, and the social world. Sartre now rejects his earlier view that man is fundamentally free in all situations; rather, we are strongly influenced by the past of our culture, by the social class we are encultured into, and by the idiosyncrasies of our family. In emphasizing the influence of the family on the early development of the individual personality (as he does in his biographical studies of Genet, Baudelaire, and Flaubert), Sartre incorporates a strong element of Freud.

Accordingly, there is now no question of individual salvation through pure reflection and authentic self-choice; rather, Sartre looks to social action, in particular to organized, "pledged" groups committed to social and political change, trying to achieve real, concrete human freedom for the oppressed. While he was a member of the Communist Party Sartre was notoriously unwilling to criticize the horrors of Stalinism, apparently because he had placed his faith in the communist movement as the only realistic vehicle of progress toward the worldwide, classless, radically democratic society that he envisaged. As he later said, he "sent ethics on a vacation," thinking it had to give way to political realism. But we may protest that it is always dangerous—and wrong—to suspend ethical constraints in the name of some supposedly greater good; and in the 1960s Sartre changed his view once more, realizing the need for a moral philosophy even in the midst of political struggles. He presented his new view of ethics in a lecture at the Instituto Gramsci in Rome in 1964, and in parts of his lengthy study of Flaubert, *The Family Idiot*. I rely again on Thomas Anderson (Chapters 7–9) for an account of this "second ethics."

Sartre hoped to find a level of ethical thought about society that is not merely conditioned by the prevailing economic structure, yet not totally abstract and unrelated to social reality. He notes, with Kant, that we conceive ethical obligations as having a peculiarly categorical force, they call us toward a "pure future," something that we accept *ought* to exist, even if it has not been the case so far. The oppressed (and those who identify with their cause) are particularly strongly aware that human life ought to be quite different from the reality for so many people under colonialist or capitalist exploitation. There is thus an implicit conception of what Sartre calls "integral humanity," human life as it should be, when freely developed and fulfilled. This, he says, is the "true ethics," the proper goal of human history. And, like Kant, he seemed to find some grounds for hope that history is moving in the right direction, with people becoming more aware of this ideal.

At this point, Sartre, who had once firmly rejected the idea of an essence of humanity, is in fact presupposing some general conception of human potentiality and its ideal fulfillment. His thought begins to move in an Aristotelean direction (much as he might hate to admit it!). He focuses on human *needs*, as setting us objective values that "demand" to be fulfilled. This notion of need is flexible enough to cover several levels, though Sartre does not seem to list them systematically. First, there are physiological needs, things we need to maintain life and health, such as air, water, carbohydrates, proteins, vitamins, medicines. But beyond mere bodily growth and maintenance, there are psychological needs—most fundamentally the needs of infants and children for loving care if they are to grow up feeling valued and believing that life is worth living (Sartre brings this out vividly in *The Family Idiot*). We might add here the typical adult needs for friendship and for sexual fulfillment (ideally, for both together in a partnership of equals), and for children of one's own.

Beyond the individual and the family, there is always the wider society: the fulfillment of even our bodily needs depends on our membership in an economic structure. We can talk here of needs for education and culture, to have one's voice and individuality recognized, to contribute one's work to society, to take part on a basis of justice and equality. Finally, Sartre recognizes a need that all humans have for a meaning and purpose to their lives. But he puts his own particular gloss on this when he says that we desire the absolute, that "finitude makes us mad for an unattainable infinite." This picks up a theme from his early period, but he now identifies this "religious instinct" not as the aspiration to *become* God, but the desire for a justification for our lives that could only come from an almighty loving God. However, Sartre continues to hold that this is an illusion and that only we ourselves can confer meaning and purpose on our lives and on the world.

Sartre hoped that some such list of human needs would provide a basis for ethics that is not tied to any particular stage of socioeconomic development, while still being concrete and realistic enough to justify ethical and political value judgments. He listed a series of conditions under which, he thought, violence on behalf of the oppressed could be morally justified—conditions that bear some resemblance to those in the traditional Christian doctrine of "just war," although Sartre does not explicitly rule out targeting the innocent.

He does not seem to have faced up to the question of how to decide what is a universal human need and what is relative to a given stage of society or a social role (e.g., contemporary "needs" for a car, a TV, a computer, or a mobile phone), or merely created artificially by advertising or fashion (such as a need for a new car every year, for cosmetic surgery, or for the latest brand of designer-label jeans). Sartre ended up appealing to a general conception of human nature or the human condition ("nude man" as he ludicrously put it!), as opposed to what is characteristic of a particular stage of society.

What Sartre was arriving at is a synthesis of themes from Aristotle, Kant, Marx, and Freud, without the transcendent metaphysics of Plato or Christianity. The vast verbiage of his philosophy issues in a challenge to us all: first, to become more truly self-aware and to use our freedom to change ourselves for the better; and second, to do what we can to work toward a worldwide society in which all people have equal opportunity to exercise their freedom.

FOR FURTHER READING

For thought-provoking introductions to existentialism generally, see William Barrett, *Irrational Man: A Study in Existential Philosophy* (New York: Anchor Books/Doubleday, 1962); and David E. Cooper, *Existentialism: A Reconstruction* (Oxford: Blackwell, 1990).

For admirable short guides to important existentialist thinkers, see Patrick Gardiner, *Kierkegaard* (Oxford University Press, 1988); Michael Tanner, *Nietzsche* (Oxford University Press, 1994); George Steiner, *Heidegger* (London: Fontana, 1978); Arthur C. Danto, *Sartre* (London: Fontana, 1975).

Those who want to read Sartre for themselves might start with his novel *Nausea* and his lecture *Existentialism and Humanism* (London: Methuen, 1948); then perhaps his short books, *The Transcendence of the Ego* (New York: Farrar, Strauss & Giroux, 1957) and *Sketch for a Theory of the Emotions* (London: Methuen, 1962).

Rather than attempting to plough straight through the huge, dense forest of *Being and Nothingness* (English translation by Hazel Barnes, London: Routledge, 2002; Secaucus, N.J.: Citadel Press, 2001), I suggest starting with Part Four (itself nearly 200 pages!), then the second chapter of Part One ("Bad Faith"), the concluding pages ("Ethical Implications"), plus some of Part Three—at least Chapter One, section III ("The Look").

M. Jeanson, *Sartre and the Problem of Morality* (Bloomington: Indiana University Press, 1980, first published in French in 1947) is an interpretation of the early philosophy that was enthusiastically endorsed by Sartre himself.

In *Sartre's Two Ethics; From Authenticity to Integral Humanity* (Peru, Ill.: Open Court Publishing Company, 1993), Thomas C. Anderson has given a very useful account of both Sartre's "first ethics" (from the period immediately after *Being and Nothingness*) and his "second ethics," especially as presented in the Rome Lecture of 1964.

Gregory McCulloch, *Using Sartre: An Analytical Introduction to Early Sartrian Themes* (London: Routledge, 1994), is a very clear interpretation of fundamental themes from *Being and Nothingness*, relating them to analytical philosophy of mind and epistemology.

10

Darwinian Theories of Human Nature

Some readers may be wondering whether it is worth giving so much attention to the religious traditions, philosophies, and speculative theories of previous centuries. Now that science has established itself as the proper way of understanding everything in the world, including living beings like ourselves, should we not look to the methods of science to find out the truth about human nature? This thought already inspired many in the seventeenth and eighteenth centuries, such as Hobbes, Hume, and the thinkers of the French Enlightenment. Since Darwin propounded his theory of evolution in the mid-nineteenth century, almost everyone has come to accept that humans are descended from more primitive creatures. And in recent decades evolutionary psychology has been widely touted as a source of new insights into human nature.

However, there has long been controversy between a variety of schools of thought within psychology and the social sciences. The contemporary academic discipline of psychology ranges from the physiological study of the brain and nervous system, through cognitive psychology of perception and language, the study of emotions, child development, and personality, to social psychology and the borderlines of sociology and anthropology—and it is doubtful whether the same methodology applies throughout this range. Many psychologists and biologists have been chary of talking about anything as general as "human nature," and have preferred to make their reputations by specialized technical studies. A few, however, have ventured to offer some sort of diagnosis and prescription for human problems; that is, a "theory" of human nature in the sense used in this book.

But when would-be scientists of human nature offer their secular schemes of salvation—or at least of progress—their claims go beyond empirical science and tend to be just as controversial as those of the other "theories" we have considered. In this chapter, I will outline some of the historical background behind contemporary would-be scientific theorizing about human nature, and I will look at several psychologists and evolutionary biologists who have offered some sort of guidance for human life and society. The centerpiece will be a critical examination (in two parts) of the approach of E. O. Wilson. Because this chapter covers such a wide area, not just one theorist, I will supply references in footnotes.

THEORIES OF EVOLUTION

"Evolution" is a term with multiple ambiguities, and it will be useful to sort them out. In its most general dictionary sense, it refers to any extended process with an identifiable end-product: we can talk of the evolution of the solar system, of the British constitution, and of the automobile—and chemists talk of substances "evolving" gases in chemical reactions. There is often a suggestion that the process is *progressive* in that the latest product is in some way better than what has gone before. But progress is not involved in the evolution of gases, and in political and technological change the latest stage may not be better than its predecessors in all respects.

The term "evolution" has sometimes been applied to the development of the *individual*, the unfolding of the potential of the embryo or the infant. Here there is a series of stages, leading up—if all goes well—to the existence of a mature individual with all the normal characteristics of the species; and it is natural to see this as progress toward adulthood. But the most famous sense of "evolution" is, of course, to refer to the development of biological *species*, expressing a vast historical hypothesis that the manifold kinds of organisms on the earth have not been fixed for all time, but that over long periods various species have evolved from their predecessors, presumably by a series of small changes.

Opposed to this would be the strongest form of "creationism," namely the claim that *all* species of organism are fixed, each having been separately created (presumably by God). The strongest form of evolutionism would say, in contrast, that all species have developed from a common origin (perhaps even in inanimate matter). In between, there are compromise views that might allow several different originating species or the special creation of the first form of life; and, of course, some religious believers still want to exempt humans from the process and claim that we have been specially created by God.

The evolution of species, including humans, from simpler forms of life is now almost universally acknowledged to be a *fact*. There is much direct empirical evidence for our common ancestry with other animals. Comparative anatomy shows the human body to have the same general plan as other vertebrates: four limbs with five digits on each. Our bodily similarity to monkeys, and especially to the great apes, is obvious. The human embryo goes through stages of development in which it resembles those of lower forms of life. In the adult human body there are remnants of lower forms; for example, a vestigial tail. The biochemistry of our bodies—blood, proteins, genes—is very similar to that of other creatures. And there have recently been discovered more and more fossil remains of creatures intermediate between apes and humans. That we have evolved from more primitive creatures is as well established a fact as anything else in science.

It is a further step from the *fact* of evolution to a *mechanism* for evolution. The hypothesis of evolution had already been propounded by many people before Darwin, including his grandfather, Erasmus Darwin. There had been speculation about the means by which species change, and in the early nineteenth century Jean Baptiste de Lamarck suggested that parents can pass on to their offspring certain traits that they had developed during their lifetimes. According to this theory of "the inheritance of acquired characteristics," an individual herbivore that had stretched its neck to eat leaves off tall trees might produce children with longer necks than they would otherwise have had—and thus, perhaps, giraffes might have evolved!

Darwin on Natural Selection

The great contribution of Charles Darwin (1809–1882) was to propose a convincing causal mechanism for the evolution of species, namely the process of "natural selection." After a long period of observation and thought (and hesitation because of his painful awareness of its worldview-shaking consequences), he published his theory in *The Origin of Species* in 1859.[1] Written for the general educated public, it supports Darwin's case with an immense range of patiently assembled evidence.

---

1. *The Origin of Species* is reprinted in Pelican classics (1982) by Wordsworth Editions Ltd., and by Gramercy Books. The full title of the book is *The Origin of Species by Means of Natural Selection: Or the Preservation of Favored Races in the Struggle of Life.*

The heart of the argument is an elegant logical deduction from four large empirical generalizations. The first two are:

1. There is variation in the traits of individuals of a given species.
2. Traits of parents tend to be passed on to their offspring.

These two general facts emerge from a wide variety of observations of plants and animals and they had long been utilized in the breeding of new varieties of plants and domestic and farm animals. Hence Darwin's talk of natural "selection" as a process that modifies species (unintentionally, of course). The remaining premises are:

3. Species are capable of a geometric rate of increase of population.
4. The resources of the environment typically cannot support such an increase.

It follows from (3) and (4) that only a small proportion of seeds, eggs, and young reach maturity: in effect, there is competition for survival and reproduction, primarily between members of the same species. This need not involve bodily confrontation, as when individuals scrabble with each other for food or males fight for females: in Darwin's sense there is also "competition" to be most efficient at finding food or at escaping from predators. From the inevitability of such competition, and from (1), we can deduce that at any stage there will be certain individuals in the population (those whose characteristics are "the fittest" in the given environment) who will have the best chance of surviving long enough to reproduce and leave offspring. Therefore, given (2), their traits will tend to be passed on into the next generation and less advantageous ("fit") traits will not.

Thus, over many generations, the typical characteristics of a population of animals can change. And, given the immense periods of past time (first realized by geologists in the early nineteenth century) and the distribution of plants and animals through the wide variety of environments around the world, different species can evolve from common ancestors. All that is needed is the constant pressure of natural selection acting on the variations within the populations in various environments. There is no need to postulate Lamarckian inheritance of acquired characteristics—though Darwin himself did some backsliding on this point because he not know the genetic basis of the patterns of inheritance summed up in (1) and (2).

The theoretical explanation of these facts was first offered in Mendel's theory of heredity, which postulated distinct, indivisible causal factors (now called "genes") that are passed on from parent to child in a process of mixing of genes from the two parents in sexual reproduction, and that remain unaffected by changes during the lifetime of an individual. Random mutations in genes account for much of the variation within populations. The biochemical nature of genes and the process of copying them was discovered in the 1950s with the elucidation of the structure of the DNA molecule.

Given this new knowledge, it is now possible to re-express Darwin's insights in terms of genes, as Richard Dawkins did in his book *The Selfish Gene*.[2] That title is a brilliantly chosen metaphor. Philosophers were right to object that genes cannot literally be selfish—only whole people (and perhaps animals) are that. But Dawkins invites us to see biological evolution not so much as species changing because of competition between individuals, but in terms of genes competing with each other for a place in the next generation. Individuals are born and die, but genes are passed on through the generations: they are relatively immortal (though they can be lost when a species becomes extinct). However, controversy continues among biologists over exactly what should be seen as the units of selection—genes, packages of genes, individual organisms, or perhaps groups of individuals, such as human tribes or cultures.

Progressive or Nonprogressive (Tree- or Bush-Shape)?

Within Darwinian theorists an interesting metaphysical division can be made between those who think the process of evolution of species is inherently *progressive* and those who deny this. The known series of life forms on earth seems to show progress, for there has been a noticeable increase of complexity over geological time (though there are plenty of primitive forms still around). And, of course, we humans tend to see ourselves as higher than all the rest! In the Victorian era, the idea of progress was part of the prevailing *Weltanschauung*, so it was natural for popularizing Darwinian philosophers like Herbert Spencer[3] to interpret both biological evolution and human history as leading the whole world onward and upward (and Darwin himself tended to go with this intellectual flow).

However, Darwinians in the twentieth century questioned whether the process of species change is necessarily progressive. As noted earlier, the word "evolution" often carries a connotation of progress, but not in every context. (In the *Origin*, Darwin usually wrote of "descent with modification" rather than "evolution.") Natural selection does not logically imply that the later forms are "better" as judged by some human

---

2. Richard Dawkins, *The Selfish Gene* (Oxford University Press, 1st ed. 1976, new ed. 1989), or his *The Blind Watchmaker* (London: Longman, 1986; Penguin, 2000)
3. Herbert Spencer wrote *First Principles* (1862), *The Principles of Biology* (1864), and *The Principles of Ethics* (1892).

criterion—only that they are better adapted to the relevant set of environmental conditions. And a species does not have to be *ideally* adapted to its ecological niche, only well enough adapted to survive and reproduce: notoriously, a species introduced from another part of the world may flourish much better than the natives. And, if the climactic conditions change dramatically, more complex or "higher" species may get wiped out. Apparently this happened to the dinosaurs, when a large asteroid hit the earth. If we humans mess up our environment sufficiently, by nuclear or biological war or climate change, we could become extinct too.

The difference between progressive and nonprogressive understandings of evolution can be represented by different shapes of the *pathway* of evolution that the two sides postulate. It has most often been presented as a *tall tree*, growing steadily upward, with many diverging branches, but some definitely higher than others, and a topmost twig on which sit (guess who?) human beings! Dawkins is a prominent contemporary evolutionist who thinks of it in this way, and he is supported by E. O. Wilson.[4] But Stephen Jay Gould has offered instead the picture of a *bush*, which tends to grow sideways and outward in all directions, according to opportunity, with no standard overall shape and no single topmost branch.[5] On this view, there was no predetermined necessity about the evolution of mammals, apes, and humans: if it had not been for that asteroid impact, the dinosaurs or their reptilian descendants might still reign supreme.

Theist or Atheist?

While we are considering the metaphysics of evolution, let us consider its relation to theism. There still are religious believers who take literally the story of God's creation in the book of *Genesis*; and for them, of course, any evolutionary account of the origin of humans is incompatible with that.[6] But there have long been theists who interpret *Genesis* symbolically, and they can say that the scientifically documented process of evolution is the way that God has brought into being all the species on earth, including ourselves. For them it is natural to interpret evolution in a progressive way, seeing it as a process intended by God to lead up to the emergence of creatures made in the image of God and endowed with rationality and free will.

But, on reflection, theism can also be interpreted in a way that is compatible with the nonprogressive, bush-like picture of evolution; even allowing that the emergence of rational, free creatures on this planet has

---

4. E. O. Wilson, *Consilience* (London: Little Brown, 1998), p. 107.
5. Stephen Jay Gould, *Wonderful Life* (New York: Norton, 1989).
6. For a critical discussion of the scientific pretensions of "Creationism," see Philip Kitcher, *Abusing Science: The Case Against Creationism* (Cambridge, Mass.: MIT Press, 1982.

been contingent on environmental circumstances. For if believers in God take seriously the thought that He is not in time, they can say that His creation does not happen at any particular moments or periods of earthly time, rather it consists in His eternally, nontemporally sustaining the world in existence. On such a view, the dependence of human evolution on contingent past conditions on this earth does not mean that our existence is contingent in the eternal order of things: there can be a Divine purpose for human life, even if we are, in terms of a scientific account of our origins, a product of random mutations and astronomical accidents. In this spirit, Gould has claimed that religion does not compete on the same empirical territory as science, but occupies the domain of meaning and purpose, rather than that of of causality.[7] But Dawkins—like the Christian creationists—interprets religious claims more literally, and because he takes them as clearly false on that interpretation, he is a crusading atheist.[8]

It appears, then, that—literalists about *Genesis* aside—Darwinians can be theists or atheists, and progressivists or nonprogressivists (hence there are four subpossibilities). There remains a tendency, however, for many theists to postulate some moments in human evolution when some absolute metaphysical change took place. For dualists like Plato and Descartes, who conceive of the soul as a distinct spiritual substance, there is a difficulty in locating a metaphysical break (the coming into existence of the human soul) in the two empirical continua of the evolution of humans and the development of the human embryo. Perhaps it is for this reason that Pope Pius XII insisted that there must have been a unique first human pair, from whom we have all inherited original sin.[9] More recently, Keith Ward has said there must have been a first moment of conscious moral choice, a point in human prehistory at which the Fall into sin began.[10] And my St. Andrews colleague John Haldane has argued that whether a mental state is a representation (i.e., a state with "content" representing things as being thus-and-so) is an all-or-nothing question, so presumably there must have been a first representation.[11]

But it seems to me that there are plenty of concepts that we now apply in an all-or-nothing way (e.g., marriage, parliament, illegal action, war, representational picture, symphony), but for which we cannot expect there

7. Stephen Jay Gould, *I Have Landed* (London: Jonathan Cape, 2002), Chapter 12 ("Darwin and the Munchkins of Kansas").

8. Richard Dawkins, *A Devil's Chaplain* (London: Weidenfeld and Nicholson, 2003).

9. Pope Pius XII, *Humani Generis* (encyclical of 1950), cited by Michael Ruse, in *Can a Darwinian Be a Christian?* (Cambridge: Cambridge University Press 2001), p. 75.

10. Keith Ward, *God, Faith and the New Millenium* (Oxford: Oneworld, 1998), p. 42, cited by Michael Ruse, in *Can a Darwinian Be a Christian?*, p. 205.

11. J. J. Haldane, in *Atheism and Theism*, by J. J. C. Smart and J. J. Haldane (Oxford: Blackwell, 1996), p. 103 ff.

to have been some exact point in history when they became applicable for the very first time. It can be conceptually indeterminate when a concept such as representation, consciousness, free will, sin, or religious faith comes into play in the gradual, messy development of human mentality and culture, but that does not mean that we cannot now apply such concepts quite determinately, in many cases. (Hegel remarked how a sufficient amount of quantitative change can become a qualitative change.) Perhaps Pope John Paul II got it more nearly right when he wrote that the moment of transition to the spiritual cannot be empirically observed,[12] though I would prefer to say that there is no single such moment in the evolutionary continuum. I do not see that a gradualist account of the genesis of some human capacity or practice implies that we are debarred from using our contemporary concepts in identifying it.

I suggest that, if theists want to avoid giving hostages to empirical and conceptual fortune, they had better divest themselves of these vestiges of creationism.[13] But that raises a question about just what meaning remains in the doctrine of Divine Creation if it is interpreted, not as a particular act of God that got the whole show going, nor as involving any particular subsequent interventions (to get evolution over the crucial metaphysical hurdles, as it were), but only as a continuous dependence of everything on God's sustaining power. What is thereby being claimed? Or is this only the verbal manifestation of an attachment to a picture of everything as being ultimately in harmony with the purposes of a superhuman and ideally good Being? The metaphysically minded theist may say that if God did not choose to sustain the universe, then nothing would exist— or if He had not intervened to add consciousness, free will, representation, or rationality to the evolution of primates, then human beings would not exist. But what is supposed to make these seemingly dramatic counterfactual conditionals true? And what is supposed to justify anyone in believing them? To debate this further would take us away from our present topic, into the realms of theology and metaphysics.

EVOLUTIONARY THEORY APPLIED TO HUMAN NATURE

Though well aware of the revolutionary implications of his theory, Darwin did not at first reveal his view that human beings are descended from ape-like ancestors: in the *Origin*, he allowed himself just one concluding remark that "light will be thrown on the origin of man and his history." But

---

12. Pope John Paul II, "The Pope's Message on Evolution," *Quarterly Review of Biology* (1997): 383, cited by Michael Ruse, in *Can a Darwinian Be a Christian?*, p. 75.
13. See E. O. Wilson, *Consilience*, p. 268.

the obvious implication aroused intense controversies, whose reverbera-
tions continue to the present day. Twelve years later, in 1871, Darwin
published his thoughts on the descent of man.[14]

In limpid, readable prose, Darwin reviewed the anatomical evidence of
our animal ancestry and theorized about the evolution of our intellectual and
moral faculties from animal antecedents—so he can be described as the first
evolutionary psychologist. His thoughts on these matters are prescient indeed, and are a classic source of the strong current of evolutionary approaches
to human nature that has flowed ever since. Darwin was clearly on the pro-
gressivist side: he wrote that "man has risen, though by slow and interrupted
steps, from a lowly condition to the highest standard as yet attained by him
in knowledge, morals, and religion."[15] He also wrote—from the point of
view of an English gentleman naturalist of the Victorian era—about the alleged differences between human races and between men and women, expressing himself in ways that are somewhat stomach-churning these days.

Darwin's theory of evolution immediately entered into the zeitgeist of
nineteenth-century thought, especially in the would-be human sciences.
Freud was obviously attempting a biological theory of human nature in postulating innate drives, rooted in our needs to feed and reproduce, and he
also speculated about how our primitive ancestors contributed to our present human psychology. But as we have seen in Chapter 8, Freud postulated
a bewildering variety of mental entities and processes that tended to become untestable by empirical observation. And at crucial points he gave a
Lamarckian rather than Darwinian account of human mental evolution.

Durkheim and the Standard Social Science Model

In the late nineteenth century, both psychology and sociology emerged
as domains of scientific study, each with its own distinctive subject matter, independent of human anatomy, physiology, and evolutionary biology. Wilhelm Wundt (1832–1900) had a hand in both. He established the
first experimental laboratory of psychology in Leipzig in 1875, in which
he proposed to investigate the external causal conditions of introspectively recognized mental states. But Wundt also wrote about "collective
psychology" from a cultural anthropological point of view.

To Emile Durkheim (1858–1917), a Frenchman of Jewish extraction,
these two sorts of "psychology" seemed radically different. He recog-

---

14. Darwin's second major book, *The Descent of Man and Selection in Relation to Sex*, first
    published in 1871, is now available in a facsimile edition with a useful Introduction by
    John Tyler Bonner and Robert M. May (Princeton, N.J.: Princeton University Press,
    1981). What is in effect a third section of the same work was published separately as
    The Expression of the Emotions in Man and Animals in 1872.
15. *The Descent of Man*, end of Chapter V.

nized the irreducibility of psychological facts to biological facts about the body, the nervous system, and the brain. But he also insisted on the irreducibility of social facts (e.g., about what is legally or morally required in a given society) to any ensemble of individual psychological facts. Durkheim saw himself as completing the program of his predecessors in the French Enlightenment—Condorcet, Montesquieu, and Comte—to establish a natural science of human society. He is recognized, along with Marx and Weber, as one of the founding fathers of sociology.

Since the end of the nineteenth century, a threefold division has usually been made between (a) the biological sciences, including anatomy, physiology, and evolutionary theory; (b) psychology (or "the psychological sciences"); and (c) the social sciences, including sociology, anthropology, economics, and perhaps "political science." However, the position and the rationale of these borderlines have been continuously contested.

Durkheim insisted that social facts are "things," in the sense that their existence is just as independent of human will as anything in the physical world. Disobey a moral or legal rule, and you are likely to find yourself faced with sanctions or penalties, whether you like it or not! Such social facts are "emergent" or irreducible; as in a similar way many facts about wholes or totalities cannot be derived from the nature of their parts (e.g., the wetness of water cannot be deduced from the properties of hydrogen and oxygen, nor can the hardness of bronze be predicted from its constituents). Social facts, Durkheim believed, can only be explained by other social facts.[16]

But he distinguished firmly between causal and functional explanation in sociology. To give the *function* of a social practice or institution is to identify the social needs that it meets, and these may be quite different from the conscious intentions of the people who take part in it. For instance, Durkheim proposed that the function of religious ritual is not the worship of a god or the spiritual exaltation of the participants—as the participants may say—but rather to sustain social unity and maintain the hold of the society's values and beliefs over its members. Thus sociologists who follow Durkheim tend to say that society is the "real" origin of the idea of God or the sacred.

Causal explanation in sociology, by contrast, involves explaining social change in terms of general sociological laws; for example, changes in moral outlook may be explained as resulting from the increasing division of labor in industrialized society. The historical causes of a social

---

16. A useful selection is *Emile Durkheim, Selected Writings*, edited with an introduction by Anthony Giddens (Cambridge: Cambridge University Press, 1972). Giddens also wrote an introduction to Durkheim in the Fontana Modern Masters Series (London: 1978).

phenomenon (e.g., the British House of Lords) may have little or nothing to do with its present function. In this there is an analogy with biological evolution, in which an organ originally selected for one function may be taken over in the service of another (e.g., legs became flippers in sea mammals).

Durkheim was an evolutionary theorist only in the most general sense of the word, believing in law-governed processes of change and development in human societies. He saw an analogy between the evolution of species and the social trend toward increasing division of labor, and hence he talked of the differentiation of "species" of economic and social roles—but he was under no illusion that this was a process of Darwinian natural selection, he held that it is subject to distinctively sociological laws.

He was all in favor of a "social scientific" treatment of ethics, not accepting ethical norms or philosophical systems simply as deliverances of human intuition or reason, but treating them as social facts that meet the needs of the relevant stage of society (like Nietzsche's contemporaneous "genealogy of morals"). But Durkheim was aware of the fact/value distinction, and insofar as he offered social prescriptions (his own preference was for a program of gradual socialist reform and secular moral education), he based them on a medical model, involving a distinction between normal or healthy and abnormal or pathological developments in society. But that raises the value-laden question of what we are to count as abnormal or deviant—a question that does not always have a straightforward answer (consider the varying standards of obesity or slimness, sedentary or active lifestyles, sexuality, aggression, or stress).

Society is not a mysterious abstract entity; Durkheim acknowledged that social rules can only affect people via other people's actions and reactions; for example, law enforcement by policemen, or reminders about etiquette from one's mother-in-law. But policemen have to be appointed by social institutions and they are supposed to have some understanding of the legal powers they are given. Mothers-in-law stand in social relations that give them opportunity to voice their views and their ideas often have a distinctively social content, revealed in comments like "what will the neighbors say?" So, as Durkheim said, there seems to be no reduction of social facts to purely psychological facts.

Skinner and Behaviorism

In reaction against both the speculative excesses of Freudian theorizing and the difficulties of the introspective method as used by the first professional psychologists such as Wundt and William James, the behaviorist movement was initiated in the United States by J. B. Watson, and came to dominate academic psychology in the English-speaking world in the mid-twentieth century. B. F. Skinner (1904–1990) became a professor at Harvard and was one of the most influential experimental psychologists of his generation.

Skinner accepted Darwin's theory, of course. And he liked to draw an analogy between his theory of behavioral conditioning and natural selection, saying that the environment (whether in nature, in society, or in the laboratory) "selects" or "shapes" behavior, rewarding or "reinforcing" some behaviors, and punishing (or not reinforcing) others, so that the former get selected over time and tend to be repeated. However, it is only in this Pickwickian sense that Skinner can be said to be an evolutionary psychologist, for behavior does not literally reproduce itself in the way that organisms do. And he signally failed to take into account the contribution of the evolutionary history of species to their different behaviors.

He firmly rejected all attempts to explain animal behavior in terms of mental states: since these are unobservable, Skinner considered them to be scientifically untestable. He had to admit the possibility of discovering physiological preconditions of behavior: the literally inner neurological state that causes a particular bodily movement. But he claimed that even when the progress of neuroscience tells us about such brain states in detail, *their* causation can be traced back to the environment, so we may as well bypass the physiology and look directly for the external causes of behavior.[17]

Skinner thus assumed that all animal behavior can be explained in terms of *environmental* variables; that is, for any pattern of behavior, there is a finite set of environmental stimulations (past and present) such that any creature to which all those conditions apply will perform that behavior. Taken to a ludicrous extreme, this would deny all innate differences between species; Skinner did not go as far as that, but he tended to assume that there are no significant innate differences between individuals of a species. Applied to humans, this would imply (as Watson boldly claimed[18]) that any healthy child could be trained to become a world-class athlete, a physicist, a captain of industry, or a thief! The fact that identical twins brought up apart are so similar, not just in body, but in personality and mental ability, is clear evidence against this. Heredity does play a considerable part.

In any case, agreeing that behavior constitutes the observable *data* for psychology does not settle whether psychologists may postulate unobservable entities to *explain* the data. Most psychologists, before and after behaviorism, have been happy to talk in terms of drives, emotions, memory, and many other "mental" entities. In rejecting all appeal to unobservables

---

17. B. F. Skinner, *Science and Human Behavior* (New York: Macmillan, 1953), Chapter III.
18. J. B. Watson, *Behaviorism* 1924, (reprinted by Transatlantic Publishers, 1997).

in explanation, Skinner was trying to be more scientific than most scientists and philosophers of science, for the physical sciences typically postulate unobservable theoretical entities such as magnetic fields, mechanical forces, and subatomic particles. Provided that what is said about such entities is testable by observation, there is no objection to them in principle.

What of Skinner's rejection of physiological states as causes? The fact that these are not easily observable or manipulable does nothing to show that they do not play a crucial role in the causation of behavior. Skinner assumes that physiological states inside an organism merely mediate the effect of its environment (past and present) on its behavior. So he thinks that psychology can confine its attention to the laws connecting environmental influences directly with behavior. But is this true of animals, or computers, let alone human beings? What a computer does in reaction to a certain keystroke typically depends on what internal state it is in at the time—there are no universal laws connecting single keystrokes with what comes up on the screen, without taking into account the present inner state.

There are two separable assumptions here. First, that human behavior is governed by scientific laws of *some* kind: "If we are to use the methods of science in the field of human affairs, we must assume that behavior is lawful and determined."[19] Second, that these laws state causal connections between *environmental* factors and human behavior: "Our 'independent variables'—the causes of behavior—are the external conditions of which behavior is a function."[20] This could be taken in a purely methodological interpretation, as expressing a program of *looking* for laws connecting environment with behavior, and there is no objection to that. But Skinner assumes that they express general facts, and we must ask whether there is any good reason to think that is true. There is a lot of evidence that human behavior depends on innate factors as well as environmental input, some of them being common to all humans, while others are dependent on individual genetic differences. Besides, it is not obvious, on reflection, that any scientific explanation of human behavior must presuppose that all human behavior is predetermined and that there is no significant sense in which we exercise free will.

Chomsky and Cognitive Psychology

One especially important area in which Skinner attempted to apply his theories is our use of language. In his book *Verbal Behavior*, Skinner proposed to show that all human speech can be explained in terms of the conditioning of speakers by their early social environment: the speech of

---

19. *Science and Human Behavior*, p. 6, cf. p. 447.
20. *Science and Human Behavior*, p. 35.

surrounding humans and their reactions to noises by the child.[21] Thus a baby born in a Spanish-speaking family is subjected to many samples of the Spanish language in use, and when its responses are reasonably accurate reproductions of what it has heard, they are reinforced by approval and reward, and thus the child learns to speak Spanish. Adult speech, too, is treated by Skinner as a series of responses to stimuli from the environment, including verbal stimuli from other people.

The crucial defects in Skinner's account of language were pointed out by Noam Chomsky, whose research has been fundamental to the cognitive revolution in psychology since the 1960s. Chomsky argued that Skinner's account of *how* language is learned pays no attention to the question of *what* it is that we learn. We can hardly ask how we learn X unless we first know what X is: we must have a criterion for someone having *succeeded* in learning X. Human language is a very different sort of phenomenon from rats pressing levers or pigeons raising their heads to peck. Chomsky suggests that the *creative* and *structural* features of human language—the way in which we can all speak and understand sentences we have never heard before—make it quite different from any known kind of animal behavior.[22]

There is another important respect in which Chomsky argues that Skinner's theories fail when applied to language. This is the matter of the contribution made by innate mental capacities to learning a language. Obviously, French children learn French and Chinese children learn Chinese, so the social environment has a major effect. But again, all normal children learn at least one language, while no other animal learns anything that resembles human languages in the crucial respect of the formation of indefinitely many complex sentences according to rules of grammar (though experiments on chimpanzees learning sign systems have been claimed to show some approximation to human ability). It seems that the capacity to learn and use a full range of human language is peculiar to the human species.

Chomsky argues that the amazing speed with which children learn the grammatical rules of their native language, from exposure to a very limited and imperfect sample of it, can be explained only by the assumption that there is in the human species an *innate* capacity to process language according to rules of that general form. Behind the impressive variety of

21. B. F. Skinner, *Verbal Behavior* (Englewood Cliffs, N.J.: Prentice-Hall, 1957).
22. For an introduction to Chomsky's theories, see his *Language and Mind* (New York: Harcourt Brace Jovanovich, enlarged edition, 1972); also J. Lyons, *Chomsky* (New York: Viking, 1970; London: Fontana, 1970, Modern Masters series). Steven Pinker gives a lively survey of recent developments in *The Language Instinct: The New Science of Language and Mind* (New York: Wiliam Morrow & Co., 1994; London: Penguin, 1995).

human languages there must be a certain basic systematic structure common to all of them, and we must suppose that we do not *learn* this structure from our environment, but process whatever linguistic input we receive in terms of it. This hypothesis has been supported by increasing evidence.

Given that we are an evolved species, this peculiar linguistic ability that we have—this so-called mental organ that humans uniquely possess—must presumably be what evolutionists call an "adaptation"; that is, a feature that has been bred into human genes by natural selection operating on hominoid populations in the distant past. At least, that is what recent evolutionary psychologists like Cosmides and Tooby (explored later in this chapter) have argued, though Chomsky himself has expressed some skepticism about such evolutionary speculations about language. Further research is being pursued at three levels: in linguistics, into further detailed specification of just what is so characteristic of human languages (what features are common to all human language); in brain science, into how language is processed and how the brain of the language-learning infant develops; and in hominoid evolution, into how our language ability may have evolved.[23] It is obvious that language serves as a uniquely effective means of communication and that this must have been adaptive in a highly social species, but there is much more detail to be empirically investigated.

Speech is not the only human activity. But it is especially important as a representative of the higher human mental abilities. This opens up the possibility that other important determinants of human behavior are not conditioned by, or learned from, the environment, but are innate. We must reckon with the thought that the evolution of our ancestors may *explain* the existence of other genetically based "mental organs" or "modules" in humans. Much detailed work has been done on the intricate, innately programmed, information-processing mechanisms that are involved in human perception; the work of David Marr on vision has led the way on this.[24]

Tinbergen and Ethology

Skinner's experimental work on animals in tightly controlled laboratory conditions was technically impressive, but his extrapolations from it were highly questionable. His discoveries about what rats and pigeons can be induced to do in Skinner boxes may apply only to those species, in those artificial conditions. And even if he identified one kind of conditioning mechanism that works in many species, there may be *other* important ways in which animal behavior is produced.

---

23. J. T. Crow, ed., *The Speciation of Modern Homo Sapiens* (Oxford University Press, 2003).

24. D. Marr, *Vision* (San Francisco: W. H. Freeman, 1982).

Niko Tinbergen (a Dutchman who became a professor at Oxford) was one of the founding fathers of "ethology," the scientific study of animal behavior in its *natural* environment. This had roots in the work of many earlier naturalists, including Darwin himself, but it developed a distinctive approach from about the 1940s onward. Other founders of ethology were Konrad Lorenz, whose diagnosis of human aggression we will examine later, and von Frisch, who studied the communicative dances of bees.

The ethologists realized that some patterns of animal behavior (those that we tend to describe as "instinctive") could not be explained in the behaviorist way: for they appear spontaneously in all individuals of the species (or in all males or females), almost independently of previous experience. In many birds, for example, the typical patterns of feeding, courtship, copulation, nest building, and care of young answer to this description. In the rutting season, male deer start to fight with other males and to pursue the females. Seagull chicks instinctively peck at the red spot on the beak of their parent (resulting in the disgorgement of food), and male stickleback fishes react aggressively to the appearance of the distinctive coloration of another male on their territory. Such behaviors seem to be innate or "fixed," in that they cannot be eliminated or significantly modified, however much the environment is varied. To explain them ethologists typically appeal not to the past experience of the *individual* animal (its "conditioning"), but to the process of evolution that has given rise to the *species*.

Tinbergen usefully distinguished four kinds of questions that can be asked about any particular item of behavior, giving four senses of the question "Why did that creature perform that behavior in that circumstance?"[25]

1. What was the immediate cause (i.e., the *internal physiological cause*) of the behavior? Here the answer may be given in terms of muscle contractions, nervous impulses, hormone secretions, and so on.

2. What in the *development* of the individual prepared the way for that behavior? Here the answer may appeal to embryology, the development of the fetus in the womb, and the normal growth pattern of individuals of the species (e.g., the hormonal changes involved in reaching sexual maturity), but is also room for the experiences of the individual to make a difference to later behavior (e.g., the detail of adult birdsong may depend on what songs the individual has heard, and primates have developed different "cultures" of tool use); there is some room here for Skinnerian conditioning by experimental psychologists, too.

---

25. N. Tinbergen, "On Aims and Methods of Ethology," *Zeitschrift Tierpsychologie* 20 (1963); summarized by R. A. Hinde in *Ethology* (London: Fontana, 1982), Chapter 1 (this book is a useful survey of ethology and its relation to other disciplines).

3. What is the *function* of the behavior? That is, what is it *for*, what goal does it typically achieve for the individual? Here the answer is sometimes blindingly obvious, indeed the very behavior itself is often described in terms of survival or reproduction, such as feeding, predator avoidance, mating, or care of young; but in other cases it is far from obvious to casual human observation what the function is of a certain behavior that may be quite distinctive in terms of the bodily movements involved. Is it a threat, or courtship, or a defense against predators, or a reinforcement of a bond between a "married" pair? Prolonged observation of such a behavior pattern in various environmental and social contexts will usually enable ethologists to arrive at an interpretation of its function, which must, on Darwinian grounds, contribute in some way to the reproduction of the individual's genes.

4. What is the *evolutionary history* of this pattern of behavior? Sometimes this seems hardly distinguishable from (3), for example, the bodily movements involved in feeding and in copulation in most species have presumably always had the same functions. In other cases, however, a distinctive behavior pattern may not always have had the same function as it has now. The evolution of behavior, as of bodily organs, often involves "jerrybuilding" (i.e., adapting inherited items to new uses) under the pressure of natural selection in changing conditions. We cannot press rewind buttons and observe the past, but in some cases ethologists can make reasonable inferences about a pathway of evolutionary history and thus distinguish (4) from (3). For example, some of the "signalling" postures of birds that now function as threats or courtship seem to have resulted from a "ritualization" of what were once merely "intention movements," preparatory to flight.

Obviously, answers of these four kinds are perfectly compatible with each other; they are all part of the complicated truth about animal behavior. If there is such a thing as a "complete" explanation of any bit of behavior, it would have to include the relevant facts at all of these levels.

Wilson and Sociobiology

Can all these different approaches—the Darwinian evolution of species by natural selection, the biochemical understanding of genes, and the explanation of behavior in terms of previous experience of the individual, in terms of the evolutionary history of the species, and in terms of distinctively social or cultural facts—be brought together and applied to the study of human nature?

Harvard biologist Edward O. Wilson boldly claimed in his book *Sociobiology: The New Synthesis* to have founded a new scientific discipline by applying the rigorous methods of population biology and genetics to complex social systems. Building on his earlier detailed scientific studies of insect societies, Wilson applied a similar approach to many other species of social animal, and in a final provocative chapter he sketched how it could be extended to humans. Wilson writes in a vivid, readable style, confidently asserting sweeping generalizations and programmatic statements; he seems either blithely unaware of the hackles he may raise or unafraid of raising them! Here is the first paragraph of that controversial chapter:

> Let us now consider man in the free spirit of natural history, as though we were zoologists from another planet completing a catalog of social species on Earth. In this macroscopic view the humanities and social sciences shrink to specialized branches of biology; history, biography, and fiction are the protocols of human ethology; and anthropology and sociology together constitute the sociobiology of a single primate species.[26]

Wilson does not stop to think whether it is either possible or desirable for us to consider ourselves "in a purely zoological spirit." Nor does he shrink from suggesting that the humanities and social sciences can become subdepartments of biological science (a view that can be labelled "scientific imperialism") and that other areas of biological and behavioral study will be absorbed into his own envisioned superscience of sociobiology (imperialism within science itself). Small wonder that the chapter generated heated debate!

The section headings of the chapter indicate the tremendous range of material that Wilson hoped to bring within his explanatory ambitions: Plasticity of Social Organization; Barter and Reciprocal Altruism; Bonding, Sex, and Division of Labor; Role Playing and Polytheism; Communication; Culture, Ritual, and Religion: Ethics; Esthetics; Territoriality and Tribalism; Early Social Evolution; Later Social Evolution; and (wait for it!) The Future. Nothing, it seems, is beyond the bounds of sociobiology! Indeed, Wilson ended the chapter on a note of prophecy, in two senses—foretelling the future:

> When mankind has achieved an ecological steady state, probably by the end of the twenty-first century, the internalization of social evolution will be nearly complete. About this time biology should be at its peak, with the social sciences maturing rapidly . . .

and interpreting what he takes to be the fundamental meaning of present and future trends:

> The transition from purely phenomenological to fundamental theory in sociology must await a full, neuronal explanation of the human brain. Only

26. E. O. Wilson, *Sociobiology: The New Synthesis* (Cambridge, Mass.: Harvard University Press, 1975), opening of last chapter.

when the machinery can be torn down on paper at the level of the cell and put together again will the properties of emotion and ethical judgment come clear.

. . . To maintain the species indefinitely we are compelled to drive toward total knowledge, right down to the levels of the neuron and gene. When we have progressed enough to explain ourselves in these mechanistic terms, and the social sciences come to full flower, the result might be hard to accept.[27]

If Wilson is right, then Durkheim and most social scientists must have been doubly wrong in thinking that sociology is irreducible to psychology, and psychology irreducible to neurophysiology. But so far we have assertion without argument, and—worryingly—without much apparent awareness of so much that has already been said about these issues by scientists, social scientists, and philosophers of science.

In his next book, *On Human Nature*, Wilson proposed to show in more detail how the evolutionary biology of humans could explain topics previously reserved for social science or philosophy. He continues to argue eloquently that the only way toward understanding human nature is to study it as part of the natural sciences. He admits that the book

. . . is not a work of science; it is a work about science . . . its core is a speculative essay about the profound consequences that will follow as social theory at long last meets that part of the natural sciences most relevant to it . . .

And, although he strikes a note of caution,

. . . I might easily be wrong—in any particular conclusion, in the grander hopes for the role of the natural sciences, and in the trust gambled on scientific materialism . . .

Wilson feels it is his scientific duty to push the sociobiological program as hard as he can, for if it has limits, that will be the best way to discover them:

The uncompromising application of evolutionary theory to all aspects of human existence will come to nothing if the scientific spirit itself falters, if ideas are not constructed so as to be submitted to objective testing and hence made mortal.[28]

27. *Sociobiology: The New Synthesis*, end of last chapter.
28. E. O. Wilson, *On Human Nature* (Cambridge, Mass.: Harvard University Press, 1978), in the preface.

Wilson is clearly a man with a mission: to apply the theories of evolution, genetics, neurophysiology, and population biology to *all* aspects of human existence! As he says himself, this is not itself a scientific theory, but a highly controversial research program—and a speculative prediction about its future success. When Wilson talks of the objective testing of ideas, he does not distinguish between the *empirical* testing of particular scientific claims by observable evidence and the *conceptual* testing of the consistency and coherence of programs that are not themselves scientific claims. What I have to say about Wilson will be at the metascientific, philosophical level.

Let us look with some critical care, then, at Chapter 1 (entitled "Dilemma") of *On Human Nature*. Wilson starts from questions that he attributes to Hume: how does the mind work, why does it work in the way that it does, and what is man's (*sic*) ultimate nature? He argues:

> For if the brain is a machine of ten billion nerve cells and the mind can somehow be explained as the summed activity of a finite number of chemical and electrical reactions, boundaries limit the human prospect—we are biological and our souls cannot fly free.[29]

As Wilson said, this is not science, but philosophical pronouncement on the wider implications of science. The trouble is that it is amateur and ambiguous. We can ask four sets of questions:

1. What does Wilson mean by "machine"? The brain is not a machine in the colloquial sense of a complex manmade device with moving parts; so one wonders what would *not* count as a machine, for him? (Is the whole human body a machine, or the solar system? Or the whole universe?) Does he mean by "machine" a complex system all of whose properties and operations can be deterministically predicted from a knowledge of its constituent parts? If so, is there any good evidence to believe that the brain is a machine in that sense?

2. What does Wilson mean by "can somehow be explained as"? Is it that every sentence describing a mental state (e.g., Oliver's falling in love with Sarah) can be *translated* into some complicated statement about chemical and electrical events in the brain, or that the existence of such a mental state somehow *consists* in such whirrings in the brain, or that it can be causally *explained* by them?

3. What does Wilson mean by saying that we are "biological"? Is it merely the truism that we are animals, or that we are *limited* by our biological nature? Or is it the implausible thesis that everything that is true

---

29. *On Human Nature*, p. 1.

of us (e.g., our ability to do mathematics or to appreciate music) can be *expressed* in the vocabulary of biology? Or is it the highly controversial claim that everything about us can be *explained* in biological terms?

4. What does Wilson mean by saying that "our souls cannot fly free"? Maybe this is just a poetic way of expressing what he has already said— Wilson is a stylish writer, and we need not be so philistine as to deny him a few rhetorical flourishes. But if we take the word "soul" seriously— as so many people have done, and still do—we would have to go back over the Platonic, Aristotelian, Cartesian, and Spinozistic ground that we have broached in previous chapters.

Next, Wilson asserts the utter incompatibility of theism and Darwinism:

> If humankind evolved by Darwinian natural selection, genetic chance and environmental necessity, not God, made the species. Deity can still be sought in the origin of the ultimate units of matter, in quarks and electron shells . . . but not in the origin of species. However much we embellish that stark conclusion with metaphor and imagery, it remains the philosophical legacy of the last century of scientific research.[30]

So he is prepared to mix it, not only with the philosophers of science and of mind, but with theologians and philosophers of religion too! Wilson takes it that the *Genesis* story, read literally, is a primitive scientific speculation about human origins that has been shown to be straightforwardly false. He leaves a chink open for Deism; that is, belief in a God who set the whole universe going in the first place but does not afterward intervene.[31] But Wilson does not seem to be aware of the position (taken by Kant and by Gould) that, properly understood, religious claims and scientific theories are not statements at the same level and do not compete. As noted in the first section of this chapter, there are plenty of theists who want to say that evolution is the way that God has created us. How much content (beyond "imagery and metaphor") that involves is a matter for further discussion, but Wilson does not seem to be aware of that version of theism.

Related points affect what he says next:

> . . . to the extent that the new naturalism is true, its pursuit seems certain to generate two great spiritual dilemmas. The first is that no species, ours included, possesses a purpose beyond the imperatives created by its genetic history. . . . If the brain evolved by natural selection, even the ca-

---

30. *On Human Nature*, p. 1.
31. See also *Consilience*, p. 268.

pacities to select particular esthetic judgments and religious beliefs must have arisen by the same mechanistic process. They are either direct adaptations to past environments in which the ancestral human populations evolved or at most constructions thrown up secondarily by deeper, less visible activities that were once adaptive in this stricter, biological sense.

... The human mind is a device for survival and reproduction, and reason is just one of its various techniques. . . . beliefs are really enabling mechanisms for survival.

... The first dilemma, in a word, is that we have no particular place to go. The species lacks any goal external to its own biological nature. . . . the danger implicit in the first dilemma is the rapid dissolution of transcendent goals toward which societies can organize their energies.[32]

In talking of "spiritual dilemmas," Wilson is not doing science, he is philosophizing—and what he says is wide open to conceptual criticism. For if it is true that the use of our human reasoning powers in forming beliefs is a technique for survival and reproduction, then that must apply to *all* human beliefs and judgments, not only in aesthetics and religion, but in mathematics, science, and the metascientific level at which Wilson himself is arguing here. But can we coherently see our own mathematical, scientific, and philosophical beliefs as mere devices for survival and reproduction? That would involve us in trying to find evolutionary causes for every such belief and not taking seriously the giving of reasons for them. I don't think Wilson (or anyone else) can suggest that abandoning all inductive and deductive reasoning is an option that is open to us. If we try to replace all reason giving by causal explanation in terms of natural selection, we would still be putting *that* forward as something worthy of rational belief (i.e., as supported by reasons in the form of good empirical evidence).

Giving reasons for a proposition is trying to rationally justify belief in it; and this is a conceptually different kind of activity from giving putative causes for someone coming to believe that proposition. The causal story tries to explain why a certain mental state of believing came into existence in a certain individual—and the relevant causal conditions may apply only to certain kinds of people, and perhaps only in certain conditions. But the rational justification offers reasons in favor of the proposition being true—and those reasons must be potentially universal in the sense that any rational being who understands them must be capable of recognizing that they are indeed reasons for belief in that proposition.

I conclude, then, that we cannot coherently treat all our beliefs—including the Pythagorean theorem, Darwinian natural selection, and the

---

32. *On Human Nature*, pp. 2–4.

content of the present sentence—as mere survival mechanisms. It is ludicrous to suggest that *all* beliefs are "direct adaptations to past environments in which the ancestral human populations evolved." Wilson will have to retreat to the second line of defense he mentions, and say that most of our beliefs are "constructions thrown up secondarily by deeper, less visible activities that were once adaptive." They are not themselves directly selected, rather they are products of underlying human *mental capacities* that presumably were selected for in the ancestral environment. It is plausible to believe that natural selection operating on our hominoid ancestors put a premium on the development of that complex level of human intelligence that now enables us to go in for abstraction, generalization, formation of new concepts, inductive and deductive argument, and critical reflection. But how exactly those selective processes may have panned out is a matter for empirical, but difficult to test, conjectures about evolutionary pathways in the long-vanished Pleistocene era.

The main point to insist on here is that the admission that our mental faculties are products of evolution is, in itself, no threat to the rationality or indeed the truth of (some of) the beliefs that we arrive at by using those faculties. Our giving of reasons for our mathematical and scientific beliefs is not undermined by the fact that our mental capacities for forming such beliefs have evolved from more primitive levels of mentality by a long process of natural selection.

But, if so, need our *ethical* beliefs be undermined by evolutionary reflections? Why shouldn't we hold that we do indeed have some objective values by which to guide our lives? (For example, Platonic harmony of soul, Aristotelian happiness, Kantian respect for all persons, Marxian social justice, Sartrian meeting of human needs, Judeo-Christian love of neighbor, Confucian benevolence—or some synthesis of these, as explored in the conclusion to this book.) It is not at all obvious, on reflection, that the mere fact of human evolution implies that the human species "lacks any goal external to its own biological nature," or "a purpose beyond the imperatives created by its genetic history," as Wilson puts it. He has provided no argument that his first "spiritual dilemma" logically follows from accepting that we are evolved creatures.

There may be some *other* good reasons for doubting the objectivity of ethics, or aesthetic judgments, or religious claims (such as the notorious absence of consensus, the implications of which philosophers have long discussed), but the mere fact of human evolution is not one of them. There may indeed seem to be a contemporary trend toward "the dissolution of transcendent goals," if by that is meant a sociological process of people ceasing to recognize the worthwhileness of any goals beyond pleasure, consumption, wealth, or power—but that is surely a result of social changes in our market-governed and media-dominated societies, not a logical consequence of the theory of evolution.

The reader should not go away with the impression that all of Wilson's writing is irredeemably confused. I have concentrated here on passages from the beginning of *On Human Nature* that are vulnerable to philosophical critique. There follows a lot of interesting material at a more empirical level, with wide-ranging thoughts about the sociobiological explanation of familiar features of human nature, notably aggression, sex, altruism, and religion. It is an enjoyable read, but it is open to criticism at the scientific level. Philip Kitcher has compiled a devastating critique, showing that many of Wilson's empirical claims are mere speculations unsupported by the evidence.[33]

Wilson's second "spiritual dilemma" concerns the choice between "ethical premises inherent in man's biological nature." I will reserve comment on it for the final section of this chapter.

The Resistance to Sociobiology

Wilson's program for sociobiology immediately generated a heated controversy in which three main strands can be distinguished: scientific, departmental, and moral/political.

Some other biologists, including Richard Lewontin, a population geneticist in Wilson's own department at Harvard, believed that his program for applying sociobiology to humans was just not "good science." Nonscientists perhaps do not realize how much room there is for different styles of thinking and writing within science. Some scientists go in for ambitious, wide-ranging, somewhat speculative theorizing; others have more austere standards, their paradigm being a well-defined specific claim backed up by hard observational evidence. The former may be good at thinking up new hypotheses, the latter may be better at testing them. There is need for both, but the different temperaments may clash. In particular, Lewontin wanted causal laws, not merely statistics, and he distrusted Wilson's simplifying generalizations, thinking that theories have to be more complex to be true to reality.[34]

Many academics—biologists in different fields from Wilson, social scientists, and those working in the humanities—resisted Wilson's "imperialist" proposal for sociobiology to take over their fields (or at least merge with them). Demarcation disputes are not unknown in academia, even in

33. Philip Kitcher, *Vaulting Ambition: Sociobiology and the Quest for Human Nature* (Cambridge, Mass.: MIT Press, 1985). Kitcher has provided a useful precis of his book in *Behavioral and Brain Sciences* 10 (1987).
34. See U. Segerstrale, *Defenders of the Truth: The Sociobiology Debate* (Oxford University Press, 2000), Chapter 3, p. 40 ff., and Chapter 11.

the supposedly "objective" sciences, and there is usually resistance to newcomers threatening to invade established territories!

But there was a larger issue at stake than departmental politics. There has been a widespread assumption—labelled "the Standard Social Science Model"—that in human beings culture completely transcends biology, so that the study of human culture and society (while not denying our evolution from hominoids) can proceed quite independently of biology. The founding fathers of social science (Marx, Weber, and Durkheim) held that, apart from a few obvious biological universals like eating, defecating, sleeping, copulating, birth, and breastfeeding, most human behavior depends more on culture than on biology (as the option to feed infants from the bottle rather than the breast vividly exemplifies). Social and cultural anthropologists have made a speciality of describing the manifold differences between human cultures all around the world (in the twentieth century there was a rush to catalog "primitive" societies before they died out or became homogenized into the global economy).

Wilson's program, with its underlying reductionist methodology seeking to explain social phenomena ultimately in terms of selective pressures, seemed to go flatly against Durkheim's postulate of the irreducibility of social facts. It threatened to undermine the disciplines of anthropology and sociology and to ignore the distinctively social aspects of human reality.

This connects with the moral and political objections to sociobiology. There was a strong feeling that, in emphasizing the biological influences on human life and apparently neglecting the social influences, Wilson was giving (perhaps unintentional) support and comfort to reactionary tendencies in American and British society.[35] If nature is admitted to be more influential than nurture in forming human individuals and societies, then it seems there would be much less possibility than many social theorists had liked to think of improving individuals and society by education, social programs, and political change. Moralists and politicians of conservative tendency could apparently say (with self-satisfaction!) that if the differences between individuals, races, and the sexes are innate, then there is no point in trying to reduce or eliminate them. Socialists, antiracists, and feminists were therefore aghast with Wilson's sociobiology! To them the only politically correct position seemed to be that, apart from our bodily physiology and a few general-purpose learning devices, human nature is basically a "blank slate" to be written on (and perhaps rewritten) by society. In the generally left-wing climate of opinion in academia in the

---

35. See Steven Rose, R. C. Lewontin, and Leon J. Kamin, *Not in Our Genes: Biology, Ideology and Human Nature* (Harmondsworth: Penguin, 1984), especially Chapters 1–2, where the authors accuse Wilson of "biological determinism."

1970s and 1980s, Wilson came in for personal abuse and "sociobiology" became a dirty word.

Tooby and Cosmides: The Integrated Causal Model

Because of the controversy that Wilson's program aroused, his term "sociobiology" has fallen out of favor, and "evolutionary psychology" has become the preferred phrase for many of those who persist in applying a basically Darwinian approach to the human mind.[36] Leda Cosmides and John Tooby, of the University of California at Santa Barbara, have provided a carefully argued programmatic statement of the evolutionary approach they recommend.[37]

Cosmides and Tooby want to replace the Standard Social Science Model, which, they argue, has misguidedly ignored the increasing evidence for the existence of many innate, evolutionarily produced cognitive mechanisms in the human mind, and they propose instead what they call the "Integrated Causal Model." Let us examine what that involves. They begin with some ambitious methodological or philosophical statements (reminiscent of Wilson's!):

> In this vast landscape of causation, it is now possible to locate "Man's place in nature" to use Huxley's famous phrase, and, therefore, to understand for the first time what humankind is and why we have the characteristics that we do.[38]
> The rich complexity of each individual is produced by a cognitive architecture, embodied in a physiological system, which interacts with the social and nonsocial world that surrounds it. Thus humans, like every other natural system, are embedded in the contingencies of a larger principled history, and explaining any particular fact about them requires the joint analysis of all the principles and contingencies involved. To break this seamless matrix of causation—to attempt to dismember the individual into "biological" versus "nonbiological" aspects—is to embrace and perpetuate an ancient dualism endemic to the Western cultural tradition: material/spiritual, body/mind, physical/mental, natural/human, animal/human, biological/social, biological/cultural. This dualist view expresses only a premodern version of biology, whose intellectual warrant has vanished.[39]

---

36. There are now several active evolutionary research programs on human nature. See K. L. Laland and G. R. Brown, *Sense and Nonsense: Evolutionary Perspectives on Human Behaviour* (Oxford University Press, 2002).

37. J. Tooby and L. Cosmides, "The Psychological Foundations of Culture," in J. H. Barkow, L. Cosmides, and J. Tooby, eds., *The Adapted Mind: Evolutionary Psychology and the Generation of Culture* (Oxford University Press, 1992), pp. 19–136.

38. *The Adapted Mind*, p. 20.

39. *The Adapted Mind*, p. 21.

> . . . the Integrated Causal Model . . . makes progress possible by accepting and exploiting the natural connexions that exist between all the branches of science, using them to construct careful analyses of the causal interplay among all the factors that bear on a phenomenon. In this alternative framework, nothing is autonomous and all the components of the model must mesh.[40]

According to this outlook, causation reigns supreme in the world. Behind any human phenomenon there will be a complicated set of chains of causation, involving:

1. natural selection operating on our ancestors over many millenia to produce a variety of innate mental modules in the human species;
2. the historical development of a variety of human cultures over many centuries;
3. the mixing of genes in sexual reproduction that gives each human his or her own unique set of genes (except for identical twins);
4. the input of the physical and social/cultural environment on the bodily and mental development of each individual;
5. the information processing involved in perception and speech recognition, the results of which join with motivational factors to be the immediate cause of particular actions.

The picture is of "a seamless matrix of causation," and the only kind of explanation or understanding that is here recognized is scientific, *causal* explanation. We should notice, however, that we will have to admit a significant element of historical contingency in the environmental conditions, both physical (e.g., volcanic eruptions, climate changes) and historical (e.g., the winning of a crucial battle may affect many subsequent cultural developments). It is this ideal, causally complete, sense of "understanding" that Tooby and Cosmides presumably have in mind when they say that only now can we "understand for the first time what humankind is." Later, they are even more explicit about their commitment to determinism and causal completeness:

> . . . every feature of every phenotype is fully and equally codetermined by the interaction of the organism's genes . . . and its ontogenetic environments—meaning everything that impinges on it. . . . the interaction of the two is always part of every complete explanation of any human phenomenon. As with all interactions, the product simply cannot be sensibly ana-

---

40. *The Adapted Mind*, p. 23.

lyzed into separate genetically determined and environmentally determined components or degrees of influence. For this reason, *everything*, from the most delicate nuance of Richard Strauss's last performance of Beethoven's Fifth Symphony to the presence of calcium salts in his bones at birth, is totally and to the same extent genetically and environmentally codetermined.[41]

So, if only we knew enough about all the relevant initial conditions and causal laws, everything could be predicted. But John Dupre has argued that this belief in determinism, or at least in *causal completeness* (the idea that there is a complete causal truth about every situation, even if some of the causal laws are probabilistic rather than deterministic), is a metaphysical article of faith that is not a logically necessary presupposition of scientific method. Dupre suggests that the absence of causal completeness provides room for a genuine sense of human autonomy, or freedom of the will, when we act (along Kantian lines) on some kind of principle; that is, for an explicitly recognized reason.[42]

Tooby and Cosmides say that to reject the picture of a seamless web of causation is to embrace one or another sort of dualism that lacks intellectual warrant. Now, I do not want to defend a dualist view of human nature, if that implies a supernatural kind of causation that occasionally (or regularly) intervenes in the natural order, when a supposedly immaterial soul affects body. But there is one distinction that is notably absent from their list of disreputable dualisms, namely that between causal explanation and the giving of reasons. And we can point out to Tooby and Cosmides (as we did to Wilson) that they themselves are in the business of *arguing* for their metascientific view and of giving *evidence* for causal, evolutionary explanations of human cognitive mechanisms—which are two kinds of reason giving.

If the web of causation is truly seamless, then it must apply to *all* human behavior, including scientists' propounding of theories, which must have its own (no doubt very complicated) causal explanation, like everything else. But the fact remains that, even if there is such a thing as a "complete" causal explanation of why someone came to hold a certain belief, to give such an explanation is quite a different thing from giving reasons for the belief. To do the latter is to give reasons for believing that the relevant proposition is *true*; but causal explanation of someone's belief formation must be equally possible whether one thinks the belief is true or

---

41. *The Adapted Mind,* pp. 83–84.
42. J. Dupre, *Human Nature and the Limits of Science* (Oxford University Press, 2001), especially Chapter 7. See also Anthony O'Hear, *Beyond Evolution: Human Nature and the Limits of Evolutionary Explanation* (Oxford University Press, 1997).

false (or doesn't know). Because everyone has beliefs, nobody—least of all the scientist, who wants to be intellectually responsible to the evidence and the arguments—can opt out of giving reasons for his or her beliefs.

This is not to deny that there are a number of innate human mental modules that have been produced by natural selection operating on our hominoid ancestors. And if some of these have to do with such humanly essential matters as language use, perception, mate selection, and parental care, that is no surprise. But, of course, it requires detailed argument and empirical evidence, not just plausible evolutionary speculations from the armchair ("just-so stories"), to establish exactly what these modules are and what the selection pressures were. In that sense, evolutionary psychology has a real subject matter and valid methods of inquiry, if sufficient care is taken.

My questions here have been about the limits of the idea of a scientific theory of human nature. Is the suggestion merely that the methods of science can tell us *many* truths about ourselves? That is something that nobody is going to deny. Or is it being asserted that the methods of science can tell us *everything* about human nature, about what it is to be human? That is something, I have argued, that there is good reason to resist.

DIAGNOSES AND PRESCRIPTIONS BASED ON EVOLUTIONARY THEORY

Over the century and a half since Darwin, there have been a bewildering variety of morals that have been suggested we should draw from the scientifically confirmed facts about human evolution. Darwin himself offered some social prescriptions based on the application of evolutionary theory to humans:

> All ought to refrain from marriage who cannot avoid abject poverty for their children. . . . Man, like every other animal, has no doubt advanced to his present high condition through a struggle for existence consequent on his rapid multiplication; and if he is to advance still higher he must remain subject to a severe struggle. . . . There should be open competition for all men; and the most able should not be prevented by laws or customs from succeeding best and rearing the largest number of offspring.

But Darwin was wise enough to recognize the limits of natural selection and the importance of human culture:

> Important as the struggle for existence has been and even still is, yet as far as the highest part of man's nature is concerned there are other agencies more important. For the moral qualities are advanced . . . much more

through the effects of habit, the reasoning powers, instruction, religion, etc., than through natural selection . . . [43]

The social Darwinists of the late nineteenth century, notably Herbert Spencer in England and W. G. Sumner in America, eagerly took up the theme broached in the first quotation from Darwin presented in this section. Here, it seemed to them, was a straightforward transition from the fact of evolution by natural selection to the value of severe struggle and competition in human society. Hence they thought they saw a justification for unrestrained capitalism, including the most extreme disparities between rich and poor. It can be replied, however, that because evolution has given us both the intelligence to pass laws and institute social programs and the sympathy to care for our fellow humans, why should we not use those mental capacities to try to steer society in the direction of greater equality? Is not that at least as "natural" to our *human* nature as unflinching adherence to "the survival of the fittest" (which was Spencer's famous phrase), implying the nonsurvival of the less fit? It would be dangerous, however, to rest the case on the very slippery concept of what is "natural"; better to appeal directly to explicit ethical principles about human equality, needs, or rights, which cannot be derived from any factual premise about evolution.[44]

Skinner on a Technology of Behavior

As we have seen, Skinner was a Darwinian theorist only in the very marginal sense that he drew an analogy between natural selection and the "selection" of behavior by experience. He is, however, an instructive example of the pitfalls of applying scientific theory to social problems. In *Science and Human Behavior* and *Beyond Freedom and Dignity*,[45] Skinner tried to apply his behaviorist theories to human society, arguing that behavioral science can solve many of our problems, if only we will give up our illusions about human free will and responsibility for action. He believed that only science can tell us the truth about human nature, remarking that science is unique in human activity in showing a cumulative progress, and he made audacious claims for the potential of science to solve human problems. Indeed, Skinner saw no clear distinction between science and technology; for him, the job of science is not just to predict but to *control* the world, and he offered "a technology of behavior" as the way forward to a better human society.

---

43. *The Descent of Man*, toward the end of Chapter XXI.
44. Subsequent vicissitudes of this debate have been explored by Carl N. Degler, *In Search of Human Nature: The Decline and Revival of Darwinism in American Social Thought* (Oxford University Press, 1991).
45. B. F. Skinner, *Beyond Freedom and Dignity* (New York: Bantam Books, 1972).

Skinner argues that we are in an unstable transitional stage between the traditional notion of free will and the scientific explanation of behavior: "We shall almost certainly remain ineffective in solving these problems until we adopt a consistent point of view."[46] Like Marx, Skinner holds that the circumstances of human life can and should be humanly formed: "Why should the design of a culture be left so largely to accident? Is it not possible to change the social environment deliberately so that the human product will meet more acceptable specifications" (as he rebarbatively puts it).[47] If we give up the illusions of individual freedom and dignity (a dangerous-sounding suggestion indeed!), happier lives can be created by conditioning human behavior in appropriate ways.

For instance, we could give up the inefficient practice of punishment and aim rather to make people *want* to conform to the standards of society. This can be done by a combination of positive inducements, education, and propaganda. In view of the increasing percentage of the population now in penal institutions in America and Britain, one wonders if Skinner had a point here. Are we serious about the reform and re-education of offenders, or do we just want to vent our anger on them?

But Skinner's utopia is open to similar objections as those to Plato's republic (see Chapter 4). Who conditions the conditioners? On what basis are the designers of a culture to be selected? What gives them the right to decide what is best for everyone? And how can misuse of their power be prevented? Skinner thought there need be no danger of despotism, provided that control is diversified between different individuals and institutions, but here he seems politically naive.

One of the most striking cases of an effective technology of behavior is the use of the mass media in commercial advertising and political campaigning. (James Watson, the founder of behaviorism, ended up in the advertising industry, after having to leave his academic post because of a sex scandal.) American corporations have led the way in applying the methods of Freudian association and Skinnerian conditioning in their advertisements, and governments have been happy to follow the lead and use similar techniques to persuade the electorate. Huge sums of money are now spent on public relations by corporations, pressure groups, and political parties, and experience shows that cleverly designed advertising and positive or negative propaganda can be very effective, in both dictatorships and democracies. Governments and corporations have become adept at using the media to create a climate of opinion, though the Internet now provides a medium by which "unorthodox" opinions can be communicated.

---

46. *Science and Human Behavior*, p. 9.
47. *Science and Human Behavior*, pp. 426–27.

Skinner is an extreme example of the "scientist" tendency to think that *all* questions—even those about human fulfillment and about what is *worth* doing or striving for—can be answered purely scientifically, insofar as they are genuine questions at all.

Lorenz on Human Aggression

Konrad Lorenz (1903–89) was, with Freud, another product of the great scientific and cultural traditions of Vienna. He made a reputation as an ethologist with his studies of animal behavior, notably the "imprinting" of ducklings on the first moving thing they see. He also wrote very readably for the general public and tried to apply his biological understanding to human problems. Like Freud, he saw a conflict between the instincts implanted in us by evolution and the moral restraints necessary to civilized society.

In *On Aggression*,[48] Lorenz describes patterns of aggressive behavior in many animal species and offers a diagnosis of human problems based on our allegedly innate aggressive tendencies. He is concerned with fighting and threats between members of the *same* species (so predation does not count as aggression for him). What is the survival value of intraspecific aggression? It can space out individuals over the available territory so that there is enough food for each. Aggression between rival males ensures that the strongest individuals are those that leave offspring. And aggressive behavior can maintain a pecking order in an animal community, which may be beneficial in that the most experienced animals can lead the group.

Lorenz suggested that humans have an innate drive to aggressive behavior toward our own species, arguing that this is the only possible explanation of the conflicts and killings throughout human history. He sought an evolutionary explanation for our innate aggressiveness and for its peculiarly *communal* nature—for the most destructive human fighting is not between individuals but between groups, in war, ethnic cleansing, and riots. He speculated that at a certain stage of our ancestors' evolution, the main threat may have come from other hominoid groups. So there would be a survival value in the warrior virtues, and those groups that banded together best to fight other groups would tend to survive longest. Thus Lorenz proposed to explain what he calls "militant enthusiasm," in which a human crowd can become excitedly aggressive against another group perceived as alien and lose all rational control and moral inhibitions.[49] Our technology of weaponry has now developed so far that

---

48. K. Lorenz, *On Aggression*, first published 1963, translated by Marjorie Latzke (New York: Bantam Books, 1974).
49. *On Aggression*, Ch. XIII.

we find ourselves in a highly dangerous situation, with both the means to inflict mass destruction and the *willingness* (on the part of state leaders and terrorists) to use those means in certain situations.

As for prescription, Lorenz believes that if we understand the nature of our aggressive drive, we can take rational steps to redirect it. Self-knowledge is the first step to salvation (another echo of Freud, Sartre, and Socrates!). One possibility is sublimation, the redirection of aggression in harmless ways: we can smash crockery to express rage and we can channel group-competitiveness into team games. More constructively, we can try to break down mistrust between groups by promoting personal acquaintance between people of different nations, classes, and cultures. Lorenz also avows confidence in our sense of humor for promoting friendship, showing up fraud, and releasing tension. Humor and knowledge are his great hopes for the future of civilization.[50]

Biologists have, however, found Lorenz guilty of an un-Darwinian understanding of evolution in terms of "group selection" operating on prehuman tribes rather than individuals.[51] Skinner also thought in this way,[52] whereas the classic Darwinian theory is that natural selection applies to a population of individuals that vary in some ways, so that those whose hereditary characteristics are "fittest" tend to pass on more of their genes into the next generation. Thus, the competition for survival and reproduction is fundamentally between individuals, not between groups or tribes of them. Debate among biologists continues, however, about the possibility of group selection in certain conditions, so perhaps we can say that the jury is still out on the defensibility of some version of Lorenz's explanation of human aggression.

The Freudian/Lorenzian hypothesis of an aggressive drive seems oversimplified.[53] Wilson has distinguished *seven* different types of aggression![54] A more plausible view, which allows a crucial role for the cultural environment, is that human genes make us predisposed to distinctively communal, intergroup aggression in certain social conditions.

Left-Wing Resistance to "Biological Determinism"
There have been allegations of ideological motivation behind theories (such as Lorenz's) that certain forms of human behavior (e.g., aggression,

---

50. *On Aggression*, Ch. XIV
51. *On Aggression*, pp. 209, 224.
52. See *Science and Human Behavior*, p. 430.
53. For criticism of Lorenz and other ethological diagnoses of the human condition, see Erich Fromm, *The Anatomy of Human Destructiveness* (New York: Holt, Rinehart and Winston, Inc., 1973); *Man and Aggression*, 2d ed., edited by M. F. Ashley Montagu (Oxford University Press, 1973).
54. *On Human Nature*, Chapter 5.

competition for resources or status, male domination, rape, or war) are innate in our biological nature. A danger is perceived of such claims being used to justify as "natural" or inevitable certain social practices; for example, the encouragement of aggressiveness, patriarchy (perhaps even rape), wars and preparation for war, and the competitive economic systems of contemporary capitalism. But equally, of course, there might be social and political motives (of left-wing "political correctness") behind some of the *resistance* to sociobiological claims. This only shows that we cannot rest content with attacking each other's motives (see the Introduction to this book). When empirical claims are being made, we have to do the hard work of investigating the evidence for the claims and, if value judgments are involved, we need to bring them out into the open and subject them to critical review.

In 1984, Steven Rose, Richard Lewontin, and Leon J. Kamin published a systematic assault on what they saw as the pernicious doctrines of reductionism and biological determinism, which they claimed to find in Wilson's sociobiological approach.[55] As open supporters of the creation of a more socially just, indeed a *socialist*, society, they argued that much of what was being presented as neutral, objective science—in studies of IQ (Intelligence Quotient), alleged racial differences, differences between the sexes, psychiatry, and sociobiology—was implicitly supportive of right-wing politics.

To be fair to Wilson, it should be acknowledged that when he discusses alleged racial differences he says "most scientists have long recognized that it is a futile exercise to try to define discrete human races. Such entities do not in fact exist"; and he concludes that "mankind viewed over many generations shares a single human nature within which relatively minor hereditary influences are recycled through ever changing patterns, between the sexes and across families and entire populations."[56] The accusation of racism against him cannot be made to stick.

In contrast, on the topic of differences between men and women, Wilson says "the evidence for a genetic difference in behavior is varied and substantial."[57] But, then, some feminists have also taken the line that there are important innate mental differences between men and women, which society should not try to eliminate ("difference feminists" thus tend to disagree with "equality feminists"). Wilson is surely right to insist that there are empirical questions here, which we can begin to answer if we suspend our prejudices and take sufficient care. He is also right to imply

55. *Not in Our Genes: Biology, Ideology and Human Nature.*
56. *On Human Nature,* pp. 48, 50.
57. *On Human Nature,* p. 129.

that, given whatever facts about innate differences between the sexes there turn out to be, we have practical choices to make about social policy (as well as about individual behavior), choices that we must make in terms of our most deeply held values.[58]

Chomsky's Argument for Human Rights

Alongside his academic work on human language and what it shows us about the human mind, its individual development, and its innate capacity, Chomsky has pursued a second career as a political writer and campaigner. He has been a relentless critic of U.S. foreign policy, from the time of the Vietnam war through the interventions in Central America and Chile, down to the new doctrine of preemptive strike without United Nations authority against any country perceived to pose a threat to U.S. interests. His main case is that for all the conventional, apparently high-minded, rhetoric about human rights, freedom, and democracy, the actual effect of much U.S. foreign policy has often been to deny those benefits to people in less-favored countries.[59]

There may not at first seem to be much connection between Chomsky's academic theorizing and his political commitment, but an interesting link emerged when Lewontin invited him to join in the moral/political campaign against Wilsonian sociobiology in 1976. In their discussion, Lewontin and Chomsky found that, although they both had left-wing sympathies, they had quite a different basis for their views.[60] They both appealed to Marx's theory of human nature, but whereas Lewontin quoted the "orthodox" Marxism of his later period, according to which there is no fixed human nature, only something malleable by social processes, Chomsky favored the theory of the young Marx (of the "Economic and Philosophical Manuscripts"), according to which man has an underlying, fixed, "species nature" (see Chapter 7). Chomsky thought that the idea of an infinitely malleable human nature gives too much scope to tyranny, and that we need a definite conception of human needs in terms of a basic, fixed, human nature, in order to know what direction society ought to move in (see Sartre on human needs, at the end of Chapter 9).

Wilson's Prescriptions

Wilson has not been shy of offering diagnoses and recommendations. The second "spiritual dilemma" he identified in *On Human Nature* concerns

---

58. See S. Pinker, *The Blank Slate: The Modern Denial of Human Nature* (London: Penguin, 2003).
59. There are Web sites about Chomsky's political writing and campaigning at www.zmag. org/chomsky/index.cfm and www.synaptic.bc.ca/ejournal/chomsky.htm. The latter site includes some material critical of Chomsky.
60. See U. Segerstrale, *Defenders of the Truth*, Chapter 10.

"the choice that must be made among the ethical premises inherent in man's biological nature." But what on earth does that mean? He tries to explain as follows:

> . . . innate censors and motivators exist in the brain that deeply and unconsciously affect our ethical premises; from these roots, morality evolved as instinct. If that perception is correct, science may soon be in a position to investigate the very origin and meaning of human values, from which all ethical pronouncements and much of political practice flow.[61]

Wilson goes on to restate the second dilemma in terms that are strongly reminiscent of Freud on civilization and its discontents:

> Which of the censors and motivators should be obeyed and which might be better curtailed or sublimated? . . . At some stage in the future we will have to decide how human we wish to remain—in this ultimate, biological sense—because we must consciously choose among the alternative guides we have inherited. . . .

And surprisingly, he asserts that biological science can answer this second dilemma:

> To chart our destiny means that we must shift from automatic control based on our biological properties to precise steering based on biological knowledge.
> . . . only hard-won empirical knowledge of our biological nature will allow us to make optimum choices among the competing criteria of progress.[62]

What Wilson says here appears deeply ambiguous and not properly thought through. Is he merely saying that empirical knowledge of our biological nature can *help* us make optimum choices? That is something that nobody will deny. Medical research tells us much about the workings of our bodies, and this knowledge can often be applied to cure or prevent illness, to repair injury, and to relieve disabilities. Some mental illnesses can be relieved by appropriate medication, and specific kinds of psychotherapy can relieve some mental distress. We know that certain disabling conditions are genetically based and, now that the human genome has been mapped, there is hope of new kinds of gene therapy.

---

61. *On Human Nature*, pp. 4–5.
62. *On Human Nature*, pp. 6–7, see also p. 120, and p. 148, where Wilson recapitulates Skinner in the optimistic-sounding—but surely deeply worrying—view that "cultures can be rationally designed."

So far, so good: there is nothing controversial about applying physiological and psychological knowledge to relieve human suffering (though there can, of course, be doubts about the effectiveness, and sometimes about the ethics, of particular methods of treatment).

A deeper philosophical problem arises when Wilson (like Skinner before him) seems to suggest that there is no question about human nature that is beyond the scope of science, so that the progress of science, and in particular, of sociobiological explanation of the evolutionary origin of human ethical beliefs and feelings, will in itself solve future ethical dilemmas. This would imply that all questions about human fulfillment, about what is good for us, about what will lead to real and lasting happiness in human life, will be answerable by the methods of science. But is it part of science to claim that every meaningful question can be answered by the methods of science? Such "scientism" is not itself an empirical claim, not something that can be tested by the scientific method of observation and experiment—and it is therefore self-refuting.

We need not deny that some sorts of evolutionary explanation of the origin of human ethical beliefs and feelings may make us more aware of their social function (remember Durkheim) and more skeptical of the unreflective deliverances of ethical "intuition," including our own. There is nothing peculiarly new in *that* kind of thought—it has been put before us in Marx's theory of ideology, Nietzsche's genealogy of morals, Freud's account of the psychological development of moral feelings, and in Durkheim's sociology.

But if Wilson is seriously suggesting that biological science will provide the answer to all ethical dilemmas, he seems to be flying in the face of the fact/value distinction. It is possible that future knowledge of the detail of the human genome and of techniques of genetic engineering may offer to people in controlling positions the power to favor, or to disadvantage, or possibly even to exterminate, people carrying certain genes (genetic "defects," blood-groups, races, or sexualities). Should such power be used? If so, in what cases? And by whom, with what safeguards? These are certainly ethical (perhaps indeed "spiritual") dilemmas, and Wilson is right to draw our attention to their importance. But I do not see that any amount of biological knowledge alone will enable us to answer them. There remain irreducibly ethical judgments that we have to make.[63]

A similar point applies to what Wilson says about "mythologies" in the chapters on religion and hope at the end of *On Human Nature*:

---

63. Wilson's treatment of ethics is elegantly criticized by Kitcher in the last section ("The Hypothalmic Imperative") in Chapter 11 of *Vaulting Ambition*.

It is obvious that human beings are still largely ruled by myth. Furthermore, much of contemporary intellectual and political strife is due to the conflict between three great mythologies: Marxism, traditional religion, and scientific materialism.[64]

Wilson dismisses Marxism as an inadequate, nonbiological form of scientific materialism. So the competition between mythologies quickly reduces to religion versus science. And for Wilson this is no contest:

> . . . the final decisive edge enjoyed by scientific naturalism will come from its capacity to explain traditional religion, its chief competitor, as a wholly material phenomenon. Theology is not likely to survive as an independent intellectual discipline. But religion itself will endure for a long time as a vital force in society. Like the mythical giant Antaeus who drew energy from his mother, the earth, religion cannot be defeated by those who merely cast it down. The spiritual weakness of scientific naturalism is due to the fact that it has no such primal source of power.[65]

Nevertheless, Wilson entertains the hope that the spiritual power of religion, based on innate tendencies in human nature to "create morality, religion and mythology and empower them with emotional force,"[66] can eventually be harnessed to the intellectually superior myth of scientific, evolutionary naturalism.[67] Somehow science is to become the new religion of humanity! (We have heard that idea before, most explicitly in the early nineteenth-century positivism of Comte.)

But it is not at all clear how this trick can be turned. Certainly, it is hard to see how any particular scientific theory, even one as wide-ranging in its implications as the Darwinian theory of evolution by natural selection, can carry the value implications and give the guidance for life that religions have traditionally offered. As we have seen, Wilsonian scientific naturalism is not itself a scientific theory, but a metascientific program for explaining everything in terms of empirically testable theories. This certainly sets standards of *intellectual* value—nothing is to be justifiably believed unless it meets this criterion of successful (i.e., observationally tested) explanation.

It does not give any more general guidance, however, for although Wilson says that "scientific materialism is the only mythology that can manufacture great goals from the sustained pursuit of pure knowledge,"[68]

---

64. *On Human Nature,* p. 190.
65. *On Human Nature,* p. 192.
66. *On Human Nature,* p. 200.
67. *On Human Nature,* pp. 193, 200–201, 204–7; see also *Consilience,* pp. 294–95.
68. *On Human Nature,* p. 207.

it seems pretty obvious that possible future human societies might pursue pure knowledge and yet vary widely in their values. Some might promote the dominance of a master race, or one powerful nation, or a fundamentalist religion, while others might value all people as an end in themselves and tolerate cultural differences, recognize worldwide human rights, and work for economic justice. That we need more than scientific materialism as a source of values to constitute ethical *reasons* for our actions is surely a conceptual truth.

Since the 1970s, Wilson has gone on to write several other wide-ranging books—clearly he is a man of tireless energy, omnivorous intellectual appetite, and a certain missionary zeal! In *Genes, Mind and Culture* (written with C. Lumsden), he offered a mathematical theory of how genes and culture co-evolve in humans.[69] In *The Diversity of Life* and *Biophilia*, Wilson campaigns to try to stop the human-caused extinction of so many of the species on this planet. In *Naturalist*, he has given us his autobiography. And in *Consilience*, he argues again for the unification, not just of science, but of all legitimate knowledge—social sciences and humanities included—under the scientific banner. The kind of unity Wilson prefers is very extreme, namely the reduction of all other scientific laws and principles to the laws of physics,[70] though, he admits, he could be wrong and that there might be genuine emergence of irreducibly new laws at higher levels of complexity. He asserts that the Enlightenment belief in the potential for unlimited human progress is being confirmed by scientific evidence,[71]—which suggests a continuing element of blithe optimism or naive faith underneath all the scientific sophistication.

I suggest that we still need an awareness of the dark side of human nature as well as a sense of the possibilities of progress, and that our sense of light and darkness needs to be inspired and educated by the great religious and philosophical thought systems of the past that we have explored in this book.

FOR FURTHER READING

In the Very Short Introduction series published by Oxford University Press, there are relevant titles on Darwin, Evolution, and Evolutionary Psychology, and on Psychology and Social and Cultural Anthropology.

---

69. For an easier introduction to this research program, see Chapter 7 of *Consilience*. It is criticized in depth by Kitcher (*Vaulting Ambition*, Chapter 10).
70. *Consilience*, pp. 58–59, 297.
71. *Consilience*, p. 6.

For philosophical overviews of sociobiology, see M. Ruse, *Sociobiology: Sense or Nonsense?* (Dordrecht: Reidel, 1979); Mary Midgeley, *Beast and Man: The Roots of Human Nature* (London: Methuen, 1980); and Kitcher's *Vaulting Ambition: Sociobiology and the Quest for Human Nature* (Cambridge, Mass.: MIT Press, 1985), which is the most technically demanding—he has written a precis of it in *Behavioral and Brain Sciences* 10 (1987).

Robert Wright, *The Moral Animal: Evolutionary Psychology and Everyday Life* (Pantheon Books, 1994; Abacus, 1996), cleverly interweaves Darwin's theories, his life, and evolutionary psychology.

Recent textbooks of evolutionary psychology include David M. Buss, *Evolutionary Psychology: The New Science of the Mind* (Boston: Allyn and Bacon, 1999), and Louise Barrett, Robin Dunbar, and John Lycett, *Human Evolutionary Psychology* (Houndsmills: Palgrave, 2002). Laland and Brown, *Sense and Nonsense: Evolutionary Perspectives on Human Behavior* (Oxford University Press, 2002), provide a useful survey of ongoing research programs.

Philosophical issues arising from evolutionary psychology are discussed by Anthony O'Hear, *Beyond Evolution: Human Nature and the Limits of Evolutionary Explanation* (Oxford University Press, 1997); Janet Radcliffe Richards, *Human Nature after Darwin: A Philosophical Introduction* (London: Routledge, 2000); John Dupre, *Human Nature and the Limits of Science* (Oxford University Press, 2001); and John Dupre, *Humans and Other Animals* (Oxford University Press, 2002).

A neuroscientist and a philosopher, Max R. Bennett and P. M. S. Hacker, have collaborated to write *Philosophical Foundations of Neuroscience* (Oxford: Blackwell, 2003).

Conclusion: Toward a
Synthesis of the Theories?

To hope to conclude this book with some final or complete truth about human nature would be foolish. Final truths do not seem to be given to us finite human beings (except perhaps in mathematics), least of all about a topic as broad and controversial as human nature. So I have no eleventh theory to offer, but offer instead an invitation to try to put together what seems most acceptable from those we have considered here (and all other sources of knowledge and wisdom).

Readers may tend to think of the ten theories as rivals (and we encouraged this in the introduction), but they are not incompatible with each other on all points. Each of them surely makes some positive contribution to our understanding of ourselves and our place in the universe. We can see each theory as emphasizing (perhaps *over*emphasizing) different aspects of the total, complicated truth. In this way, they may begin to add together to form a more adequate conception of human nature.

In this concluding chapter, I will risk sticking my neck out by trying to sketch how the main lines of such a composite picture might go, using our familiar four-part structure of metaphysical background, theory of human nature, diagnosis and prescription. For this irenical project, I suggest that Kant's system of thought (with some modernizations) provides a comprehensive and hospitable framework that offers a basis for integrating what we find acceptable in the other theories into one coherent overall view.

I prefer *not* to start with cosmic metaphysics, however. That is an area where agreement is least likely, especially when we consider the differences between naturalist and supernatural worldviews and between different supernatural religious beliefs. One of the most persistent metaphysical disputes is over the existence of God or other quasi-divine or supernatural beings such as angels or devils, spirits or ghosts (supposedly with mental powers, but without material embodiment). There is unclarity, too, over the nature of those more impersonal, but quasi-divine realities spoken of by other traditions, such as the Heaven of Confucianism and the One or *brahman* of Hinduism. And there are more purely philosophical disputes over the existence of abstract entities such as Platonic forms, including the objects of mathematics. Not only do we disagree about these matters, we do not seem to have any reliable method for *resolving* such disagreements. All in all, then, this is not a promising place to begin. If we have to settle on a generally acceptable metaphysics before anything else, we will never get going at all!

A PRIORI THEORY (OR METAPHYSICS) OF HUMAN NATURE

If we look for an irenical theory of *human* nature, the prospect is perhaps a bit more hopeful. Kant's distinction between different levels of thinking, resulting in different kinds of truth (a priori and a posteriori) allows us to find a place both for philosophical reflection and argument, and for empirical facts based on observation and experience in the sciences and in history and anthropology.

Thus, we can formulate an a priori conceptual definition (influenced by Plato and Aristotle, as well as Kant) of what criteria any creatures (anywhere in the universe) have to meet to count as rational thinkers and agents. They are to be capable of giving reasons for their beliefs and their actions, and their giving of reasons has to be done in language of some sort. It is not implied that such rational creatures *always* give such reasons (for most of the time we judge and act without explaining why), nor is it required that they are always *capable* of stating their reasons (we may be unable to give rationally plausible reasons for some of what we do!). All that is required for this most basic notion of rationality is that the subjects be *able* to formulate intelligible reasons for *some* of what they believe and do.

What is it about human beings that makes such (minimal) rationality possible? Plato and Descartes believed that we are essentially immaterial souls and that our most distinctive rational nature hence lies beyond scientific investigation. This issue of dualism or materialism has to be faced. Are minds, consciousness, and rationality essentially nonmaterial, or are we made of matter alone? Are mental states (sensations, emotions, beliefs, desires, etc.) and brain states (the electrical and chemical goings-on investigated by neurophysiologists) two different sorts of thing or two aspects of one set of events?

I make bold to suggest that this metaphysical issue about human nature is more tractable than the cosmic disputes mentioned earlier, because Aristotle and Spinoza have supplied us with the outlines of a more promising approach to it. As we explored in Chapter 5, Aristotle saw the rational mode of mental functioning that is distinctive of humans as superimposed on the animal way of functioning (perception and self-movement), which is itself superimposed on the most basic functions that all living things have (metabolism and reproduction). We are animals and we are necessarily embodied, but we are animals of a special rational, language-using kind.

What, then, makes our linguistic and rational abilities possible? It is surely our brain, which is enormous and highly complex compared with those of other animals. Even if we reject a Cartesian dualism of substances and roughly identify the mind or soul with whatever the brain enables us to do, we find an unavoidable duality of *aspects* (or properties, or vocabularies)—as Spinoza saw. There are mental descriptions in terms of the content of our beliefs, desires, hopes, fears, and other emotions (which figure in our reasons for action), and there are physical descriptions in terms of neuron firings, chemical changes, and so on (which figure in scientific explanations of brain functioning), and these different descriptions are irreducible to each other. There is no necessity that the same belief or desire, identified in terms of its content, involving the concepts of the subject, is embodied in exactly the same physiological kind of brain state, in different species of rational being, in two individuals of the same species, or even in the same individual at different times.

As Kant said (in his own idiosyncratic vocabulary), and as emerged in our discussion of Freud, Sartre, and Darwininian theories, we use a seemingly irreducible duality of *kinds of explanation*. On the one hand are explanations of human actions (and beliefs) in terms of *reasons*, appealing to intelligible conceptual connections between premises and conclusions in a piece of theoretical or practical reasoning. On the other hand are explanations (typical of the physical sciences) in terms of *causes*, appealing to universal (or probabilistic) laws of nature plus particular preceding initial conditions.

But neither Kant nor the other theorists resolves all the philosophical puzzlements in this area. Further discussion of these issues is a central topic in contemporary philosophy of mind and action and the issues are fundamental for psychology and the social sciences. There is a connection with the traditional problem of free will, too, for if we can understand how there is conceptual room for *rationality* in a physical world (how creatures whose brain-functioning consists in electrical and chemical events can also be said to have reasons for their beliefs and actions), then there may be hope of understanding how there is room for free will in a world of determining (or merely probabilistic) causes.

Perhaps the conceptual and empirical complexities of our mental functioning will require us to distinguish more than one level of *mental* functioning and description. Our notion of "the mental" is wide and ambiguous. Aristotle can be seen as distinguishing animal and human levels of mentality, Freud offered a distinction between primary and secondary mental processes in us, and recent psychology and cognitive science make more subtle distinctions of level.

EMPIRICAL THEORY OF HUMAN NATURE

Into this a priori conceptual framework we can fit all sorts of empirical facts about human nature (and perhaps some different facts about other rational beings elsewhere in the universe). There are plenty of such facts about our bodies and about our human mental capacities (e.g., for facial recognition and for interpreting other people's motives) and emotional dispositions (e.g., a tendency toward pair-bonding, and the need of infants and children for attachment to parents or other caretakers and for loving care from them).

Kant wrote before Darwin, of course, but we can integrate evolutionary theory into the empirical side of his thought. We can offer a scientific, basically Darwinian account of how the most basic physical and mental commonalities of humans have evolved on this planet. With the aid of evolutionary theory, genetics, and study of the fossil record, we can begin to piece together the complicated story of how the faculties of rational thought and agency have come to be embodied in the human species (the evolutionary pathway that led to us). But, as we have seen in Chapter 10, we have to be very careful in our application of Darwinian theory to human phenomena. Not every aspect of human behavior has a direct evolutionary explanation—not, surely, the fashionablity of jeans, the interest of some of us in philosophy, or the decision of America and Britain to conquer Iraq in 2003. Determining just which kinds of human mental functioning are appropriate topics for evolutionary explanation is itself a delicate issue—and only the most basic and ancient seem to be plausible candidates.

Our reasons for action involve our beliefs and values, and are expressible in terms of our systems of culturally developed linguistic concepts. Culture is at least as crucial to the realities of our contemporary human nature as evolution. It is superimposed on basic human biology, of course. That there are *some* innate tendencies in human nature is indisputable, for example, our sexual behavior is obviously rooted in our biological nature. But even that inescapable example immediately raises problems and questions, for the forms sexuality takes vary considerably between societies and over time, and in devotedly celibate individuals like monks and nuns its expression may be deliberately suppressed. We have some innate biological drives, certainly, but we seem to be unique in the extent to which the detail of our behavior depends on the particular culture we have been brought up in. And it also depends on individual choices.

Rudimentary cultural differences have been discerned in some of the apes, but to nothing like the human extent. Although Skinner was wrong to see cultural influence in terms of the mechanisms of operant conditioning he imposed on his experimental animals, he was right to recognize the enormous difference that the social environment makes to the development of every human being from birth onward. Freud made us realize just how crucial the influence of parents and other caretakers is on the infant and young child. After that, peer groups and the wider society begin to take over education and socialization. In the high-tech capitalist economy that now dominates the world, much of the social influence is exerted through the power of money, advertising, and the media.

In the empirical study of archeology, anthropology, and history we can come to understand how the expression of the basic human faculties has developed through a great variety of human cultures. We can thus widen our sense of the options that evolution leaves open for cultures and, indeed, for individuals.

DIAGNOSIS

Any diagnosis of something wrong presupposes some standard of how things ought to be. Like Plato and Aristotle, Kant offers an objective, nonreligious (or not explicitly religious) basis for ethics, appealing both to pure reason and to empirical facts about human nature. The particular ethical systems of these great philosophers differ, and the interpretation of them leads into deep issues of scholarship, but this broad-brush description applies to all three.

Kant often seems to want to derive morality from rationality alone, but I see him as appealing to a fundamental *moral* principle of respect for all rational beings. In this, he was surely influenced by the Judeo-Christian ideal of love for one's neighbor as oneself—unlike Plato and Aristotle, who were more aristocratic or meritocratic in their bestowal of value or care on others. Confucius's notion of benevolence, and the Hindu and Buddhist programs of detachment from ego or self, seem to point in the same direction of universal compassion. Marx's burning sense of injustice was surely inspired by the Judeo-Christian ideal. In his "second ethics," Sartre also presupposed a universal conception of human potentiality and its ideal fulfillment in "a city of ends."

Kantian respect for all rational beings as ends in themselves implies recognition of the rights and needs of human beings. Rights imply corresponding obligations on other people and, much though the rhetoric of human rights has expanded in recent decades, it seems to me that the most appropriate place for talk of rights is in the negative cases: the rights *not* to be killed, injured, tortured, enslaved, imprisoned without trial, or exploited for someone else's benefit—where the corresponding negative obligations (on everyone) are generally acknowledged.

As we saw in Chapter 9, Sartre thought of human *needs* as objective values that "demand" to be fulfilled if human beings are to flourish. Put another way, given a basic value attached to human flourishing and facts about what human beings need to flourish, we attach a derived, but objective, value to those things. The notion of need applies at several levels. First, there are things we need to maintain life and health—air, water, protein, vitamins, medicines. There are also psychological needs—most fundamentally the need of children for loving care if they are to grow up feeling valued, and there are typical adult needs for friendship, for sexual fulfillment, and for children of one's own. Beyond the family, there are needs for education and group membership, and to work, or contribute in some way to society. We sometimes talk of a need for a meaning and purpose to life—but it needs clarifying how distinct this is from the rest.

If we can agree on most of these (surely not very controversial) conceptions of human rights and needs, a diagnosis immediately follows, given the facts about the world. Throughout history and into the present, human rights are all too frequently abused, and crying human needs are even more frequently unfulfilled. But *why* is this the case? Why is there so much human suffering in the world? The question is ancient and enormous—and it arises not only for theists.

One part of the answer is sheer accident. Earthquakes, volcanic eruptions, and asteroid impacts are beyond all human control. Epidemics, famine, floods, drought, and climate change have usually been in the same category (though we are now realizing that in some cases human activity contributes to these disasters). And, of course, there are accidents and diseases on a smaller scale, which kill or disable individuals. So there is a category of events beyond human control that is traditionally called "Fate" (Confucius talked of "Destiny"). Theists may call them "the Will of God" (or, at least, events that God does not prevent), but that does not necessarily make them any easier to bear.

Another part of the answer is economic scarcity. The world, rich in resources as it is, does not provide enough for unlimited numbers of human beings to grow to maturity and reproduce themselves. Of course, human ingenuity in science and technology often finds ways to utilize more of the resources of nature and thus makes economic and social advance possible, as Marx analyzed in some detail. But growth in population and economic development generates new needs or demands (it is a nice question whether there is a conceptual difference there!), not all of which can be met at any one time. So there will always be some degree of scarcity, some competition for resources, and awkward questions of economic justice.

However, a further large part of the answer must be human culpability. When a human need is not met, it does not follow that someone is to blame—though it is true in some cases (perhaps many). But when a human right is abused, then someone is responsible for that abuse: someone, or some group or social agency, has ordered or done the killing or torture, the enslavement or exploitation. And why have they done it? (We are asking here for reasons; that is, for beliefs and desires that make the action intelligible, even if not admirable.) The answer will typically involve their seeing some advantage to themselves.

No doubt there are a few perverted, sadistic individuals who take an intrinsic pleasure in causing pain, and there may be some who are prepared to inflict suffering in the name of some "greater" cause (e.g., the Nation, the Party, or the Church), but surely in most cases people do what they see as best for themselves (sometimes, just avoiding the unpleasant consequences of disobeying orders); they put other people's interests second, if they recognize them at all. As Kant said in his reformulation of the doctrine of original sin, there is a "radical evil" in human nature that consists in the tendency to prefer one's own interests over those of everyone else as represented in the fundamental principle of morality.

However, we should not see this entirely in terms of *individual* culpability, for because of our social nature and the immense influence of culture upon us, there is an important social dimension to sin, pride, and selfishness. It only needs a charismatic but perverted individual to gain influence or power, and many people will follow, motivated by some mixture of perverse inspiration and crude self-interest. Often there is *struc-*

tural injustice, enshrined in economic, social, or legal systems, the exploitation of one set of people by another, whether distinguished by class, race, nationality, or simple vulnerability (e.g., to sweatshop conditions of labor imposed by the market forces of global capitalism).

Those born into a favorable position in such a system, and acculturated into it (including its conceptions of superiority and inferiority, rights and lack of rights), bear no direct responsibility for the system. It may need a feat of imagination, or a stimulus from some other ethical or political or religious ideal, even to realize that something is morally wrong. But insofar as some such realization hits home, then the person has some responsibility to do something about it—whatever little they can. And I am thinking here not just of the extreme cases in the past, such as Nazi Germany, South Africa under apartheid, or our slave-owning ancestors, but of those who are presently oppressed, whether in the third world, in Palestine, in Chechnya, or indeed in the rich countries.

PRESCRIPTION

In the light of scarcity, and individual and social evil, can we entertain any hope, like Kant, for ethical and social progress in future? And what, if anything, can we do about it? More enormous and ancient questions, which arise both for theists and atheists! I hesitate to presume to have anything to say about them, but since I am sticking my neck out in these concluding reflections, I will try to say what little I can, which will not be particularly original. What answers there are, are likely to be quite ancient too!

As noted, scarcity can be alleviated by scientific discovery and technological ingenuity. If we can find an effective way of harnessing the energy that continually pours down upon the earth from the sun, then our present energy shortages may be solved. But, as I also noted, new affluence breeds new needs or demands. And this is not just an economic truth, but a psychological one as well. As Kant and others have noted, there is an inherently competitive streak in human nature; we constantly compare ourselves with others and want to do as well as them, or better. There is a moral point in the offing, too, for though our competitive tendencies may be acceptable, and even laudable, in sport or in scientific, scholarly, artistic or other professional achievement, they all too easily go "over the top" into ruthlessness, cheating, and greed. They may help drive social and cultural progress (as Kant realized), but they stand in need of limitation by higher ideals of unselfishness and compassion.

What remedies can we see for individual and social evil? The first step is surely to name the evils for what they are, to try to make everyone plainly and vividly aware of what is wrong, both in ourselves and in society. We human beings are adept at finding good names for what we do: there are almost infinite possibilities of self-justification, self-deception, Freudian repression, or Sartrean bad faith, with similar moves at the social level, especially what Marx called "ideology" that covers up or tries to justify the underlying exploitation. Of course, there are dangers in "preaching." None of us can lay claim to unique or infallible insight into right and wrong, and our first duty must always be to look to "the beam in our own eye." But there is surely a second duty, when (by our own best lights) we recognize an evil: to identify it as such, with all due sensitivity and respect to people who may be in some way enmired in it. And public, institutional evils may deserve a public, organized campaign of dissent.

Besides naming and opposing evil, we can do something more positive by putting forward and upholding standards of goodness, expressing our ideals of how human life ought to be. Again, "preaching" can be objectionable, and the first duty is to try to embody or emulate those ideals ourselves: as the old saying has it, "actions speak louder than words." But, given our social nature and our individual fallibility, there is a need for some attempt at institutional, permanent, or ongoing presentation of ideals and some kind of spiritual practice to help people rise to them. This, in outline, is what Kant called "an ethical community."

The Christian churches and the other world religious traditions (including Confucianism and Hinduism, which figured in Chapters 1 and 2) have to some extent played this role, each in their own peculiar way, overlaid or underlaid with various historical traditions and metaphysical beliefs. Kant hoped that these differences would come to be seen as optional, and that a common set of moral duties and ideals would be emphasized as the essential ethical core of all religion. But it has to be admitted that in the two centuries since Kant there has been little sign of this happening (with the possible exception of the Unitarians and Quakers, who appeal to minority tastes). Religions, in their traditional metaphysically supernatural forms, seem to have a hold over many human minds.

At any rate, there is always a need for education in the widest sense, including moral education—as Plato and Aristotle showed us. This applies to children and young people, especially, but we all remain capable of learning throughout life. None of us is omniscient or perfect and each of us may need teaching or reminding, at any time in our lives, about what is true, or good, or beautiful. There are always spiritually enlightening resources available, outside each frail and fallible individual. There are immense riches (as well as a good deal of dross!) to be found in the sciences, the philosophies, and the arts—as well as the religions. I hope this book will help readers appreciate some of these resources.

This book has concentrated on general *theories* and has hardly mentioned the arts. In closing, let us remember how literature, painting, opera, and dance present us with imaginary—but in another sense very "real"— particular cases of men and women displaying their nature in feeling and thought, action and song. In the greatest works, our understanding of human nature is extended and deepened, though not perhaps in ways we can put into explicit words. In contrast, many of the movies or "soap operas" that enjoy wide contemporary popularity present shallow, stereotyped characters and social situations, and restrict rather than deepen our understanding. (Plato realized how influential the arts and the "media" of popular communication can be—for better or for worse.) Understanding, wisdom, and sensitivity to the complex ethical dilemmas of life *can* be enhanced by attention to particular cases, whether factually described in biography, history, or anthropology, or presented imaginatively in the arts. We can thus achieve some liberation of our imaginations from the tyranny of the familiar and the contemporary.

The religions offer various forms of spiritual practice, some of which are described as leading us out of this world; but most of them are also expected to make us better persons in this world. There will be disagreements about the metaphysics, but perhaps we are more likely to agree about the test for being "a better person"—remember St. Paul's writing that "the harvest of the Spirit is love, joy, peace, patience, kindness, goodness, fidelity, gentleness, and self-control."

Human nature is a topic that breaks down the boundaries between the sciences, the humanities, and the religions. Social, and political problems in our own societies, and all around the world, cry out for better understanding of other human beings and cultures. Often the technical problems are soluble, but what seem insuperable are the political, social, and psychological problems. Some foreign policy analysts and governments assume that nations or "civilizations" are going to remain enemies indefinitely, and so continue to develop new technologies and strategies of "defense" instead of looking for ways of reducing tensions, addressing injustices, and making conditions for lasting peace. And, even in situations of affluence and peace, individual existential dilemmas, relationship problems, family tensions, illness, and death remain. There is no contradiction between Kant's hope for social progress and his recognition of the need for each person to come to terms with his or her individual destiny.

FOR FURTHER READING

Two thought-provoking histories of psychology are G. A. Millar and R. Buckout *Psychology: the Science of Mental Life*, 2d ed. (New York: Harper & Row, 19⁻ and L. S. Hearnshaw, *The Shaping of Modern Psychology: An H˙*

Introduction (London: Routledge, 1987), which covers the whole story since ancient times. In *Acts of Meaning* (Cambridge, Mass.: Harvard University Press, 1990), Jerome Bruner reviews the progress of psychology and recommends "cultural psychology." An innovative introduction to a variety of approaches in personality theory and social psychology is *Understanding the Self*, edited by R. Stevens (London: Sage Publications, 1996).

A reference book full of fascinating articles on a huge variety of topics is *The Oxford Companion to the Mind*, edited by R. L. Gregory (Oxford University Press, 1987). A comprehensive set of philosophical readings is *Philosophy of Mind: Classical and Contemporary Readings*, edited by David J. Chalmers (Oxford University Press, 2002).

There are many good modern introductions to the philosophy of mind: George Graham, *Philosophy of Mind*, 2d ed. (Oxford: Blackwell, 1998); John Heil, *Philosophy of Mind* (London: Routledge, 1998); Samuel Guttenplan, *Mind's Landscape* (Oxford: Blackwell, 2000); Tim Crane, *The Mechanical Mind*, 2d ed. (London: Routledge, 2003); Margaret A. Boden, *The Creative Mind*, 2d ed. (London: Routledge, 2003).

Iris Murdoch, *Metaphysics As a Guide to Morals* (London: Chatto & Windus, 1992), though long-winded and a bit wandery, is full of fascinating, unconventional insights into the basis of ethics and religion, inspired especially by Plato and Kant.

Roger Scruton's *Intelligent Person's Guide to Philosophy* (London: Duckworth, 1996) is an unconventional introduction, fired by his conviction that "scientific truth has human illusion as its regular by-product, and that philosophy is our surest weapon in the attempt to rescue truth from this predicament"—a message that I hope this book has reinforced. See also Scruton's *Intelligent Person's Guide to Modern Culture* (London: Duckworth, 1998).

Mary E. Clark, retired from a Chair in Conflict Resolution, has written a wide-ranging interdisciplinary book, *In Search of Human Nature* (London: Routledge, 2002), in which she offers hope for the future, despite our manifold problems.

John Cottingham, *On the Meaning of Life* (London: Routledge, 2003) is a delightfully clear, concise, and balanced discussion that ends up recommending some form of nondoctrinal spiritual practice to develop our responses to objective truth, goodness, and beauty, and our faith, hope, and love.

Index

Other Recent Work by Leslie Stevenson

At a Similar Introductory Level to this Book:

The Many Faces of Science: An Introduction to Scientists, Values, and Society, 2d ed., with Henry Byerly (Westview Press, 2000)

"The Arms Trade and the Slave Trade," *Journal of Applied Philosophy* (1999)

"A Two-Stage Life after Death?" *Theology* (2001)

"Kant's Philosophy and Quakerism," *The Friends' Quarterly* (2002)

At an Intermediate Level:

"Kant's Many Concepts of Appearance," *Cogito* (1998)

"Is there any Hope for Kant's Philosophy of Religion?" *Proceedings of the 9th International Kant Congress,* (2000)

"Twelve Conceptions of Imagination," *British Journal of Aesthetics* (2003)

At a More Advanced Level:

"Six Levels of Mentality," *Philosophical Explorations* (2002)

"Knowledge, Belief or Faith, and Opinion," *The Kantian Review* (2003)

"Freedom of Judgment in Descartes, Spinoza, Hume and Kant," *British Journal for the History of Philosophy* (2004)

Other Recent Work by David L. Haberman

The Bhaktirasamrtasindhu of Rupa Gosvamin (Indira Gandhi National Centre for the Arts in association with Motilal Banarsidass Publishers, 2003)

"River of Love in an Age of Pollution." In *Hinduism and Ecology,* edited by Christopher Chapple and Mary Evelyn Tucker (Harvard University Press, 2000)

"Textual Intimacy: Benefits and Techniques of Academic Translation." In *Notes From a Mandala: Essays in Honor of Wendy Doniger,* edited by David L. Haberman and Laurie Patton (Seven Bridges Press, 2004)

"Forty Verses in Praise of 'The King of Mountains,'" *Journal of Vaishnava Studies* 12, no. 1 (Fall 2003)